California BASS angling guide

Joni Dahlstrom

California BASS *Angling Guide*

Photographs • Adam Zetter
Maps • Esther Paleo

Frank Amato Publications
P.O. Box 02112 • Portland, Oregon 97282 • (503) 653-8108

Copyright 1991 • Joni Dahlstrom • Printed in U.S.A.
Book Design: Joyce Herbst • Typesetting: Charlie Clifford • Maps Esther Paleo
ISBN 0-936608-93-5

Dedicated to: Good Fishing in California

About the Author and Photographer:

Joni and Adam are a writer/photographer team living in Santa Barbara. They are members of the Outdoor Writers Association of America.

CONTENTS

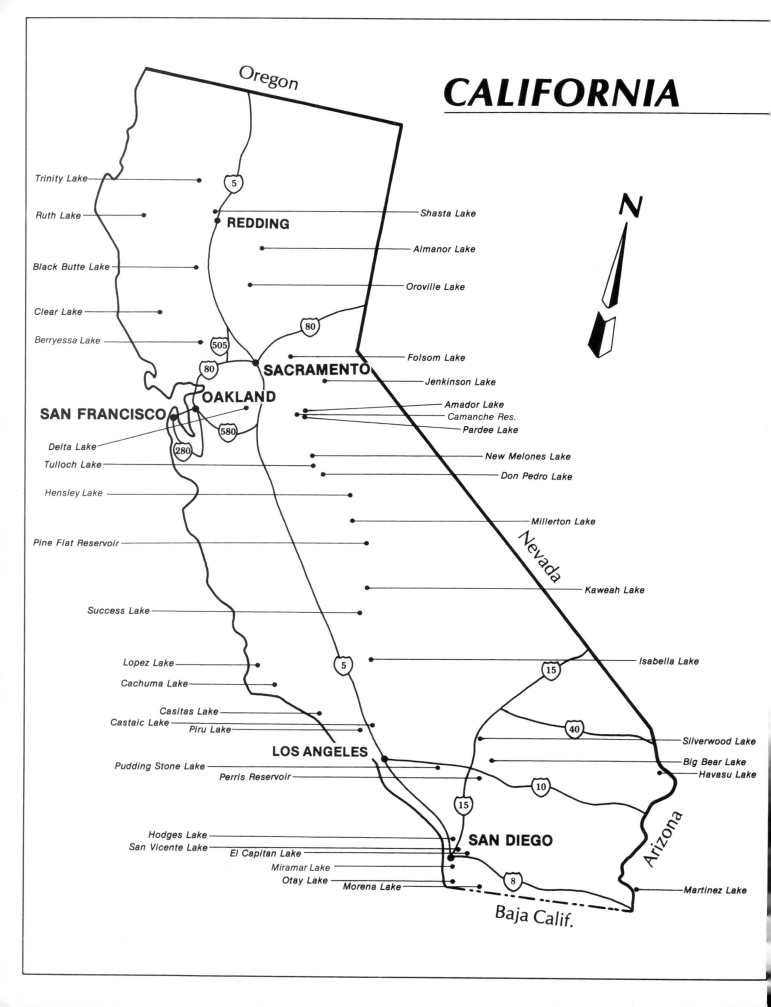

INTRODUCTION

How many times have you traveled a long distance to fish a new bass lake only to arrive in the worst possible season and with the wrong tackle—or at the end of the day, realize that all of your time was spent on unproductive structure?

Bass fishing is a sport which strongly favors the local fishermen. Sure there are general rules that govern bass movement and behavior, but each lake has its own character. Lakes vary in terms of temperature, structure types, forage base, bass species, and climate, to name just a few possibilities. Often it is difficult to piece the whole puzzle together, from the deck of a boat, without years of experience on a single body of water. You may know your home lakes like your own backyard, but still be left without a clue as to how to approach a new lake.

This book is designed to give you the basic information needed to catch bass in 40 different California lakes. Pros, guides, tackle shop owners, and other good fishermen were interviewed on their home lakes. We believe that fishermen know their home waters best. When a lifetime of bass fishing experience is combined with intimate knowledge of a particular lake, it is hard to go wrong.

These fishermen share how they approach each lake — what types of structure they look for, how deep they fish in each season, what type of lures they use, and how fish are affected by short term weather patterns. We didn't ask for a list of their favorite spots on each lake because these change with water level fluctuation, season, and fishing pressure. Instead we tried to learn what clues they look for each time they go out on the water.

To make the information easy to find, we have divided each lake chapter into five parts: map, text, key, facilities, and guide information.

The maps are bathymetric whenever possible. They provide a picture of the general features of the lake bottom. These maps will indicate where the lake is shallow and flat, or where there are steep walls. Take the water level fluctuation into account when reading these maps, they are all drawn as if the lake was full.

The key is a quick recap of the most important items discussed in the text—so you won't have to reread the whole chapter to find out what color grub the guides recommended.

Facilities are included to give information on campgrounds, launch ramps, tackle shops and other essential services. Phone numbers for the agencies in charge of the lakes are provided, to help you obtain up-to-date information about weather and water levels.

The section on the guides provides information about how to reach the licensed guides that were interviewed for this book. We also wanted to tell you a little about the credits of these fishermen, to give you confidence in their information and abilities. In those cases where the address and phone number of guides are not printed, it was done at the fisherman's request, but we still wanted to let you know who they are and why we felt confident in interviewing them.

California Bass Guide will give you an edge when exploring new waters, and in the long run, help you bring more fish to hand.

ALMANOR LAKE

There was a time when Almanor was known primarily as a trout fishery. Though fishermen knew the lake held smallmouth bass, almost no one actively fished for them. First and foremost, this lake was a trout spot.

Then word got out about smallmouth that averaged better than two pounds, topped by the occasional lunker that topped eight pounds. Better yet, Almanor didn't hold only a few big fish, there were a lot of quality bass in this "trout" lake. "It isn't uncommon to catch 20 or more bass in a long, spring day. Not uncommon at all," said Roger Keeling, "and practically all of them will be over three pounds."

Almanor is one of the largest man-made lakes in California, with 28,000 surface acres. Located in the Lassen National Forest, at 4,500 feet the lake is at a fairly high elevation for a bass lake, but it turns out to be an ideal environment for smallmouth, which prefer cooler more sterile water than largemouth.

The lake has a wide variety of smallmouth structure spread throughout the entire lake. The structure in Almanor includes: well-defined ledges, flats, cuts, creeks, coves, stumps, and grassbeds. This is the difficult part of fishing Almanor.

Use smaller lures on this lake. Crawdad colors work best in spring and fall. Smelt colors work best in summer.

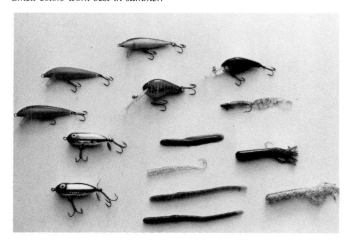

"There is a lot of water that looks like typically good smallmouth water," said Keeling, "but it will be devoid of fish. You need to know the right structure to look for at different times of the year."

On any water at high elevation, the changing seasons become one of the most important factors to consider. Water temperature is one of the main factors governing the movement and activity of bass on any lake. Yet temperature becomes paramount on waters that range from 40 to 80 degrees in a normal year. On Almanor, the spring and fall bites turn on with a vengeance; in the heat of summer it is slow. The smallmouth fishing shuts off completely around the end of October, when the surface temperature drops below 46 degrees; the fish may still bite reluctantly, but not well enough to make it worth braving the cold. When planning a trip consider the season; and while on the water use a temperature gauge to locate the best spots.

In early spring, before the water reaches the low 50s, the best lures are slow-moving baits, like Gitzits and small plastic worms. Work them snail slow, in 10 to 15 feet of water, on the migration channels from the deep ledges to shallow spawning flats. Crankbaits worked very slow can produce fish too, though they work better after the water warms a bit. This is a pre-spawn bite, it won't be wide-open action, but the fish tend to be good quality.

"By spring the spawning bass are using the shallow flats with old stumps and root systems," Keeling said. "You'll find the fish in less than five feet of water. You can really do a job on them, because you can see them real good on sunny days wearing polaroid glasses."

"They seem to like a slight difference in the water depth," added Joe Mason, "like a little dip in a shallow area, or a little drop-off in the middle of a flat, covered with stumps and gravel." These are prime areas to look for spawning smallmouth. The bite begins a little later than on low elevation lakes, in a normal year the spawn will be well underway by mid-April.

Ripping is a popular tactic in spring. Use any shallow-running lure and fish it by making fast, jerky, three- foot retrieves. Grubs, jigs, and worms all bring in fish that hold on beds in the shallows, especially when bass won't take the fast-moving baits. The fish are feeding primarily on crawdads early in the year, use lures with color combinations of green, brown-red, and orange.

"I like to fish an area called the Fox Farm," said Ralph Schattenburg. "It is a shallow stumpy area on the west shore. There is also the boat ramp where the diversion canal feeds water into the lake — this is a real shallow stretch with a lot of stumps. Both sides of the peninsula are good too. On average the east side of the peninsula has larger fish than the west side. All these spots have pretty consistent shallow-water fishing by April."

Almanor's water is clear, except when the wind stirs up the mud on the flats. It isn't unusual to have a slow morning of fishing — while the lake is still and the water is very clear — then when the wind comes up the bite turns on in a flash. Water clarity in the shallows can change from clear to muddy within about 15 minutes. Fish the murkier water whenever possible.

"By mid-June, the water is warm," said Schattenburg, "the surface temperature is in the 70s at the end of June, it'll be about 65 degrees around the first of the month. The fish will have moved back out a little. They are a bit deeper, but you still don't have to fish below 30 feet. They are in groups of five or six fish. There is a big cove on the east side about 100 yards wide where the water goes from 0 to 60 feet. I have seen bass stacked up back in there, that is a good summer spot."

The larger bass hold in 15 to 25 feet of water, off the tips of main points. The straight rocky shorelines may hold a lot of bass, but these are smaller fish. For big bass, head for the primary structure.

Log booms around the resorts are good summer spots for big fish. The booms are tied around swimming and marina areas, and anchored to the bottom with cables. Moss grows on the cables, and that attracts baitfish, which attracts the bass. The logs also provide shady structure that bass relate to.

In extremely low water years, underwater springs may be the best place to find fish. The reason is that when the water level drops, the lake reaches higher than average summer temperatures. There are several underwater springs beneath the lake that can cool the surface water by as much as two degrees and make an even more significant difference at depth. In the cooler water there is more dissolved oxygen, so these spots attract both the bait fish and the bass. The springs are marked on some maps and known to local fishermen. However, springs are a hot spot only in low water, hot weather years; in cool, high water years, the bass may stay on the bite all through the summer at depths from eight to fifteen feet.

There is a good top-water bite on Almanor, from post-spawn through the summer. For the most part, this is a morning bite, starting when the sun rises and lasting until about 9:00 a.m. The bass hit Rapalas, Tiny Torpedos and Baby Spooks. Work just off the stump flats, where the bottom

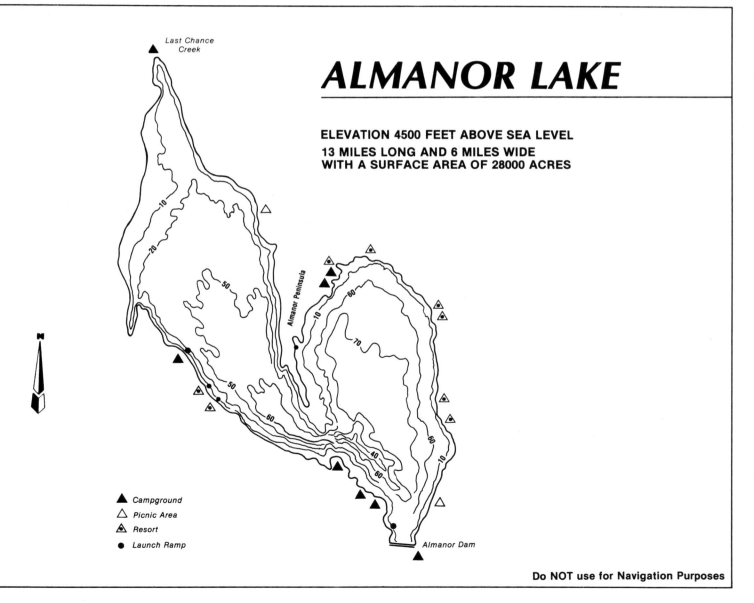

ALMANOR LAKE

ELEVATION 4500 FEET ABOVE SEA LEVEL
13 MILES LONG AND 6 MILES WIDE
WITH A SURFACE AREA OF 28000 ACRES

Last Chance Creek

Almanor Peninsula

▲ Campground
△ Picnic Area
▲ Resort
● Launch Ramp

Almanor Dam

Do NOT use for Navigation Purposes

drops off into deeper water.

Imitations of pond smelt are better than crawdad colors in summer because the fish will have switched over and started chasing the smelt. The smelt will bust the surface in the morning and go deeper after the sun hits the water. Smelt were stocked in the lake because threadfin shad don't do well on a lake with such extreme temperature fluctuations.

"As fall first comes on, the fish are really scattered," Schattenburg said. "Some guys will fly fish for them from the banks at this time of year, but I usually go deeper and crank about 15 or 20 feet from the bank. I like to hit the east shore. The fish could be deep, shallow, almost anywhere. You'll get shallow feeding late in the day."

By the time the water hits 52 to 54 degrees, fall is in full swing and the fishing is best on slow moving lures. There is a possibility of a top-water bite, but this isn't a standard fall pattern. As the water continues to cool, the fish move to deeper holes off points adjacent to the main lake. When the water drops below 46 degrees, it marks the end of the good bass fishing until next spring.

"Most people aren't aware of it," said Mason, "but the largemouth are coming back a bit. Their numbers are increasing. The lake record is six pounds, eleven ounces, and we have caught a few in the five pound range this past summer. The largemouth are holding in the same areas as the smallmouth, and they hit Gitzits well.

"The trick on this lake," he added, "is to be there when the bass are hitting. Don't be discouraged if you don't get anything. This is sort of an 'on and off' lake. Some days, guys get 60 fish in a day, and they'll all be two or three pounds. Another day or another spot, it could be slow. But the good fish are in there. You can get them if you are patient."

Roger Keeling with a four-pound smallmouth. Fish of this size are not rare on this lake if you know the spots and fish hard.

ALMANOR GUIDES

Roger Keeling (916) 258-2283
P.O. Box 11, Chester, CA 96020
Roger has guided on Almanor for 18 years, he also guides on some of the other lakes in the area. He has appeared in six televised video programs on bass fishing.

Joe Mason
Joe has fished on Almanor his whole life. He didn't start fishing for bass up here until about 10 years ago. But, then again, hardly anyone fished for bass on Almanor until about 10 years ago.

Ralph Schattenburg (916) 256-2311
P.O. Box 256, Westwood, CA 96137
Ralph has had 20 years of experience fishing for bass and has fished Almanor for 12 years. For the past three years he has guided for bass, as well as trout and salmon.

The solitude is rare and wonderful.

ALMANOR FACILITIES

At this high elevation, winter is pretty cold. Many of the campgrounds and resorts are not open all year-round, and the exact opening dates depend largely on the variable weather. Call before planning a trip.
• U.S. Forest Service, operates Almanor campground, on the west side of the lake. It has 101 sites and the fee is $7 per night. There is a launch ramp in the campground. There is no charge for day use or launching. Open from May 1 to November 1. Call (916) 258-2141 for information.
• Pacific Gas and Electric (PGE): Operates three campgrounds on the lake, as follows. Fees are charged during the summer.

Springtime fish will hold on flats. Work top-water bait around the tree stumps.

Fox Farm, has 44 sites, a boat launch and RV dump.
Mountain View, 20 sites and a launch ramp.
Rocky Point Campground, 20 sites and a launch ramp.
• Lake Haven Resort, has cabins, campsites, full RV hook-ups, marina, store, and docks. Located on the east shore, 7329 Hwy. 147, Westwood, CA 96137. Call (916) 596-3249.

• Wilson's Camp Prattville is an RV park, with marina, restaurant, groceries, boat launch and boat rentals. Located on the west shore, Canyon Dam, CA. Call (916) 259-2464.
• Lassen View Resort, has cottages, RV hook-ups, snackbar, gas and propane, launch ramp, boat rentals, and a store. On the east shore, 7457 Hwy. 147, Lake Almanor, CA. (916) 596-3437.
• Almanor Lakeside Lodge, offers furnished housekeeping units on the lake, docks and a launch ramp. 3747 Eastshore Dr., Hwy. 147, Lake Almanor, CA. (916) 284-7376.
• Big Cove Resort, has camp sites and RV hook-ups, marina, boat rentals, propane, and bait and tackle. 442 Peninsula Dr., Lake Almanor, CA. (916) 596-3349.
• Lake Almanor Resort, has a lodge, housekeeping cabins, launch ramp, boat rentals, bait and tackle, and grocery store. 2706 Big Springs Rd., Lake Almanor, CA. (916) 596-3337.
• Dorado Inn, has lake-front housekeeping units, on the beach. But no launch ramp. 4379 Eastshore Hwy. 147, Lake Almanor, CA. (916) 284-7790.
• Timberhouse Restaurant and Lodge, in the town of Chester, isn't on the lake, but they allow dogs in the room, and the restaurant is a good place for steak and to watch televised sporting events on a big screen TV. On Main Street, Chester, — Call, (916) 258-2729.

• The Sports Nut, sells bait, tackle, and all sporting goods. They are open year round. Call (916) 258-3327.
Chester/Lake Almanor Chamber of Commerce: For additional information on Almanor resorts call, (916) 258-2426.

KEY TO ALMANOR

Best Season: April and May, everything works. Good top-water fishing from May through the summer, primarily early morning. By the end of October, the water is too cold for any decent action, forget about fishing the winter bite.

Lures To Use: Smaller worms and grubs, as well as jigs. Crawdad colors are good in spring and fall. Through the summer go with smelt or shad imitations. All types of ripping baits produce fish. For top-water use Tiny Torpedos, Rapalas, and Baby Spooks.

Primary Structure: In spring, the stumps on flats around the Fox Farm and the flats off the Peninsula. For summer, fish the edges of main points and wood or rock near deep water, but there is no need to fish below 30 feet. In a warm year, look for cool, underwater springs. To be effective the springs should make a difference in the surface temperature of about two degrees. The log booms around the resorts can hold fish in summer.

Other: Very clear water for the most part, unless wind or water skiers stir the mudbanks up. Fish with light lines and small baits. The water temperature fluctuates greatly, so the lake is seasonal. Use a temperature gauge to key in on the best spots.

15

AMADOR LAKE

Bob Trippe said, "Amador is the place to get your wall-mount." It may be a small lake, it covers only a little more than 400 surface acres, but Amador holds big fish.

The lake record, caught in 1986, is 17 pounds, 1 ounce, and was the Northern California bass record for three years. "We have more and bigger fish," said Bob Lockhart. "We host an annual night tournament every year, with 50 boats. In one night we had 20 bass over seven pounds. We probably had a 100 bass over five pounds."

The typical situation that occurs on many Southern California lakes is that a small heavily fished lake becomes dominated by a few huge bass that grow fat on stocked trout. This isn't the case at Amador. Here the bass population is well-balanced, with fat healthy fish of all year classes represented. Acre for acre, Amador may surpass any lake in the state for numbers of quality bass.

But, that doesn't mean Amador is an easy lake to fish. The

A lot of people on Amador just use jigs and spinnerbaits. Although surface baits will produce good quality fish in the pre-spawn and through summer. Later in the year the surface bite is limited to morning and evening.

lake is located in the foothills east of Stockton. It is fed by rain-water from the surrounding foothills rather than snow-melt. For this reason the water is rich in nutrients and that leads to an abundant food supply for forage fish. The result is a food-rich environment that allows bass to become lazy, selective feeders. They won't chase a bait and they may not bite, because they just plain aren't hungry.

The other complication is structure. Fishing on Amador is like working a lure through the Black Forest. The steep-sided canyon walls are completely covered with trees. Finding bass among those tangled, gnarled branches is one thing, getting them out is another matter.

The pre-spawn bite begins in late February. At this time bass are active in the top 25 feet of water. In a wet year, when the water is muddied from heavy run-off, use large jigs in the top five feet of water. The Jackson Creek Arm is the top producer of large bass. Concentrate on fishing trees near creeks and drop-offs; look for a combination of structure types — rock and wood or breaks and wood — since timber is everywhere.

If the water is clear use four-inch worms. Green Weenies, salt and pepper, and purple worms are always good. Lockhart recommends line of at least eight to ten pounds, even on relatively small worms since large fish break off too easily with lighter line. There is far too much brush to fish an open-hook, so go Texas style with 2/0 hooks and a bullet sinker that will come easily through the branches.

"One good thing about the spring is that the forage fish have not come up yet," said Lockhart. "Our Florida bass come up about 30 days before everything else. The bass are shallow and hungry because their metabolism has kicked up; but there is no food for them in the shallows. This is the one time of year when you can have 50 fish days. The bass won't all be big, but they are nice fish. You'll get the big fish two or three days after a storm, look for them in the warmer coves and fish with a jig. That's when you have the best chance of getting a real big one."

The only way to get fish during the spawn is by fishing beds. Bass are literally all over the lake, packed into the shallows. Throw eight- to twelve-inch worms for the larger fish.

"After the fish move off the spawning beds, I like to use spinnerbaits on 17-pound test," said Trippe. "Use chartreuse or white, with number five or seven Colorado blades. Cast into the ugliest snarls, because the spinnerbait will come out of them. Work the bait close to the surface. The strike is absolutely awesome when a six pounder comes up and inhales a spinnerbait right under the surface."

Surface plugs produce bass beginning in the pre-spawn and continuing on through summer. Bass topping 13 pounds have been taken out of Amador on Devil's Horse and Rapala lures, though Trippe prefers large buzzbaits and Zaras, because he targets trophy bass. Before the heat sets in, the top-water bite can last all day; later on in the year, it becomes an early morning and late evening bite. Surface lures don't seem to work well at night, this is primarily a dawn and dusk tactic.

The best all around lure over the years has been a six-inch ring-worm, in black with a chartreuse tail. "One thing a lot of guys do up here," said Lockhart, "is to put two worms

LAKE AMADOR

ELEVATION 460 FEET ABOVE SEA LEVEL
CONTOUR INTERVALS 20 FEET, &
INDICATE DEPTH OF WATER

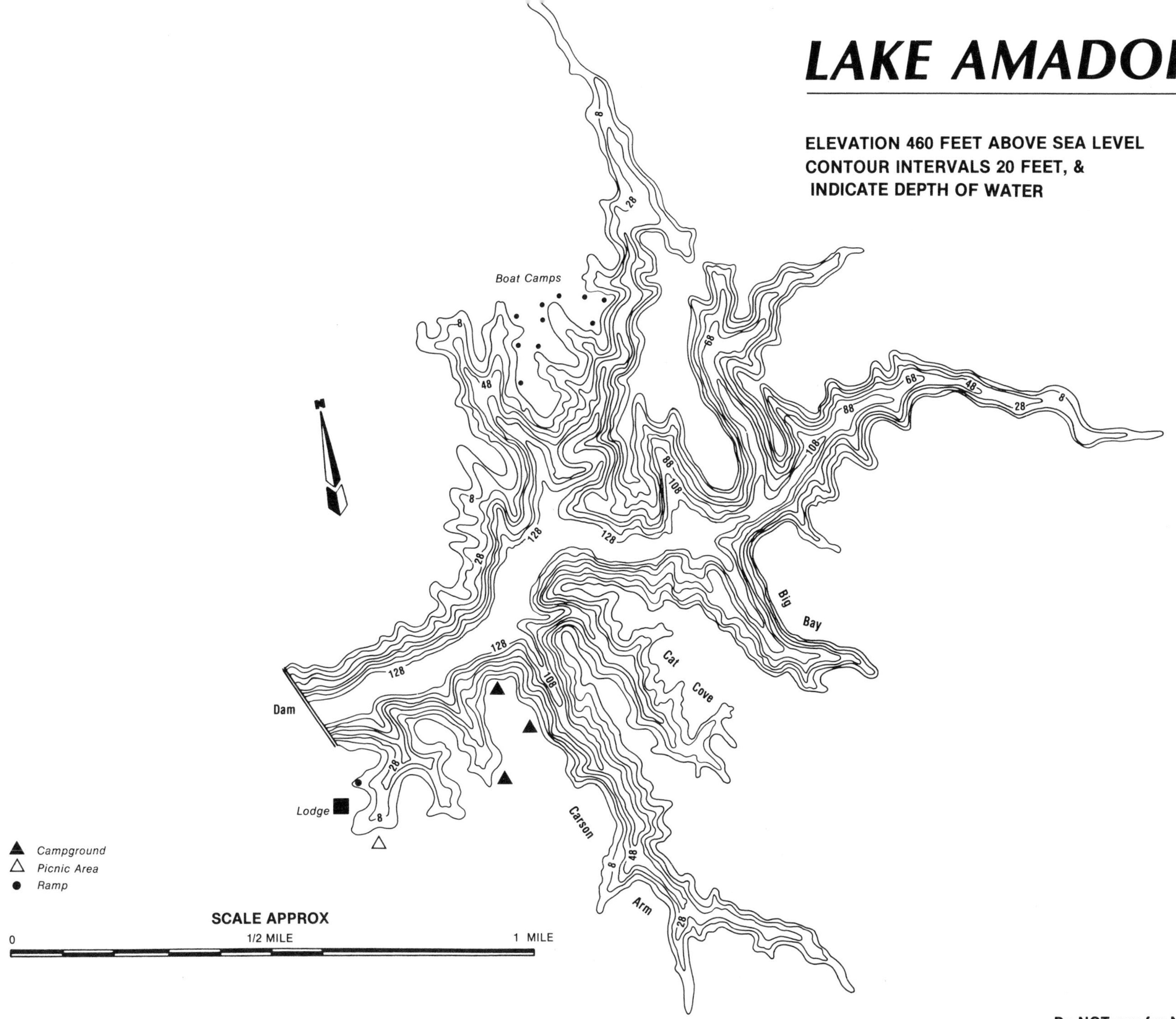

Do NOT use for Navigation Purposes

Big Bay

Cat Cove

Carson Arm

Boat Camps

Dam

Lodge

8
28
48
68
88
108
128

Campground
Picnic Area
Ramp

▲
△
●

SCALE APPROX

0   1/2 MILE   1 MILE

together by heating them with a match and then holding them together for about four seconds. This gives fishermen the ability to create any worm they like with only a match and a handful of plastics. The guys will put two or three tails on one worm, to get more vibration. This works well at night, when the fish feed by motion and vibration rather than sight. With the vibration of a ribbed worm and three tails they can really do something."

Rocky structures and stick-ups usually pay off.

From June to September the fishing is best early and late in the day, or at night. Summer bass hold in 20 to 30 feet of water during the day. At night they come up to 15 feet, but not all the way into the shallows. Amador is 200 feet deep when full, with wood structure from top to bottom. The bass tend to stay 15 to 30 feet deep all year long; the spawning season is the only exception. During summer look for bass on points off the main lake, with rocky structure. When fishing is real tough, move to submerged islands in 25 feet of water. Use worms and fish slow, letting the tail action of the worm do all the work.

"Even though there is a lot of structure, you can't flip on this lake," Trippe said, "because it is too deep. We do a lot of vertical jigging in summer, working right in the trees. A graph is useless, there is just too much structure. We'll go up to the trunk of a tree, drop a big jig down through the branches and let it fall to 30 feet alongside the trunk. Then jig it back to the top, lifting a few feet at a time. The bass are suspended and relating to the trunks."

Fall offers very good top-water action. Throw a spinnerbait or buzzbait past the trees, and let it land close to the shore. Then work the lure back over the surface, through the branches. Work the lure all the way back to the boat, since fish may be holding near the surface in the tree-tops, in spots where the bottom is 25 to 30 feet deep.

Plastic worms and jigs, worked along the shore in shallow water are the most reliable lures in fall. The jigs are better after rainfall muddies the water.

Amador is a virtual ghost-town in fall, even on weekends there may not be more than five boats on the water. Trippe

thinks that this is the time of year to catch a trophy, since fall is when he caught his 14-pound, 8-ounce fish; but Lockhart thinks that though fall is good for catching quality bass, May is the big fish month.

During winter, November through January, bass move down to 30 foot depths. The best way to catch them is on six-inch worms or jigs, worked slow. Look for warmer water, near rock and trees that absorb heat, in the northwest coves. This is a midday bite, so don't bother getting on the lake at dawn.

"Amador is not an easy lake to fish," said Lockhart, "because these bass have everything they need." Spring is the only time of year when large numbers of fish are easy to catch. The rest of the year, success on Amador requires persistence and patience. And the lake can shut off for days at a time. "When the fish are off the bite," said Trippe, "you won't catch them anywhere on the lake. Don't feel bad, even the best fishermen have blank days on this lake. But, when it is on, you get good fish."

The water in Amador lake is owned by a small collective irrigation district, rather than a huge municipal corporation or the state. The resort with complete RV and tent camping facilities, as well as lodge and restaurant, is owned and operated by the Lockhart family. This means the lake is run in a different way than most facilities. Four dollars of the entrance fee goes directly to fishery programs. The Lockhart family currently stocks trout and catfish. In the future they plan to stock one-pound, Florida-strain bass in the lake. The bass hatchery is currently under construction. Skiing and jet-skis are not allowed on the lake, though swimming is permitted. There is a swimming pond, playground and game room for kids. This is an ideal fishing and family vacation spot.

Bob Lockhart displays an Amador bass. Amador has a healthy population of largemouth in all sizes. This is not a lake that just has a few giant fish. While fishing for a 10 pounder you will be kept busy with two- and three-pound fish.

This shows the type of structure in the lake—trees and rock everywhere and all holds fish.

AMADOR GUIDES

Bob Lockhart (209) 274-4739   7500 Lake Amador Dr., Ione, CA 95640

The Lockhart family have owned and operated the Lake Amador Resort for 17 years, and Bob has been fishing the lake for this entire period. He guides only occasionally, but his brother guides during the season.

Bob Trippe (916) 782-8778

247 Fig St., Roseville CA 95678

Bob is a licensed guide who considers himself an instructor; he likes to teach people how to fish. He guarantees a fish on his guide trips, or the client doesn't pay. His sponsors are: R and B Tackle, Hal's Weenie Mania, Joe's Marine and Water Sports.

AMADOR FACILITIES

• Fanbasstic, the resort at Amador, is owned and operated by the Lockharts. It is a full-service camping facility. There are 150 camping sites and 75 RV sites with full hookups, that are next to the water (when the lake is full). There is also a restaurant and store with tackle and supplies, boat rentals, launch ramp, swimming pond, and playground for kids. The fees are: RV sites, $15 to $18 per night; camping $12 per night; day use $4; boat use $4; fishing permit, $2 per person. Call (209) 274-4739 for reservations.

• There is a good restaurant, bar and general store in nearby Buena Vista. They are all in the same building, and it is basically the only commercial building in town, so you won't have a tough time finding it.

• Glory Hole Sporting Goods: Complete bait and tackle 20 minutes away. At 2892 South Highway 49, Angels Camp. Call (209) 736-4333,

KEY TO AMADOR

Best Season: February and March, as the hungry bass begin to come shallow, prior to the shad moving up. The fishing stays pretty good through the spawn. Summer is good for fishing at night.

Lures To Use: Eight- to twelve-inch ring-worms in black with a chartreuse tail. Also larger worms with multiple tails. Larger double-bladed spinnerbaits are good. Lures need to be able to come through trees and brush.

Primary Structure: There are trees everywhere so concentrate on rock and breaks. Jackson Arm produces the largest fish. Except during the spawn, fish in water from 15 to 30 feet deep.

Other: A turbid lake, use line of eight to twelve pounds. This is a feast or famine lake, the fish are either biting or they are not. Unlike many lakes it is very rich in food and nutrients, these bass aren't hungry all that often.

BERRYESSA LAKE

Lake Berryessa is a temperamental lake that is frustrating for many bass fishermen. It is a typical boom or bust lake, fishermen either catch limits or nothing. With 13,000 surface acres that hold bass, an unlucky fisherman can easily spend the entire day fishing close to bass, but never hit those magic spots. Berryessa was clear cut which leaves only the bottom characteristics as structure. To be successful fishermen must learn to read the bottom and pay attention to the temperature and season.

Yet, for those who take the time to become familiar with finesse fishing on a clear-water structure-poor lake, Berryessa can provide daily limits almost year around. There are smallmouth, largemouth, and spotted bass in the lake. Since the aggressiveness of each species peaks at a different water temperature, at least one bass species should be biting in any given season.

Good spring fishing gets underway by March and lasts through May. The first largemouth areas to turn on are Putah and Pope creeks. Early in the year, work the creek channels, off the points closest to the main lake, from five to thirty feet deep. Look for smallmouth on points in the main lake, and follow the fish to the nearby coves later in the season.

"If you go up into Putah Creek," said Jim Munk, "stay up

Lure selection should primarily target smallmouth.

there all day long. Putah and Pope hold most of the largemouth. It is too big an area to cover in only one day, there are so many little feeder creeks at Putah. You've got the best of everything in there, stumps, drop-offs, rock, flats, creeks, and aquatic vegetation. Catching bass is just a matter of finding the concentrations of fish. A lot of times I go up the secondary creek channels and look for where two creeks join. There is usually a little wood or a drop-off on a spot like that. These are the kind of places where I like to throw spinnerbaits and cranks."

As the water warms through the season, follow the bass from the points, back into the coves. Munk said, "It is sort of a seasonal movement from the point to the backs of bays on the flats. Early in the year I try to find fish on the points, then I can stay with them as they move to the spawning beds. To find fish, I start out by hitting four or five points, I work them until I find the depth fish are at. If I don't find fish on the points, I start moving in until I do."

Early in the season Munk likes to use 1/4-ounce jigs with pork, in black/brown combinations. Grubs are also good on split shot in deeper water or fished with dartheads over the shallow flats. When the water gets to 60 or 65 degrees in April and May, switch to crankbaits, spinnerbaits or top-water plugs. Work the spinnerbaits slow, with just enough speed to keep the vibration going. Try chrome crankbaits, like Rat-L-Traps. For top-water, the Devil's Horse is one of the best lures on this water, from the spawn through the post-spawn period.

In June, July and August, the best action is in the early morning hours. There is a good spinnerbait bite back in Putah and Pope creeks until mid-morning. A shallow jerkbait can also produce fish around creek channels where water is flowing. Munk said, "Look for that movement in the water before throwing a jerkbait, it's a real good sign that there should be feeding activity."

At midday go down to the big islands in the main body of the lake. These islands have deep water around them; smallmouth will hold in less than 20 feet of water on the shady side of steep shelves and points. Fish with jigs and grubs, in 10 to 20 feet of water.

Late in the day, fish the mud banks on the east shoreline. The afternoon water-skiing activity forms good mud lines off the banks and points that can bring the bass up into less than 10 feet of water. Crank along the mud lines with silver DB3s and Rat-L-Traps, or DB2s in crawdad color with a little spot of chartreuse.

Because the lake is clear, fishermen need to use six-pound line with spinning gear, and 10-pound line for cranks and top-water.

The fall fishing pattern is similar to spring. In September and October the bass move back into the creek beds and adjacent flats and hold in 12 to 15 feet of water. The bass are aggressive and actively feeding; to capitalize on it, fish primarily with crankbaits like those used in summer. The bass also hit smaller spinnerbaits fairly well. If the weather is mild, the good fishing of fall can hold through November, it usually lasts at least through October.

In winter, the pattern is deep water fishing with slow moving baits. "I use a lot of three- to five-inch grubs, and 1/4-ounce jigs again," said Munk. "On this lake, the brown or black jigs are your year around bait. We don't use many worms in the spring, if you could only have one lure on Berryessa, it should be a jig. You have to fish slow in winter, in water from 25 to 35 feet, or even down to 40 feet deep. When you are fishing slow enough, it could take 10 minutes to make one retrieve.''

Steep banks, points, and deep creek channels are the primary spots to fish in winter. There is a deep creek channel down by the dam, called the Narrows that will often hold winter fish. There is no point in getting on the water before 9:00 or 10:00 a.m. in the winter.

The smallmouth are likely to be more consistent in winter than the largemouth, because they don't seem to be affected by cold fronts as much as the largemouth. In general, Munk recommends moving up and back into the coves when a warm front passes, and out to the deep water points or channels when a cold front passes.

Wes Sheehy uses entirely different tactics than Munk for catching smallmouth on Berryessa. Sheehy said, ''Typical California bass fishing does not apply on Berryessa, it is a very different lake. I started trolling, deeper and deeper, and I found that this is where the larger smallmouth are. They stay below 15 feet year around. They only come up that shallow when the water is down to 50 degrees, in the winter season.''

Sheehy trolls a three-inch walleye lure, dragging it on the bottom, so that the bill of the lure will wear out after a day of use. The lure has to plow into the lake bottom, to attract the attention of the bass.

He trolls at about six mph, over deep gravel flats. He says that because of the clear water, going slower than six mph won't get a reflex strike out of the bass; a smallmouth doesn't have trouble nailing a lure moving at this speed. If the water is murky, slow down because the fish can't see the lure from

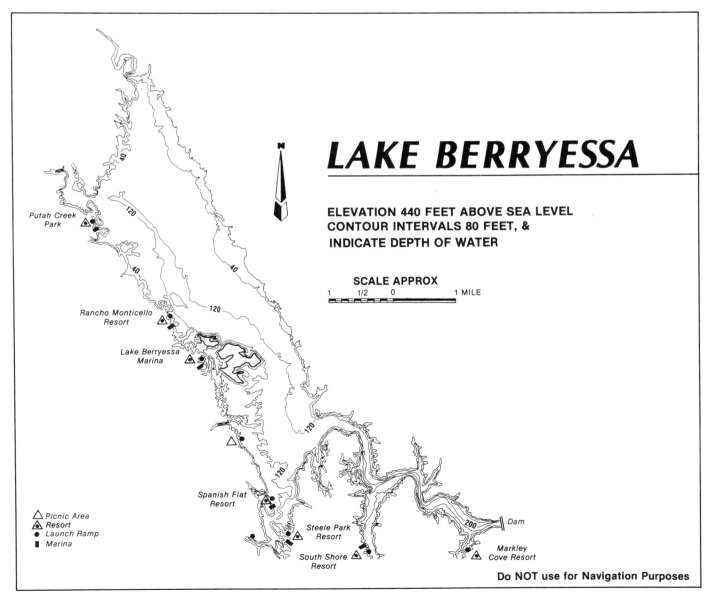

LAKE BERRYESSA

ELEVATION 440 FEET ABOVE SEA LEVEL
CONTOUR INTERVALS 80 FEET, &
INDICATE DEPTH OF WATER

SCALE APPROX
1   1/2   0   1 MILE

Putah Creek Park

Rancho Monticello Resort

Lake Berryessa Marina

Spanish Flat Resort

Steele Park Resort

South Shore Resort

Dam

Markley Cove Resort

△ Picnic Area
▲ Resort
● Launch Ramp
▮ Marina

Do NOT use for Navigation Purposes

as far away, so they need more time to strike.

This isn't a method that tournament fishermen can make use of, but from January through March it can easily produce limits of smallmouth bass for recreational fishermen. The key is to get the right trolling speed, keep the lure on the bottom at the correct depth, and look for a surface temperature of 50 degrees.

"This is a superb smallmouth lake, with fish that average 13 or 14 inches," Sheehy said. "At the top of the season, from February through April, the fish average 2 1/2 to 3 pounds. Berryessa is unusual, in that it has a strong forage population of threadfin shad and crawdads, so you have heavy bass."

Jim Monk with a couple of smallmouth bass.

Water near long points is always worth fishing at Berryessa.

In spring, tree covered shallow coves can be great for spinnerbait fishing.

BERRYESSA GUIDES

Jim Munk (707) 995-0438
Jim has been fishing on Berryessa for over 20 years, he has been a licensed guide for the past two years.

Wes Sheehy (707) 433-5933
Wes has guided for the past four years. He has been fishing for fresh and saltwater fish for his entire life.

BERRYESSA FACILITIES

There are many private camping and RV parks on Lake Berryessa, with launch ramps, tackle shops, groceries, and restaurants. Most of the private RV parks have boat rentals, though they may be oriented more towards water skiers and trout fishermen than towards bass fishermen.

The Bureau of Reclamation operates a public boat launch ramp at Capell Cove.

Following is a partial list of Resorts. For more detailed information contact the Lake Berryessa Chamber of Commerce, (707) 226-7455.
• Putah Creek Park: launch ramp, full service marina, campsites, RV park, and a small motel. (707)966-2116.
• Lake Berryessa Marina Resort: launch ramp, RV Park, camping, boat rentals, and restaurant. (707) 966-2161.
• Spanish Flat Resort: launch ramp, boat rental, boat repair, bait and tackle, gas, deli store, restaurant and bar, camping for RVs and trailers. (707) 966-2101.
• Steele Park Resort: launch ramp, full-service marina, boat rentals, RV and trailer sites, motel, cottages, restaurant, bar, and pool. (707) 966-2123.

KEY TO BERRYESSA

Best Season: February through May, followed by September and October. The smallmouth will be biting by February, but the largemouth fishing doesn't really get going until about March.

Lures To Use: The most consistent lure throughout the year is a 1/4-ounce jig in black or brown, with 101 pork rinds. Silver Rat-L-Traps, shad-colored DB3s, crawdad-colored DB2s, and Devils Horse for top-water — 1/4-ounce spinnerbaits are good too. For plastic worms, go with clear or smoke colored bodies, with a flake, smaller grubs in three to five inch sizes are the most reliable.

Primary Structure: In the main body of the lake, the only structures are the cuts, points, and drop-offs formed by the bottom. Mud lines are the only other possibility. In Putah Creek, there are a lot of creek channels, some stumps, rocks, and quite a bit of aquatic vegetation.

Other: This is a clear water lake, use six-pound line on spinning gear, and 10-pound line on baitcasting gear.

BIG BEAR LAKE

Elevation: 6,000 feet. That sounds a little high for a good largemouth bass fishery. But they say the exception proves the rule, and Big Bear lake is definitely the exception.

This mile-high alpine lake offers excellent largemouth and smallmouth fishing. The largemouth are strictly northern-strain and they don't reach terrific sizes, but the lake holds plenty of quality bass. The smallmouth were introduced in the mid-80s and some are now reaching sizes of over three pounds. In time, Big Bear should offer a dynamite smallmouth bass fishery, given the preference of smallmouth for cooler, clearer water.

Big Bear is a popular, busy resort. In summer the lake borders on crowded. But, most of the fisherman are after trout. Bass fishermen will find little competition for the best fishing spots and the best fish.

Because of the high elevation, spring fishing at Big Bear takes off about three weeks later than on lowland lakes. The fish don't begin moving up until late March or April. "Basically we have to wait for ice-out," said Jim Hall. "We always get some ice on the lake, but it doesn't always freeze solid. Still, you can't get your boat onto the lake until the ice is gone. Although you can bank fish in the holes around the lake even earlier. Go slow and use a small lure, and you can be successful."

This is a selection of lures that will produce fish at Big Bear. Flipping jigs and spinnerbaits around the docks is often a good place to start.

Also, because the maximum surface temperature on Big Bear is about 72 degrees, the bass have become accustomed to cooler water. They spawn at slightly lower temperatures than largemouth in lowland lakes.

The east end of the lake, where the water is shallower, turns on first. This is simply because the water over the flats warms more quickly. There are flats on the east side of Eagle Point that hold fish in early spring and through the spawning season. "In the mornings, the west side of a bay is best," said Dick Rangel, "where the sun hits first. As the sun comes up the bass start moving around a bit more. Head for the warmer water."

In early spring, the local fishermen have the best success on smaller lures, using larger baits in fall as the forage fish grow and the bass become more aggressive. Hall suggests small spinnerbaits, in white/chartreuse or chartreuse/blue with a single, number 5 blade. Rangel recommends both jig and pig and spinnerbaits, worked shallow and flipped near docks. The spinnerbaits work best along the shoreline. He adds that the fish will be shallow in the morning, but move down to about 15 feet as the sun hits the water. Keep moving out and deeper with the spinnerbaits as the day wears on.

Hall does a lot of top-water fishing in spring. Even though he prefers smaller baits when it comes to most categories of lures, he almost always begins the day with a larger surface lure and works down in size until the lure starts getting bit. Hall prefers to concentrate on larger fish when fishing on the surface; he sacrifices a few bites for the chance at a big bass. Zara Spooks and number nine Rapalas are his most successful lures.

Spring fishing is best around the shorelines. Look for sandy bottoms and areas that are clear of weed. It is fairly easy to find pre-spawn fish in the shallows, they are often lying in plain sight. The flip side of this is that the bass are skittish and timid; don't try motoring a boat up on top of the fish, instead use long casts and stay well off the banks. After weed begins to grow and fish actually begin to spawn, they are not as easily spooked and more aggressive tactics will catch fish. As the weed begins to come up, Rangel suggests using a shallow running crankbait that only dives about two feet, a lure that runs shallow can come over the top of weeds that grow from the bottom.

"We have milfoil, spyro gyra, coontail, and moss. When we get a lot of weed it is difficult to fish around the shoreline," said Hall. "As the conditions worsen, you can pull the boat into the weed-mess itself, look for holes and drop the bait right down to the bottom, you'll have pretty fair success. The weed gets heavy by April or May."

Summer is more difficult on Big Bear. The bass move to deep water off points and structure, from 10 to 40 feet deep. The docks can be good in summer, but they are inconsistent. They can be worth a few casts, to see if fish are holding on them, but don't spend a lot of time here. A graph is almost essential to locate the deeper water sanctuaries and migration routes. Hall adds that if you can find a good break in a migration route, one that leads to a deep water fish sanctuary, it is almost guaranteed to produce some good fish, even on a tough day.

Hall likes Cordell Spots in summer, used as countdown lures. Rangel prefers small, curled tail grubs. Both guides prefer darker colors for their plastics, though there are days when the bass will only hit a light-colored lure. Top-water will continue to produce fish all summer, fished in the early morning or late evening, or when wind creates a slight ripple on the surface of the water.

Because this is a clear water lake, light lines are the rule, from four- to eight-pound test. "We do have quite a few submerged trees and other structure, of course then you need a little heavier line," Rangel added. "I like to use a spinning rod. When you are using a lighter lure, like a grub, it is easier to cast."

By October, the fish are moving into a fall pattern. This isn't exactly what most bass fishermen would refer to as a feeding frenzy, but the fishing is easier than in summer. The weed begins to die back and the water is usually very clear in fall, light line becomes even more critical than at other times of year.

When it comes to the depth bass hold at in fall, a split seems to occur. "Fish are shallow and deep," said Hall. "We have done it both ways. Most of the areas we fish are 10 feet deep or less; the outer edges are most productive. We also try

deep water structure fishing and of course you are fishing deep off points too. I always make an initial run with my graph, it eliminates a lot of water quickly. If you have the misfortune of finding all the bass suspended, you have real problems, they aren't relating to anything then, they are just taking up room."

On Big Bear, fall lures are similar to spring, with the standards being spinnerbaits, jig and pig, and six-inch worms. Light-colored spinnerbaits are most popular, because the water is clear in fall. Pig and jig flipped around docks is productive in fall, especially docks in bays where the water is still warm.

There is usually skim ice forming around the lake by the end of November. The lake won't freeze solid until the end of December or middle of January; many years it doesn't freeze solid at all. Bank fishing can be fun, work in the open patches between ice, with small spinnerbaits and grubs, but Hall and Rangel add that they don't catch large fish in winter. Think of winter fishing as a way to kill a lazy Sunday afternoon while the rest of the family goes skiing and plays in the snow.

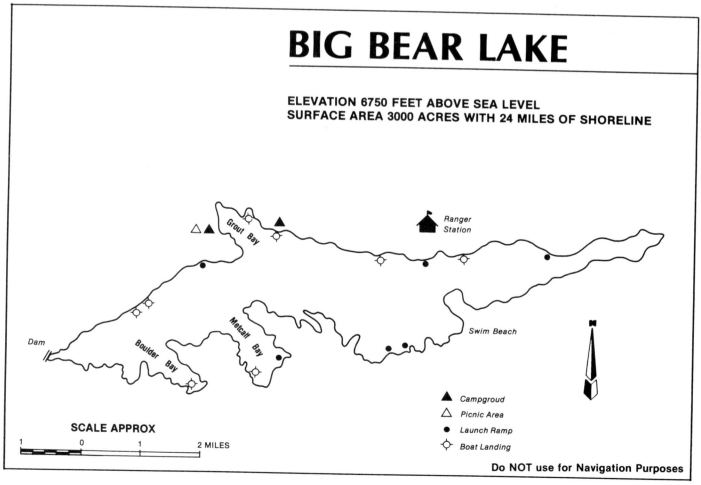

BIG BEAR LAKE

ELEVATION 6750 FEET ABOVE SEA LEVEL
SURFACE AREA 3000 ACRES WITH 24 MILES OF SHORELINE

Grout Bay
Ranger Station
Metcalf Bay
Dam
Boulder Bay
Swim Beach

▲ Campgroud
△ Picnic Area
● Launch Ramp
◇ Boat Landing

SCALE APPROX
1   0   1   2 MILES

Do NOT use for Navigation Purposes

Dick Rangel holding two typical Big Bear bass. This is not a lake where you will catch a world record, but for scenic beauty and lots of one-pound to three-pound bass, this is the place.

Rocky areas like this one near the dam can also hold good numbers of fish. A Texas rigged worm is preferable to split shotting because it will not hang up in the thick weed that flourishes.

Floating docks like this can produce fish. If you try them in the morning without success, they may be worth trying later in the afternoon.

BIG BEAR GUIDES

Jim Hall (714) 866-3466
Box 1539, Big Bear City, CA 92314
Hall is not a licensed guide, but he has been fishing the lake for 40 years — since he could barely hold a rod. He is currently a broker with Spencer Real Estate.

Dick Rangel (714) 585-2623
737 Silvertip, Box 6801, Big Bear Lake, CA 92315
Rangel has lived at Big Bear For the last 15 years, though he has been fishing on the lake for most of his life. He is not a licensed guide, but he has appeared in bass fishing videos filmed for Japanese television.

KEY TO BIG BEAR

Best Season: The spring bite doesn't get going until late March or early April. The fishing stays real good through June, with a hot top-water bite. It slacks off a bit in summer, but is definitely worth the trip until about October. In winter you can't get on the lake with a boat because of ice.

Lures To Use: Smaller lures early in the year, four-inch plastics, and white/chartreuse or chartreuse/blue spinnerbaits with a single, number five blade. Zara Spooks and number nine Rapalas for top-water. For summer use Cordell Spots and curled tail grubs. Jigs are good for flipping around docks, and deep water in fall.

Primary Structure: Flats east of Eagle Point in spawn. Breaks on migration routes leading to deep water sanctuaries, especially those below 20 feet the rest of the year.

Other: This is a clear water, high elevation lake. Go with line of four- to eight-pound test, and stay well away from the fish by using long casts.

BIG BEAR LAKE FACILITIES

Big Bear could be thought of as a full-service lake. For a lake of its size, Big Bear has a lot of campgrounds, marinas, launch ramps, hotels and tackle shops. Because there are so many businesses catering to fishermen, this is only a partial list.

Big Bear Chamber of Commerce, for information on facilities: 41647 Big Bear Blvd., Big Bear Lake, CA 92315, (714) 866-4607.

Big Bear Ranger District, for information on campgrounds: Box 290, Fawnskin, CA 92333, (714) 866-3437.

Central Reservation Service, for reservations in local hotels: P.O. Box 3050, Big Bear Lake, CA 92315, (714) 866-4601.

Pleasure Point Landing, 603 Land Lock Landing, Big Bear Lake, CA, (714) 866-2455.

Holloway's Marina and RV Park, Edgemoor Road/Metcalf Bay, Big Bear Lake, CA, (714) 866-5706.

Big Bear Marina, Corner of Paine and Lakeview, Big Bear Lake, CA, (714) 866-3218.

Boulder Marina, 39080 Big Bear Blvd., Boulder Bay, CA, (714) 866-7557.

Gray's Boat Landing, Fawnskin (northshore), (714) 866-2443.

Juniper Point Marina, 41380 Northshore Dr., Fawnskin, (714) 866-2433 or (714) 866-8555.

Lighthouse Trailer Resort/Marina (714) 866-9464.

BLACK BUTTE LAKE

Black Butte is never going to be famous. *Outdoor Life* is never going to suddenly declare Black Butte the best kept secret of the bass fishing circuit. This lack of publicity has less to do with the quality of bass fishing at the lake, than with its location, mid-way between Shasta, Oroville and Clear lakes. Black Butte is simply overshadowed by the larger better-known lakes. No matter how much press Black Butte gets, it will always be something of a privileged secret, fished mostly by locals and a few fishermen who value solitude as much as a wall- mount.

This is a great lake for top-water action, with a buzzbait bite that turns on in April and holds right through Indian summer until the end of November. With the exception of winter, it isn't much of a trick to land a limit of keeper bass in a few hours. Actually, it isn't uncommon to catch and release 20 bass in an evening of top-water fishing.

There is a good population of largemouth bass that average one to two pounds, with a few fish that get up to eight pounds. And there are also smallmouth that top five pounds. The bass may not reach record sizes, but there are enough decent fish to keep any fisherman busy.

Black Butte is not well known and fishing pressure is light. Through the summer spinnerbait and buzzbait fishing can be sensational.

This is a typical lowland reservoir. It is shallow, with the deepest water about 60 to 65 feet. The lake covers 4,500 surface acres with two main arms. All around the lake there are rolling hills, dotted with oak trees and grasslands. The backs of the arms are shallow and almost completely overgrown with willows and tules, while the main body of the lake is mostly flats covered with small broken rock.

The lake bottom is not much different than the surrounding hills, with lots of sloping flats, low-profile islands, and sandbars. In the two main arms there are almost no sharp breaks, with the exception of the main river channel in the Stoney Creek Arm. Back in these shallow arms bass structure is mostly rock piles, weed beds, and miles of channels that wind through the willows. Near the dam and Black Butte Campground, there are steeper banks and rock walls.

"Because of the type of lake this is, there are flats everywhere that hardly ever hold fish," said Hal Huggins. "You have to look for something more. There is good fishing around the marina, on the little points and stuff. And on the right side of the Stoney Creek Arm there is an old roadbed, this is a really superb spot, the fish really hold on that. And there are a lot of stumps, foundations and culverts right next to the old road that the bass seem to like."

The buzzbait bite is one of the best things going on the lake. The place to go for this action is in the Stoney Creek Arm, in the channels around the willows. In spring and fall bass will hit top-water all day. In summer, surface action occurs early morning and late evening, but it can produce on the shady side of points at midday. Always keep a buzzbait ready to go on this lake, no matter how hot the air temperature is.

In early spring, four-inch plastic worms are good. Jack Hendershot prefers to fish worms on a darthead hook, so he can swim them through the willows and around brush piles. "But, my old reliable in all seasons is a chartreuse spinnerbait," he added. "When nothing else works, go with the spinnerbait."

During the spawn, bass hold in three to ten feet of water. Concentrate on flats near deeper water access, in areas with brush. If the water level is rising, flats with newly submerged vegetation back in the arms of the river channels often hold spawning fish.

Wind is a big factor on this lake. Black Butte isn't a clear water lake to begin with, there is usually a green tinge to the water, but after a day or two of cool spring winds, it can turn real muddy. During windy periods fish the sheltered water around Eagle Pass, near the dam. The muddy water conditions clear up almost as fast as they come. Within a few days of calm weather, the lake will be back to normal.

By May or June, there is a good flipping bite where the small willows and older growth willows meet and form what amounts to a break. Huggins said, "It is best when the water level is rising and beginning to cover the smaller willows. Use a jig and pig on 20-pound line. Back in Stoney Creek is where you are going to find this combination of willows, and there is deeper water nearby. I've gone in there and flipped a fish off of every one of those small willows."

Hendershot fishes medium-running cranks during the hot summer months. Fish don't go deep in summer. They are still in less than 15 feet of water; use a crankbait that works well

BLACK BUTTE LAKE

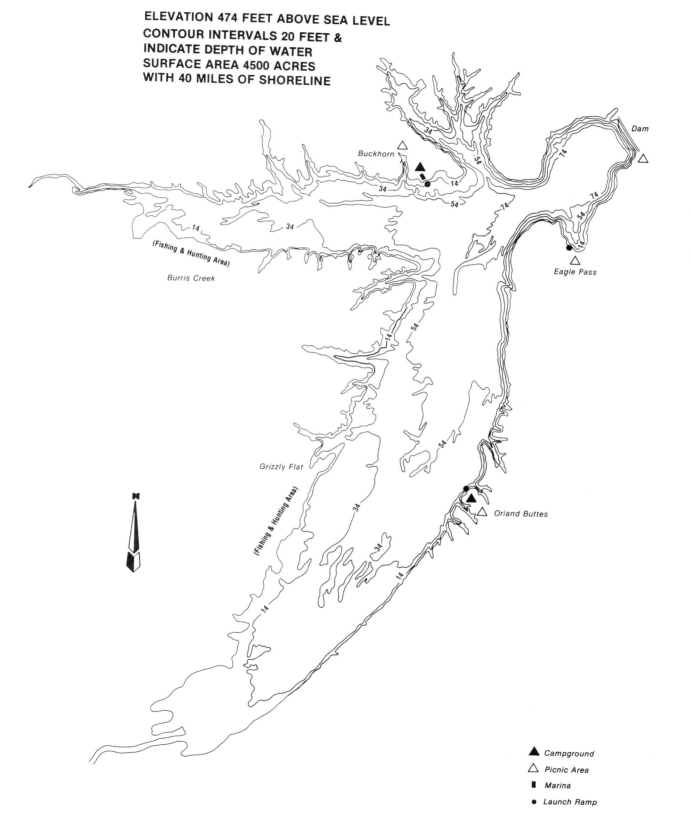

ELEVATION 474 FEET ABOVE SEA LEVEL
CONTOUR INTERVALS 20 FEET &
INDICATE DEPTH OF WATER
SURFACE AREA 4500 ACRES
WITH 40 MILES OF SHORELINE

Dam

Buckhorn

34

54

74

34

14

54

74

74

54

14

(Fishing & Hunting Area)

14

34

34

14

Eagle Pass

Burris Creek

54

14

54

Grizzly Flat

(Fishing & Hunting Area)

34

54

34

14

Orland Buttes

14

▲ Campground
△ Picnic Area
▮ Marina
● Launch Ramp

Black Butte is like two lakes in one. One end is all willows, the other is islands, rocks, and points. Often when one end of the lake is not producing the other is.

at 10 to 12 feet. Crawdad colors are the standard. At this time of year, bottom structure becomes more important, look for rocks, sandy bottom, and any type of drop-off. Work the crank so it bumps along the structure.

In the heat of the day, live bait can make the difference between catching fish and not catching fish in summer. "I use live bait a lot in the summer," Hendershot said. "Use large minnows, hooked through both lips, that way they stay alive longer. This is a relaxing way to fish when it's real hot. You have to look for shade. Fish on the shady side of the points and even down near the dam. Then later towards evening, fish Tiny Torpedoes on top-water. You'll get lots of fish and it's fun."

Fall is more or less a continuation of the summer pattern. Santa Ana winds keep the region around Black Butte fairly warm until late October or November. It sometimes helps to look for bass in slightly deeper water after a cold spell, but generally feeding fish will stay in less than 10 feet of water and hit surface lures or spinnerbaits.

"You'll see a lot of threadfin shad in fall," said Huggins. "They'll go up the two arms in large schools and just bust on the surface. Go into there with a Baby Spook, throw it in the school and shake it. Leave it in one place for a few seconds,

then twitch it, and the bass'll come and hammer it. You need a flat period for this pattern to turn on, but it can be great."

In winter, bass move to a depth of 20 to 40 feet. The only lures that work well are worms, spoons and jigs, on steep rocky points and over brush piles in deep water. A Rat-L-Trap can be good too, fished on the same spots. Use rattling lures by counting them down — let the lure sink till it hits the bottom, then rip it.

The weather makes winter fishing tough, it becomes windy and the lake turns muddy. Five-foot waves aren't uncommon. But, after a few warm, calm days in a row, look for bass feeding in shallow water, near the banks and willows.

There are two campgrounds on the lake, though only Buckhorn Campground is open in winter. Many of the campsites at Buckhorn are on the lake and boats can be tied off the bank alongside the camps. At Buckhorn there is a full-service marina and small grocery and tackle store. Both campgrounds have free launch ramps. Black Butte is popular with water-skiers in summer. At this time of year it can be crowded on the lake during the day. When school is in session there are few boats on the water, as a matter of fact, during the week in spring and fall there may not be any other boats on the water.

30

BLACK BUTTE GUIDES

Jack Hendershot (916) 534-6466
7415 Reservoir Rd., Oroville, CA 95966
Jack is a taxidermist and as such gets to see some of the nicest fish caught in central California. He has been fishing the local lakes, including Black Butte, since he was a kid.

Hal Huggins (916) 865-4020
Hal's Marine and Tackle Distributor
56 Huggins Dr., Orland, CA 95963
Hal has lived near and fished on Black Butte for 25 years. He has been in tournament fishing for 17 years, and is currently Tournament Director for WON Bass. He manufactures and distributes tackle throughout California. His sponsors are: Ranger, Yamaha, Berkley, MotorGuide and Humminbird.

While the lake is known to be best for largemouth, Hal Huggins holds up a pair of smallmouth. The lake holds a good population of smallmouth which very few take advantage of.

If the buzzbaits and spinnerbiats are not catching fish in the trees move to the other end of the lake and try split shotting on points and work parallel to rock walls and on breaks.

BLACK BUTTE FACILITIES

At Black Butte there are two campgrounds with launching facilities and a picnic area with a launch ramp, all are run by the U.S. Army Corps of Engineers. Some of the campsites are on the lake, so you can tie your boat up for the night by your camp. Camping fees are $8 per night; there is no launching fee. Reservations are not taken, first come, first serve is the way it works. For information call, (916) 865-4781. Hotels are available in Chico. There aren't many tourist services, except for a good pizza parlor and a Mexican restaurant over the freeway in Orland.

Black Butte Campground: Open year-round, 65 sites for tents and RVs, and a day use area. There is a full-service marina, with boat rentals, mooring slips, gas, bait and tackle, and supplies; the marina facility is open only from March 1 to October 1.

Orland Buttes Campground: Thirty-five sites for tents and RVs. This campground is open only from March 1 to September 30.

KEY TO BLACK BUTTE

Best Season: Spring and fall are the times to fish, at this time there are few fishermen or skiers, and the top-water bite is dynamite. The spring bite gets underway by March. The top-water action is hot by May, with fish biting all day long in spring and fall. In the heat of summer it may be more of an early and late bite. Winter fishing is good in shallows after a few calm days, but the lake is prone to heavy winds at this time of year.

Lures To Use: Four-inch plastics early in the year, and four- to six-inch plastics later in the year. Also buzzbaits and Baby Spooks.

Primary Structure: The backs of the arms with willows near creek channels. Look for the newly inundated willows, and the breaks where small willows are next to the older willows. Also, broken rock banks and offshore humps. There are lots of flats, so that doesn't mean much, look for a flat with some kind of distinguishing structure.

Other: A murky turbid lake most of the time, use line from 10 to 20 pounds depending on the type of structure fished. There are lots of skiers during the day in summer, but the lake is scarcely used in spring and fall.

One of the many structures found on Black Butte.

CACHUMA LAKE

Cachuma Lake has a mixed reputation among bass fishermen. Those who are not experienced on this lake may find the bass fishing tough. It is a different story with local fishermen, who consider Cachuma to be one of the better lakes in Southern California.

The Cachuma guides agree that this is not a typical Southern California bass lake and this may be at least part of the reason why many bass fishermen have a difficult time here. The guides also point out that Cachuma holds a healthy population of quality bass.

Five- and six-pound fish are caught frequently, and Cachuma holds a lot of three- to four-pound fish. This is one of the few lakes where fishermen stand a good chance of landing a fish that tops seven pounds. Northern largemouth were originally stocked in the late-50s, but Florida-strain were illegally introduced some time ago.

The Cachuma largemouth fishery has been on the decline in recent years, but it has the potential to recover when the water level rises. An experimental juvenile habitat program may significantly increase the survival rate of young bass, a factor that should increase total numbers of fish over the years. A severe drought and population growth in Santa Barbara have drawn Cachuma's water level down dangerously

Some of the best lures to use on Cachuma Lake.

low. At this time there is a possibility that the lake could go dry in 1991. That would obviously destroy the fishing in the short-term, however in the long run, when the lake fills, the fishery should recover strongly. All of the ingredients necessary for a great fishery are there, stable water is all that is lacking.

Though Cachuma is famous for its largemouth, the smallmouth fishery is the rising star. The reason is very few anglers target smallmouth. According to Jay Carter, "The smallmouth fishery at Cachuma is the best fishery in Southern California. I have the experience and know the techniques that work on this lake. When I guide, we have days with over 40 fish, and we easily catch limits on average, for each fisherman."

Cachuma is unusual for several reasons. First, these bass seem to prefer larger lures, compared to fish in other Southern California lakes. Though plastic worms and light line have their place, the guides agreed that Cachuma is a big lure lake. Crankbaits, spinnerbaits and jigs are favored over small plastics. Phil Whittemore may flip plastics into holes in the weeds and vegetation, but this is partly because it is one of the few ways to reach fish that are holding in heavy cover. Plastics are not his first choice on Cachuma.

Also, at Cachuma the large fish do not migrate from very shallow to very deep water in normal years. The bass hold at a constant depth, of about eight to fifteen feet. Finally, there is a lot of structure and a great variety of structure types including: submerged trees, aquatic vegetation, creek channels, bays, ledges, and submerged islands. This can make it difficult to determine exactly which areas hold bass, because most of the shoreline looks like good bass habitat. "But, at Cachuma, just because a spot looks good at first glance, doesn't mean it holds fish," Whittemore said. "A lot of those areas are marginal for bass. There is more structure in the lake than largemouth, fish will be found only on the primary spots."

There is no single pattern for fishing Cachuma. Each of the guides interviewed had their own method for finding and catching fish. However, all were in agreement that the eastern end of the lake holds the greatest concentration of fish. The Narrows, Cachuma Bay, Jack Rabbit Flats, Arrowhead Island, and Bobcat are reliable largemouth spots. But, as in most lakes that receive heavy fishing pressure, the less obvious, off-shore structure can produce the greatest chance of a large fish.

The west end of the lake near the dam is the place to look for trophy smallmouth, but there are fewer fish overall. The water is generally clearer, requiring longer casts, and it takes more skill to find and catch fish in this half of the lake.

No matter what the season, look for fish in eight to fifteen feet of water. In general, bass move shallower on windy or overcast days, or when the water is off-color. The only exception to fishing at this depth is during a long, cold winter, a rare occurrence at Cachuma, when the fish may go deeper. At that time fish jigs and spoons near broken rock or on vertical walls, working the lure from 10 to 50 feet, because on steep walls fish can be dispersed vertically from shallow to deep water.

Though there is relatively little seasonal variation at Cachuma, windy or rainy days will turn the lake on. About a

LAKE CACHUMA

ELEVATION 750 FEET ABOVE SEA LEVEL
CONTOUR INTERVAL INDICATES DEPTH OF WATER
SURFACE AREA 3200 ACRES

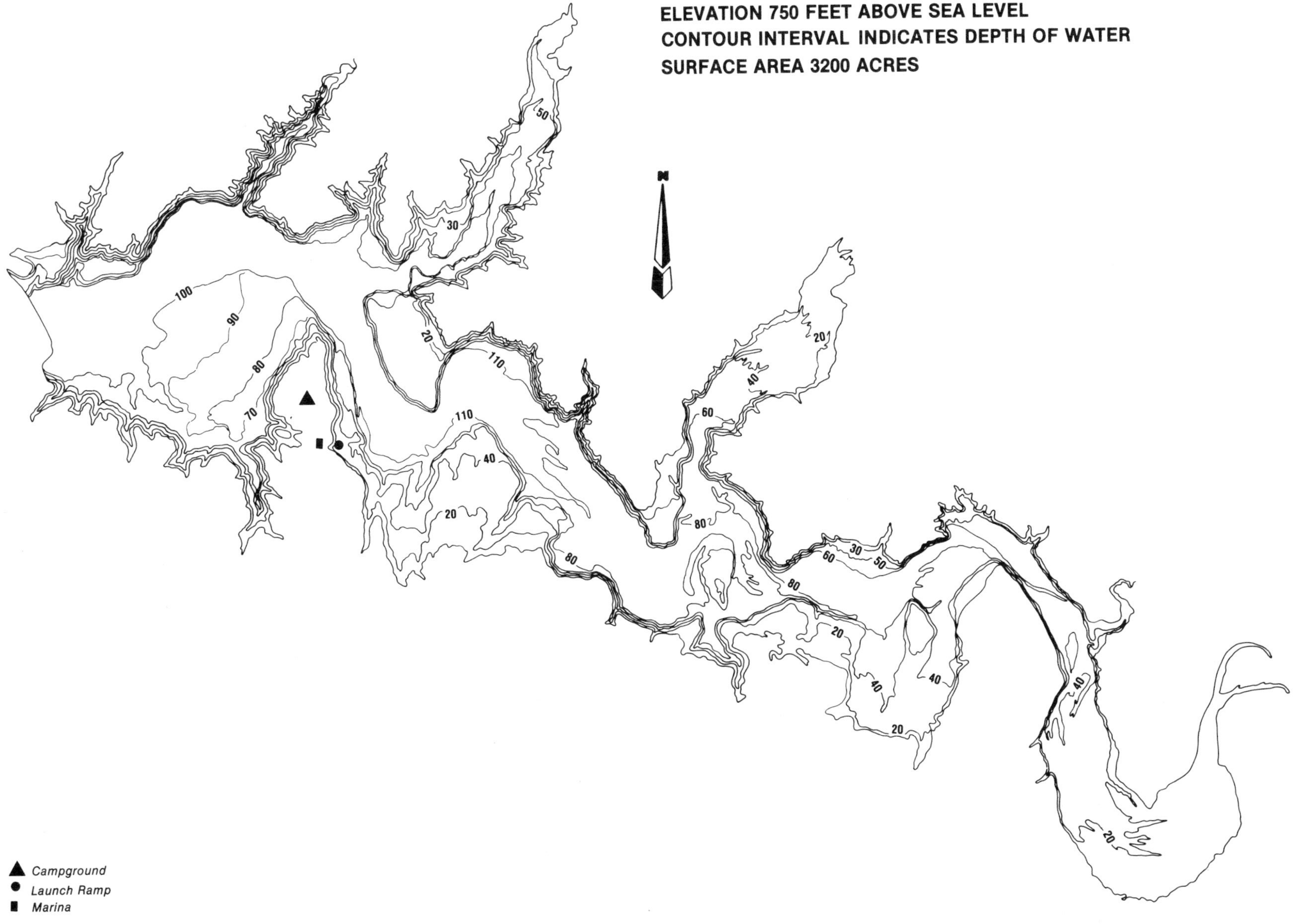

▲ Campground
● Launch Ramp
■ Marina

Phil Whittemore, nationally known fishing pro, holds up two quality Cachuma bass.

half an hour after the wind begins to blow hard, fish along walls or points where the water breaks onto the shore. "The wave action on the shore aerates the water and knocks nutrients into the lake, and that causes plankton production," said Whittemore. "That draws baitfish to the area and the baitfish will attract the bass."

As far as other specific signs of bass, the guides have several suggestions. At Cachuma, the walls and points covered with baseball-sized rocks are likely to hold largemouth. Look for fish on submerged trees, in vegetation, and over ledges, providing that the other factors, such as appropriate depth, oxygenated water, and deep water nearby, are all present. There must be deep water nearby even though these bass hold in relatively shallow water; they won't stay shallow if there isn't water of greater than 20 feet to escape to. Fish in the off-color water, where the bass may be shallower and are less skittish.

Whittemore uses a standard pattern on Cachuma, starting the day with top-water and working gradually deeper, if he has to, in order to catch fish. In the early morning he throws a top-water lure, usually a shad imitation. Later in the day he switches to a crankbait or spinnerbait; he likes white in clear water, and chartreuse in dirty water. He works these lures over flats with a steep drop-off, along the southeast side of the lake, and in spring he uses the spinnerbait on the east side of the Narrows. "If I still don't get bit," Whittemore said, "it is time to go to a deep-water finesse bait, like a jig or worm. Then I'll work it at the depth where I find baitfish, or very slow and close to structure."

Dennis Wright changes his lures with the season, but he still concentrates on fishing offshore structure, like rows of submerged trees that are parallel to the shoreline, points, and breaks in walls covered with baseball-sized rock. In January and February he may concentrate on the chalk bluffs on the northwest side of the lake and fish as deep as 20 feet with a brown or brown/purple jig and pig. In spring, the water is usually rising and off-color, so he favors the chartreuse spinnerbaits worked over prime spawning flats at two to ten feet. In fall, he uses a medium-size crawdad crank. Summer is the toughest time of year as far as Dennis is concerned, but he cautions against moving to very deep water. "More fish may be deep, but the big ones will still come shallow in morning and evening to feed. In summer I use a variety of lures until I find something that works, fishing along weed lines and points."

"But, if you want to have a great time catching a lot of fish," Jay Carter said, "use live crawdads and go for smallmouth. You don't need a lot of fancy equipment for it, any $12 rod and reel will do. And, once you get the hang of it, you can catch a limit in a matter of hours." The crawdads should be less than 1 1/4 inch long. Carter prefers to fish without any added weight, but if the bait won't reach the bottom, he uses a split shot. The crawdads are fished on a No. 12 or 14 Mustad live bait hook, with two-pound line. "Fish may break off," he said, "but getting bit is no problem, the two-pound line is the only way to make it a challenge."

He usually works the crawdad slowly uphill or along a ledge. If the fish are hitting the bait as it falls, let it lie on the bottom, when the bass are in this mood they probably won't take a bait that is moving. If there is a good wind, Jay anchors the boat with a long line so that the wind swings the boat back and forth along the ledge. The movement of the boat drags the bait along with it. Carter also catches smallmouth on fairly large jigs that resemble crawdads, but he has never caught a smallmouth on a crawdad/jig combination.

"To find smallmouth," Carter said, "look for a hard-bottom with broken rocks, especially over humps, breaks, or creek channels. I use my flasher, and look for a double reading that indicates a hard rock bottom." The depth to concentrate on all year-round is 15 feet, near a drop that goes to 50 or 60 feet. "At Cachuma, if you don't get a bite in 20 minutes, move," Carter added, "and you don't have to motor all over, the best spot on the lake is about 500 yards south of the marina, at the Indian Burial Site."

March is big fish month at Cachuma, prior to the start of the spring spawn. Most of the lake records have been caught in March. November and December can also be good times to catch large fish, and the fishing stays good until the water gets cold in January. The current lake record for largemouth is over 16.7 pounds, taken on a salt and pepper grub, March 1988.

"Wear polaroids and bring a graph if you can, for finding off-shore structure like the creek channel near jack rabbit flats," Wright said. "Bring plenty of your favorite lures, because there is so much structure you are bound to loose some of them. This is a beautiful lake, not just for fishing, but simply to be on. You will see lots of deer coming down to the water, and even bald eagles. And be ready for big fish, I have caught nine and ten pounders out of this lake."

CACHUMA GUIDES

Jay Carter
Carter is a licensed guide who specializes in smallmouth fishing trips. He has won many major tournaments all over California, and has lived and fished in the area since these lakes were built.

Phil Whittemore
Phil was a licensed guide and professional tournament fisherman in the Santa Barbara area for many years. He recently pulled up anchor and headed to Texas, to be closer to the larger professional tournament circuits.

Dennis Wright (805) 967-5101
Dennis is a licensed guide who specializes in fishing on Cachuma. For many years he was the captain of the salt water charter fishing boat, *Condor*, out of Santa Barbara Harbor. He has lived and fished in Santa Barbara his entire life.

KEY TO CACHUMA

Best Season: Fairly consistent year-round due to a mild climate. Probably a little better in spring. Good during rain.

Lures To Use: Larger lures are favored over small plastics popular on other lakes. White, double-bladed spinnerbaits in clear water, chartreuse in murky water. Medium to full-size crankbaits in crawdad or shad colors, as well a stickbaits and top-water plugs. Large jigs are good for bottom fishing. Carter likes to use live crawdads with little or no weight.

Primary Structure: Points and breaks covered with baseball- sized rocks. Stay in the east end of the lake for largemouth, and look for breaks and structure in eight to twenty feet of water, year-round. For smallmouth, head for the west end of the lake and fish points with broken rock over hard bottom.

Other: A clear water lake, use lines of eight to twelve pounds. The heavier lines should only be used with large jig and pig, or big blades.

CACHUMA FACILITIES

Cachuma Lake Park: This is a county park, with complete boating and camping facilities. There is a launch ramp, marina, boat rentals, bait and tackle shop, snack bar, store with groceries/camping supplies, and showers. Swimming in the lake is prohibited, actually, touching the water is prohibited. There are 82 full-hookup sites and 25 partial hookups for RVs. The price for these spots is $15 per night. There are 500 tent campsites, at $11 per night. Day use fee is $3 per vehicle and launching is also $3. Reservations are not accepted. Call (805) 688-4658 for information.

Other: There are complete services, such as motels, restaurants, and tackle shops in Santa Barbara, 30 minutes away.

This lake is becoming better known for smallmouth. Rocky banks with baseball sized rock are a good place to target when aiming for smallmouth bass.

CAMANCHE LAKE

Camanche was once one of the finest bass lakes in Central California. The lake was known for producing lots of largemouth bass in the eight- to ten-pound range. In recent years, the fishing at Camanche has fallen off a bit. Fishermen still catch plenty of four- to five-pound bass in spring and fall, but the big northerns are increasingly rare. Camanche now holds smallmouth and spotted bass as well, and threadfin shad were introduced at the same time as the spotties.

The decrease in numbers of quality largemouth may simply be due to the three year drought, which brought the lake down to about one-tenth of its normal surface area. If this is the case the lake should rebound when the water level rises. However, a variety of other factors may be influencing the bass population, for instance competition with other strains of bass may be having a negative impact on the northern-strain largemouth. Or fishing pressure may be taking its toll. Nonetheless, even if this is no longer the "best lake in the whole country," as G.B. Riechter claimed it was when he moved here from Florida in the early seventies, it is still one of the better bass lakes in California.

All standard lure patterns work on this lake. Large jigs are popular for big fish.

Camanche is located in the motherlode region of the Sierra foothills, east of Stockton. It is a large, shallow impoundment of 7,700 surface acres, with a maximum depth of about 120 feet. There are full service resorts on both the north and south shores of the lake.

"The key to finding largemouth on Camanche, is finding their migration routes," said Chris Cantwell. "Then look for a long slow grade on a point that leads to deep water. Bass will be near areas like this all year. They move along the migration routes as the seasons change. Then you need to find the structure they prefer, that can change day to day. In warm weather they generally like rocky structure, especially in late summer and fall, because the water there is cooler and holds more oxygen. In winter and spring they like the grassy structure better. From that point it is a matter of experimentation."

Spring is the prime time for fishing on Camanche. Two-to three-pound bass are caught consistently. On good days it is no trick to catch and release three limits of quality fish. In a normal year, fish move into the shallows after the middle of February. Concentrate on water from five to eight feet deep.

"In a drought, cottonwoods grow in the coves and on the islands," said Troy Brawley. "These are great when the water is rising and really good for the spawn. The fish will be back in there." There isn't a lot of vegetation and wood in lake Camanche, with the exception of newly submerged grasses and willow trees in rising water. Because there is so little of this type of structure, it is a virtual magnet to shallow water bass.

In early spring bass hit top-water lures, jigs, worms, and grubs, equally well. Riechter likes to use floating surface plugs, like Poe's and Bagley's that are about five inches long. For the jigs, go with a full-size lure, like the Brawley Bug. (The Brawley Bug was invented by Troy's brother, Wayne.) Small worms and grubs seem to be the best all around baits during a slow bite. With all of the shallow sloping flats and grassbeds, the lake looks like it would be perfect for spinnerbaits, but they don't seem to produce as well as other lures.

Camanche is not a clear-water lake. Riechter and Cantwell both use lines of about eight to twelve pounds, while Brawley prefers to go with lighter line weights of six-pound test on finesse lures. Riechter said, "You can go with light line on this lake, because there isn't a lot of stuff for the bass to get hung up in. I landed a 10-pound, 5-ounce bass on 10-pound line, and my wife landed a 9-pound, 8-ounce bass on 8-pound line; you can only do that if it is mostly open water."

By summer, fishing gets a little tougher. There is still a good top-water bite early in the morning and late in the day. Use surface lures over shallows and on points or ledges where the water is less than 15 feet deep. Concentrate on shallow areas near deeper water.

There are breaks all over Camanche, even far from the shoreline. What were once rolling hills now form underwater islands with vertical and steep structure. There are dozens of creek channels, old building foundations, and roadbeds in the lake that provide good deep-water structure for bass.

"The fish will waive a little comfort as far as temperature

CAMANCHE LAKE

**ELEVATION 236 FEET ABOVE SEA LEVEL
CONTOUR INTERVALS INDICATE DEPTH OF WATER
SURFACE AREA 7700 ACRES WITH 53 MILES OF SHORELINE**

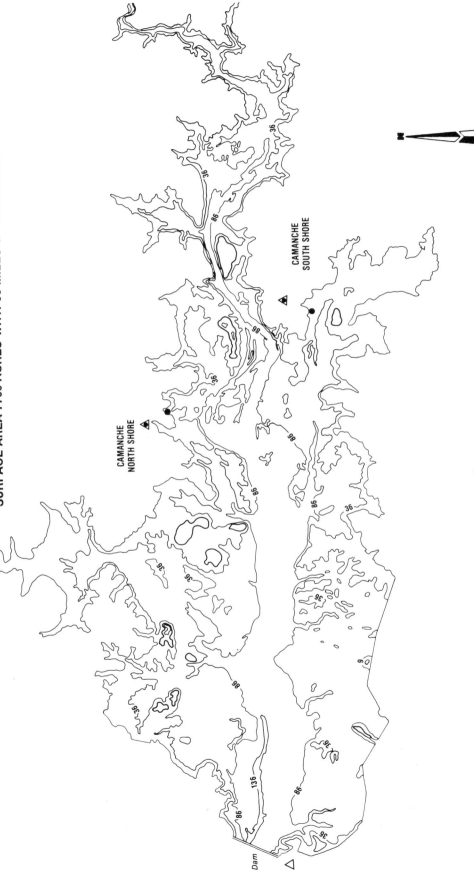

CAMANCHE NORTH SHORE

CAMANCHE SOUTH SHORE

Dam

▲ Resort

● Launch Ramp

Do NOT use for Navigation Purposes

Fish submerged trees and brush.

goes, for a good break," said Troy Brawley. "They'll go up and down in summer. I don't believe in a morning bite, I have caught more fish overall between 9:00 a.m. and 2:30 p.m. Go fishing when you want to go. But, you have to get deeper in the heat of the day. Look for offshore breaks, you want nice steep points. There are good breaks and cover in the creek channels and around old roadbeds."

Brawley adds that the bass slow down in summer. It is important to work baits as slowly as possible, right on the bottom. He is a firm believer in slow tactics for inactive fish. Bass will pick a lure that is hardly moving up off the bottom. There isn't any reason to move a lure fast when the bite is slow. And don't be afraid to fish below 35 feet when it is tough.

"I go back up the river during the hot summer months," said Riechter. "Up in the river the water is cooler. There are all kinds of drop-offs, because they used to mine (for gold and copper) up there and that left dredger tailings. These spots are real good for both smallmouth and largemouth. Fish up in the river at depths of 20 to 25 feet. Go slow with finesse baits, like jigs and small worms."

October to Christmas offers very good fall fishing. The fish orient off rocky points in less than 15 feet of water. The top-

water bite can last all day, with jigs and worms as a back-up. Brawley said, "there is a two to six week period when it is just like spring. The fish are shallow and everything works."

"I basically fish one lure, at one depth," said Cantwell. "It's a purple Brawley Bass Bug, a big jig, worked from the bank to 10 feet deep. This is the only lure I fish. It does not imitate any bait, it is just huge and it intimidates the bass. When you stick it in their face, they either attack it or pick it up and try to move it out of the way. They do spit it out, and of course, most guys usually only feel it being spit out. Work this lure real slow, it flares on its own. Sometimes the bass really attack it, a five-pound fish can practically knock the rod out of your hands."

Cantwell adds that he doesn't fish much in summer when it is hard to find shallow fish. But, he also goes along with the theory that there are always at least a few shallow fish that come up to feed. And when they are feeding on the flats, his is there, waiting for a bite.

The winter fishing season is short on this low elevation lake, lasting only from January to February. In winter, the bite is slow after the surface action of fall, but the solitude on the lake makes up for it. "The fish bite good in winter," said Cantwell, "you just have to use deep water methods. Fish slow on submerged islands in 25 feet of water. It all comes down to touch and sensitivity."

"The fish don't go as deep in winter on this lake as on some others," Brawley added. "They don't just keep on moving down deeper like they do in summer. They will hold pretty much at 25 feet. You'll get the good solid fish on plastic jigs, by fishing the vertical shoreline and going slow, slow, slow. Get the motor set and run along the breaks at depth without even moving your jigs. I've caught real big fish that way."

"In your first week on this lake it might be tough," said Cantwell, "but once you learn it, it's consistent. A good bass fisherman can catch fish 364 days a year on this lake. You need to have at least one day out of the year without fish, so your ego doesn't get too bad."

Points and brush are good areas to start fishing.

The main structure on the lake is rock, old foundations, and road beds. This lake used to be one of the best in the country but has declined in recent years.

CAMANCHE GUIDES

Troy Brawley
Troy is known as the "grandfather of Northern California jig and structure fishing." He has a long history of guiding, tournament fishing, and appearing on television in bass fishing shows. He no longer guides, but can be reached at South Shore Marina where he works part time.

Chris Cantwell (209) 763-5166
Chris has lived at Camanche for 11 years, and fished the lake for 16 years. He runs the marina facility at North Shore on Camanche.

G.B. (Rick) Riechter (209) 763-5370
P.O. Box 297, Ione, CA 95640
Rick has fished Camanche regularly since he moved here in 1970. He only guides for his wife. He puts her on the points and she catches the big fish.

CAMANCHE LAKE FACILITIES

North Shore Camanche, is currently being renovated. There are 215 numbered campsites planned, none of them will have hook-ups. There will be hot showers, a launch ramp, boat rentals, gas, slips, coffee shop, and a marina tackle and sundries store. Camping fee is $10 per night. Day use $4. Launch fee $5. (209) 763-5121.

South Shore Camanche, has over 500 tent campsites, plus 120 full hookups. There are three launch ramps, a general store, bait and tackle, and gas. The day use fee is $4. Launch fee is $5. Camping in tent sites $10, for hookups $14. Reservations are taken on the RV sites only. (209) 763-5178.

KEY TO CAMANCHE

Best Season: By March the spring bite turns on and will stay good through late May. Summer is the toughest time, except for very early and late in the day on top-water. October to Christmas is very good, with fish coming shallow again. Winter lasts only from January to February, and the bass don't go deeper than about 25 feet.

Lures To Use: Brawley Bass Bugs, a large plastic jig. Poe's and Bagley's surface lures, as well as shallow crankbaits. Four- to six-inch worms and grubs are the old reliables. This looks like a good spinnerbait lake, but it isn't.

Primary Structure: The lake bottom is like the surrounding countryside, all rolling hills. This means lots of flats and long sloping points. Look for the migration routes leading from deep to shallow water. There are plenty of old roadbeds, creek channels and building foundations around the lake. Early in the year, try newly inundated vegetation and wood. When it is hot weather, head for rock and gravel.

Other: Fish slow on this lake. Slow down, then slow down more even more.

39

CASITAS LAKE

When Raymond Easley caught a 21-pound, 3-ounce largemouth at Casitas Lake, it made news. The lake near Ojai became famous among bass fishermen, almost overnight. The whopper was the second largest largemouth bass ever recognized for a fishing record. The current world record bass was caught prior to World War II, so that makes the Casitas bass the largest caught in recent history.

It may come as something of a surprise that a lake which can turn out world record size bass, covers only 2,700 surface acres. But, in many ways Casitas has the ideal bass environment.

The lake has over 32 miles of shoreline, with loads of points, tiny coves, and bays. In spring, terrestrial grasses are covered by rising water, and in summer extensive aquatic grass and weed beds grow in the bays and coves. The lake is absolutely loaded with crawdads, which provide an excellent forage base. The mild coastal climate keeps the lake from becoming too hot or cold, allowing Casitas bass to grow throughout the year.

Other factors may be of even more importance. The water level at Casitas fluctuates, but not as drastically as many

Top water baits work well in the summer, the rest of the time soft plastics are the most reliable fish catchers.

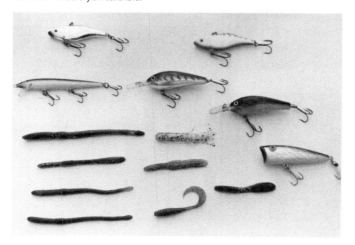

other California bass lakes; the stability may increase the survival of the spawn. In addition, there are extensive areas that are closed to fishing. Bass could live their entire lives in these closed bays without ever coming within range of a fisherman's hook. When one of those big guys finally does come into fishable water, there is real potential for a world record.

Casitas is a classic feast or famine lake. When the bite is on, limits can be landed in a matter of hours. On the other hand, the lake can shut down cold as stone. This is one of the best winter fisheries on the South Coast, but limits can be taken almost any time of year. On the other hand, even the pros have blank days at Casitas.

"It can be excellent one day, and shut down the next. You might go a whole weekend without getting bit. The next week, you'll get bit on the exact same pattern and catch limits," Glover said, "but if you can hit the lake during a spring rain, it's awesome."

Around February or March, the bass move into a pre-spawn pattern. There are a couple of different approaches to fishing the pre-spawn at Casitas. Don Iovino doodles in deeper water through early spring. He said, "The fish will be deep early in the season, on any outside major point with rock, between 30 and 50 feet. In spring, I use a 4 1/2-paddle tail worm, in crawdad or black color. I always use six-pound line on Casitas."

Brakebill said, "When the water temperature is in the mid-50s, say 53 to 57 degrees, stay with the main and secondary points only. As the water temperature gets up around 63 degrees, start moving back a little farther in the coves. In that colder water, I'll work at about 15 feet; by the time it gets warm, look for fish in two to three feet of water. Shake that worm hard, to make it quiver."

All of the guides agree that a depth finder can be very important at this time of year. A depth finder will provide the best indication of the points and secondary structure, it is also crucial for locating fish. Actually, whenever the bass are not feeding in the shallows at Casitas, a good graph could mean the difference between fish in the boat and a blank day.

Later in the year, when the water temperature is between 63 and 67 degrees, number 7 Fat Raps and Rat-L-Traps begin to produce. This pattern is best after the grass has started to come up, and bass move into the shallows chasing shad. Colors like Tennessee bleedin' shad, and bright chrome with a blue back, are good all day — use chartreuse later in the day.

Brakebill adds, "The fish may not hit worms very well after the shad have come into shallow water. But, they'll hit a fast moving crank. They'll blaze it. They'll practically rip the rod out of your hand."

From about May until late fall, Ron Glover uses a top-water pattern at Casitas. "I love a surface bite, there is nothing more exciting," Glover said. "Fish it in the heat, when it is 95 degrees, it doesn't matter. "If the fish are there, they'll hit anything, cause they're hungry. I might not catch as many with top-water, but the fish are all quality fish. In general you'll catch bigger bass on top-water.

"The moss beds at Casitas hold fish inside of them," Glover added. "Bass come right up through the moss. Just because you can't see any fish doesn't mean they aren't

LAKE CASITAS

ELEVATION 567 ABOVE SEA LEVEL
CONTOUR INTERVALS 50 FEET, AND INDICATE DEPTH OF WATER

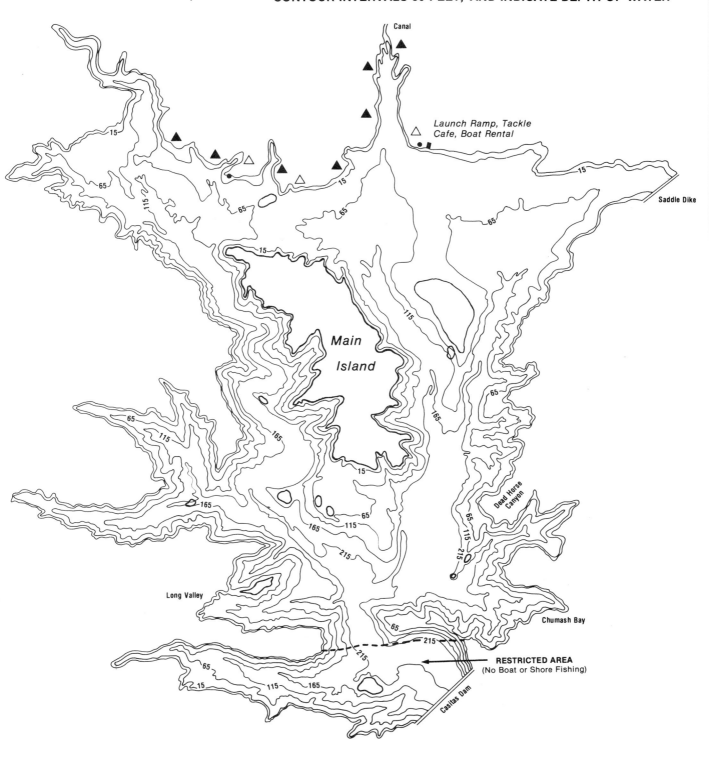

▲ *Campground*
△ *Picnic Area*
● *Launch Ramp*

Do NOT use for Navigation Purposes

there. In summer, the fish seem to orient over points and structure. I'll use top-water where the bottom is as deep as 60 feet. The fish will just come up if the water is clear enough.''

Glover feels that Zara Spooks get the largest fish. To work a Zara, fishermen should extend the index finger of the hand they hold the rod with, along the rod butt. The idea is that the rod tip should move back and forth from left to right, through an arc a foot or so wide, so that the Spook is turned from right to left. Use the extended finger as a lever that moves the rod tip back and forth. When retrieving the lure, pause between turns on the reel handle and press on the rod, the tip will move to one side, when pressure is released the tip bounces back. It takes a little practice to get the timing down, however this method is less tiring than flexing the wrist.

Iovino also likes top-water on Casitas in summer. Pop-Rs are good, along with Spooks, buzzbaits and Rattling Rogues. If top-water isn't productive, split-shot a straight-tail worm or a small grub. He points out that on a worm bite fish are caught out of the grass beds all day long. This pattern can produce one fish after another.

Because of warm Santa Ana winds, September and October are not properly considered fall, it is better to describe this period as an extension of summer. The fishing gets tougher. Stick with the same patterns as summer, until the water begins to cool. Through fall, look for fish in the shallows first, then move out to deeper water to doodle if

shallow patterns don't bring in fish. This slow, early fall season lasts for two or three months.

By late fall, the fish migrate back to the points, to depths of 30 to 50 feet, this occurs by mid-November. Iovino said, "This is a great time to fish at Casitas, right through to March. In the dead of winter, any warm weather storm can turn the lake on. The biggest stringers ever caught here, were caught during storms.''

For fall/winter, the guides go back to using split shot and doodling techniques. "Fish are coming back to the outside points,'' Brakebill said. "Fish the breaks. The old roadbed runs next to a 'nothing bank' that drops from five down to fifty feet. The fish will move along that roadbed in fall. There is also a long ledge off Deer Slope. These are the types of structure to look for at this time of year, a long point or break leading from shallow to deep water.''

A graph is essential in winter. If it is a cold year, bass may be deeper than 50 feet. However, often winters are very mild, and bass may be holding at depths closer to 20 feet. This is where the graph comes in. Slow finesse lures are most productive 90 percent of the time in winter, either a small jig or straight tail worms. Because these techniques aren't good for covering a lot of water quickly, stick with concentrating on areas where bass show up on a graph.

At this time of year, bass may suspend, then the best technique is doodle sliding with worms. "Shake it as it falls,'' Iovino said. The most consistent pattern in winter, is to find

Fish the points

rock and steep walls where fish can move from deep to shallow water, without covering a lot of distance.

Casitas is a clear water lake, this is why lines of less than six pounds are the rule. Heavier lines may be used, but only for top-water. Casitas fish prefer clear water, and even if there are mud lines along the banks, the bass don't often associate with colored water. These bass are far more likely to hold near rock or grassbeds in clear water, than hang beneath a mud line.

The entire East Bank is considered a prime area during the spring and summer, and perhaps it is the best place to start at any time of year. There are also a number of off-shore submerged islands, that can hold lunkers. However, as fishermen who have been on Casitas in the past know, almost every mile of shoreline holds a few fishable areas. There are literally dozens of spots that could hold bass.

Mike Brakebill with a Casitas largemouth bass.

Fishermen at dawn on a point.

CASITAS GUIDES

Mike Brakebill (805) 525-2315
165 Salas St., Santa Paula, CA 93060
Brakebill is a licensed guide. He has fished on Casitas since he was 10, and at age 13, Mike had fished in, and won, his first tournament. His dad, Bob, gets the credit for bringing him into the sport. Brakebill is sponsored by: Cajun Boats, Evinrude, Lowrance, Hooker Worms, California Worms, and Limit Worms.

Ron Glover (818) 349-1757
Glover was Angler of the Year 1988, for the Southern Division River Circuit, in west coast. He has fished tournaments for 11 years. He enjoys teaching people how to fish and has been a licensed guide for the past three years. He is sponsored by: North Hollywood Marine, D.K. Spinners, B.C. Tackle, and C and L Tackle.

Don Iovino (818) 848-6180
Don Iovino Products
3220 Wyoming St., Burbank, CA 91505
Don was World Champ for U.S. Bass in 1984. In 1985 he was Angler of the Year. Don invented the doodling system for deep, clear water worm fishing. He markets doodling equipment, and has created a video to explain the finer details of how to use the technique.

CASITAS FACILITIES

Casitas Recreation Area, is a full-service fishing, picnic and camping park. There are 450 regular campsites and 300 additional sites in an overflow area. The fee is $9 per vehicle, per night, $3.50 per boat. Day use is $3 per day, per vehicle. The park offers a complete bait and tackle shop, gas, boat rental, snack bar, and a grocery/camping supply store. The lake is open every day of the year, but the gates are shut for two hours prior to sunrise. Reservations are not accepted, but fishermen can call (805) 649-2233, for information. The bait shop number is (805) 649-2043.

Other: The town of Ojai, nearby, has restaurants, shops, and motels.

KEY TO CASITAS

Best Season: March through May, though the fishing is also good from December through September. In winter, until February or March, fish the water below 50 feet by doodling. In spring, go for the shallows, bass can be caught on almost any lure. In summer, fish top-water over the grass beds.

Lures To Use: Four- to six- inch straight-tail and paddle-tail worms, in blue, shad and crawdad colors. Shad colored crankbaits, Zara Spooks, buzzbaits, Rattling Rogues and Pop-Rs over the grass and moss beds when fish are less than 20 feet down.

Primary Structure: Points, roadbeds, offshore islands, and bays with vegetation. When fish are in water less than 20 feet deep, the vegetation is the best bet. During the spring and fall migrations, look for the points and cuts on migration routes. When the bass are deep, take advantage of the roadbeds, offshore islands, and main-lake points.

Other: The lake record on Casitas went to a bass that weighed 21 pounds, 3 ounces, the second largest bass ever officially recognized for an angling record. The fish was caught by Raymond Easely.

CASTAIC LAKE

Castaic is known as a big fish lake, with good reason. When it comes to 16- and 17-pound bass, Castaic is one of the top producers in the country. A bass over 20 pounds was caught in 1990. For a real trophy largemouth, this up and coming lake is a contender. As Don Iovino said, "There could be a world record in that lake."

But, don't go and get the heavy duty bass tackle off the garage shelf. The old story about big baits for big fish simply doesn't hold true on Castaic. The standard lure is a split-shot four- to six-inch worm. Small worms, grubs, and tiny jigs account for most of the big fish caught from the lake. Gary Harrison calls it, "a mini-bait lake." Finesse fishing is the only way to go.

That means fishermen can forget about dragging trophy fish in on 25-pound line. The absolute maximum line weight that any of the regular guides on the lake use is 12 pounds. Most of the time they suggest using lines of six- to eight-pound test. Not only is there a possibility of hooking up with a monster bass that tops 15 pounds, fishermen are also going to land those bass on eight- pound line.

Castaic Lake is located near Six Flags Magic Mountain, 3 1/2 miles north of the junction of Interstate 5 and Highway

Shad imitation lures and light line are the ticket on this lake.

126. The lake covers about 2,500 surface acres. For structure, Castaic has little variety, just miles of red mud banks with lots of points and ledges, all of it covered with broken rocks and shale. There is almost no wood, though willows have been planted near the flats in recent years. In summer, there are grass beds in the shallows. That is not a great variety of structure by the classic definition of a trophy bass lake, yet Castaic turns out good fish.

The lake is divided into two distinct arms, the Ski Arm to the west, and the Fishing Arm to the east. "Fish the Ski Arm in summer," said Iovino, "and the fishing arm in winter. The water temperature varies in the two arms, those are the times when each arm is most favorable to bass. And always fish the hard bottom with broken rock."

"Water clarity is important," said Jack O'Mally. "Often these bass seem to show a preference for the dirty water. I should really call it stained, like strong tea. They thrive on that in Castaic."

In spring, the fish will hold relatively deep, in about 30 to 35 feet of water. The spawn takes place later on Castaic than on other lakes in the area. Iovino says that the fish don't spawn at Castaic until June or July, and he has seen them spawning as late as August. "You'll catch big fish in early spring on Castaic," Iovino said, "but they will be in pre-spawn at 35 or 40 feet."

Look for pre-spawn fish on long ledges and near steep drop-offs that lead to deep water. The active fish are in the more sheltered areas, where the water is cleaner and warmer. "And particularly around newly submerged vegetation," said O'Mally, "the bass will hold real tight around this stuff."

Both O'Mally and Iovino, say that split-shot plastic worms are their first choice on Castaic. Iovino recommends straight-tail worms, four inches for winter and spring fishing, and six inches for summer and early fall. Small crankbaits of less than three inches, thrown parallel to the banks along ledges, or perpendicular to points also catch fish, but nine days out of ten, small plastic worms catch the greatest number of fish.

Shad colors seem to work best on Castaic, since shad is the primary bass forage in the lake. The best colors for almost every type of lure are: silver, blue, gray, and smoke. Cinnamon-blue, pearl, and blue thunder have also always been good colors on this lake.

Harrison prefers to fish with a small jig, rather than split-shotting worms. He uses a jig that was originally designed for smallmouth bass, called the Skinny Bear. This jig has a very thin-wire hook, and a short skirt that "quivers" as it bounces over the rocks. He believes the thin-wire hook penetrates the mouth of fish more easily and when he is fishing with 30 to 50 feet of line in the water, that makes a big difference.

Bottom lures on Castaic must be worked at a snail-slow pace. Harrison lets his jig sit on the bottom, without retrieving at all, and then he drifts with the wind or uses his trolling motor to cover water. This tactic can be more effective when the fish want a slow moving lure, than constantly retrieving and casting. Harrison calls it, do-nothing fishing. "I move the lure very, very slowly," he says.

In the summer, bass may hold in deep or shallow water. To cope with this, be prepared to fish two completely different patterns, depending on the conditions. One pattern relies on

CASTAIC LAKE

ELEVATION 1500 FEET ABOVE SEA LEVEL
CONTOUR INTERVALS 80 FEET &
INDICATE DEPTH OF WATER

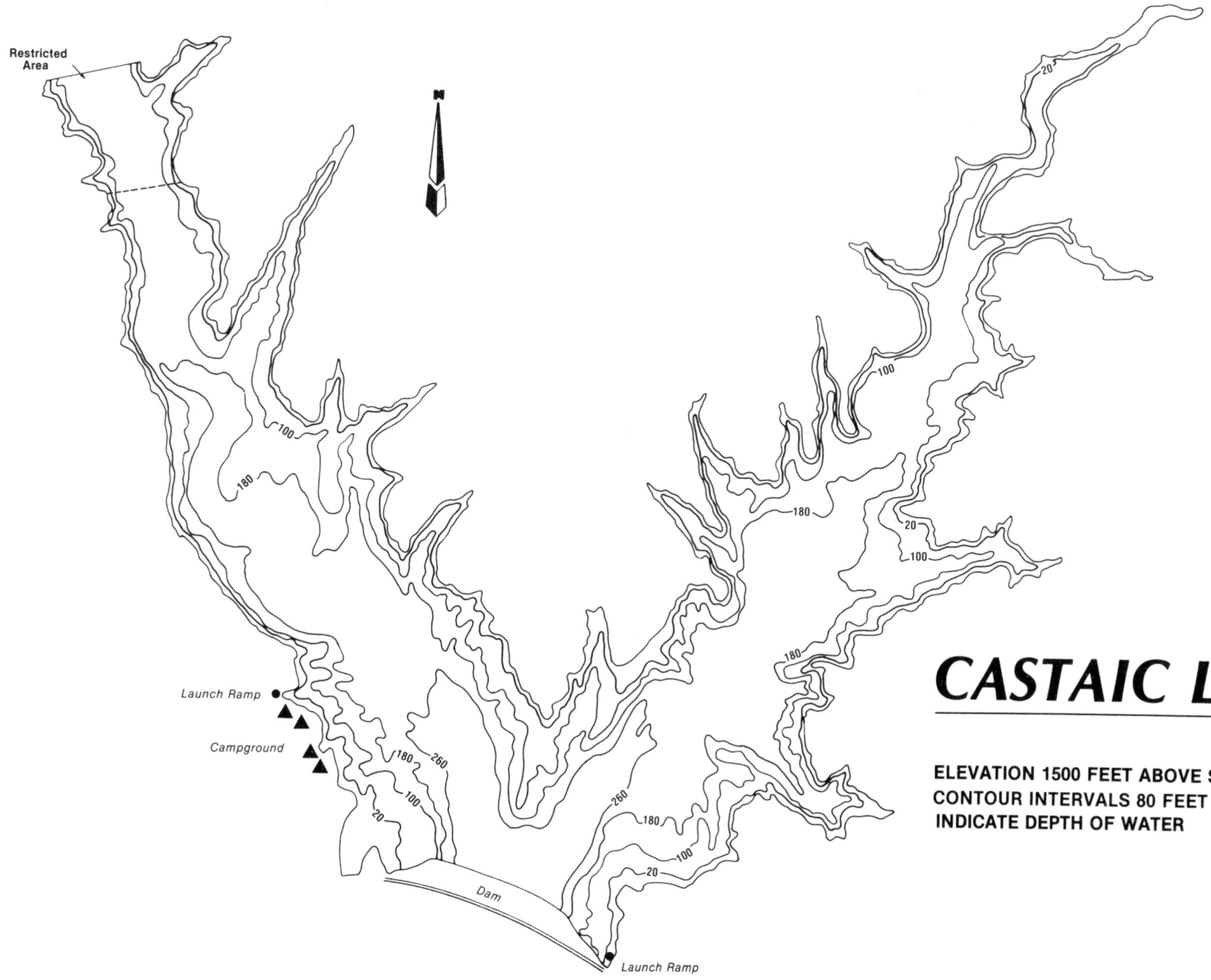
Restricted Area
N
100
180
Launch Ramp
Campground
180
260
100
20
Dam
260
180
100
20
Launch Ramp
180
20
100
180
100
20

Do NOT use for Navigation Purposes

Finding bait on your graph will tell you the difference between structure that is good or just looks good.

fishing deep-water structure where fish or bait balls show up on a graph; the second pattern targets shallow water mud lines, that can be near points, ledges, grass, or deep water.

To go after the deep-water bass look for underwater islands, rock piles, and balls of shad. If the bass are deep usually they will be at least 50 feet down. The best lures for deep fish are spoons or jigs. Even when fish are deep, they remain fairly active in the summer season. As a matter of fact, Castaic may be one of the better summer lakes on the South Coast, since the bass seem to continue feeding in hot weather, even after moving into deep water.

The shallow water summer pattern produces bass primarily in early morning or late evening. Though the guides consider it a shallow pattern, it is closer to what most people think of as mid-range, targeting depths between 12 and 25 feet. Work the mud lines, by doodling worms or cranking small plugs. Mud lines can form where wind is blowing across a point, up against a ledge or wall, or where there is fast boat traffic. It doesn't matter a great deal what the structure around the mud line is, or what formed it; Castaic bass are attracted to the edge of that dirty water no matter what the cause. O'Mally adds that he has caught 15-pound fish in mud lines, where the bank didn't look like it would hold any fish at all. Harrison said, "You can often catch fish in the mud lines formed behind ski boats that have been pulled up onto the beaches. The motor activity churns the water and brings the bass up."

"Fall is the toughest time of year on this lake," O'Mally said. "After the peak season earlier in the year, it is real tough. The fall slump can mentally destroy some of the fishermen."

The trouble with fall is that the bass often suspend. They may be in the same general areas, around points or ledges that they were on during summer; but the fish move away from the structure. They may hold at 20 feet, in a spot where the bottom depth is closer to 40 or 50 feet deep. It is hard to target these fish without a graph to clearly show exactly where they are.

The toughest part to accept is that getting these fish to bite is often as difficult as finding them. These bass may be more interested in finding an appropriate water temperature, than in feeding. Try swimming baits near the bass, or use vertical jigging techniques.

By late November or early December, fishermen may graph clouds of bait at 65 to 100 feet. The bait and the bass can stay in this super-deep water for as long as three months, and the best fishing depths may be well below 65 feet for the entire winter.

They may be deep, but these winter bass are catchable. Use lures that are easy to maintain contact with in deep water; worms rigged Texas style, spoons, or jigs are preferable to split-shot. A lure that is fished with a direct straight line from the rod tip to the eye of the hook, makes it easier to feel a pressure bite and provides a more direct and forceful hook-set. Hooks must be sharp for easy penetration.

"The depth and activity of the fish varies with passing storms," said O'Mally. "Get out there when the barometer is falling. After it starts to rise, stay home and sleep late; the fishing is very tough for three to five days after a front has passed."

At Castaic, a strong north wind is dangerous. The marina is completely exposed to the north wind, which builds strength as it funnels down the canyon. It can be impossible to get a boat out of the water safely in a relatively moderate blow. When north winds may be a problem, bring a fishing partner to help with launching, and be cautious, several boats sink at the ramp every year.

CASTAIC GUIDES

Gary Harrison (805) 294-0036

Harrison moved to Castaic, for the sole purpose of fishing the lake on an almost daily basis, in his search for a truly big bass. He has caught a number of fish over 15 pounds and is a licensed guide.

Don Iovino (818) 848-6180

Don Iovino Products

3220 Wyoming St., Burbank, CA 91505

Don was 1984 World Champion for U.S. Bass. In 1985 he took Angler of the Year. He is the only angler who has succeeded in taking both titles in U.S. Bass. Don also invented the doodling system for fishing deep water. He markets tackle for doodling, and has a video tape on the market that explains the finer points of the technique.

Jack O'Mally

Jack has been fishing these South Central California lakes for years. He has had a lot of experience on both Isabella and Castaic. He now fishes Castaic on a regular basis.

There is not that much wood on Castaic but when you find it, it can be great.

Gary Harrison with a typically healthy Castaic bass.

CASTAIC LAKE FACILITIES

• Castaic Lake, operates a launch ramp, snack bar, and small tackle store, on the main lake. The county is in the process of opening a 60 site RV Park on the afterbay, below the main lake. The cost will be $4 for day use and a $4 launching fee. Call (805) 257-4050.

• Castaic Lake RV Park, is in the town of Castaic. They have 103 full hookup RV sites, a pool, Jacuzzi, and hot showers. The price is $20 a night. Located at 31540 Ridge Route Rd., Castaic, CA 91310. Call, (805) 257-3340 for reservations.

• Mobil Mini Mart, is the place where fishermen meet on their way to the lake. The Mini Mart sells bass tackle and gas. Located on the road to the lake, at 31752 Old Ridge Rd., Castaic, CA. Call (805) 257-3717.

• Other: There are motels and restaurants in Castaic, as well as in the area around Magic Mountain, south of the 126 junction.

KEY TO CASTAIC

Best Season: March to August. In spite of the fact that Castaic is back in the hills, where air temperature is scorching, it is a good summer lake. Winter is good too. Fall is the pits.

Lures To Use: Straight-tail worms, four inches in winter and spring, six inches in summer and fall. Use lures in shad colors. Small crankbaits can work around the mud lines and rock. Also Skinny Bear jigs, a small jig with a fine-wire hook designed for smallmouth fishing. Six- to eight-pound line is the only way to go in this clear water, finesse fishery.

Primary Structure: Points, rock piles, cuts and ledges. The lake has little structure, except for physical characteristics of the rock-covered red mud banks. Fish the hard-bottom. There are grassbeds in spring and summer, and these can be good areas to get fish.

Other: The bass spawn later on Castaic than at other lakes on the South Coast, in about May or June. This is an up and coming lake that may produce a world record.

The main structure on the lake is deep cuts and points.

CLEAR LAKE

Dan Hannum said, "Clear Lake is the finest bass fishing lake in California. There are more five pound bass per acre, than on any lake in the U.S." And Hannum isn't the only guy who thinks Clear Lake is great. Ask any California guide or tournament fisherman to list their favorite lakes in the country, and Clear Lake almost always ranks near the top.

The reason is obvious, this lake holds a lot of quality bass. There are more two pound and better fish in Clear Lake than barely-legal fish in most other lakes. The water is extremely rich in food and nutrients, creating an incredibly productive lake.

Clear Lake is also a fairly easy lake to fish. Many big fish lakes are difficult, with selective fish that demand just the right bait and perfect presentation. However, Hannum said, "Clear Lake is a great place to take somebody who has never caught a fish before. They can throw darn near anything and still catch good bass."

What the lake is not, is a serious world record contender. Now that may seem irrelevant, since the chances of landing a world record-size fish on any lake are darn slim. But, the fishing press often describes Clear Lake as likely to hold a world record, and it just doesn't seem to be so. A commercial

Almost any lure will catch fish at Clear Lake. Choose lures according to the type of structure you want to fish.

carp fishery nets the lake, which may affect the bass; they have netted bass up to 17 pounds. Whatever the case, the lake record is 17.5 pounds and almost every tournament weighs in a few seven to eight pounders. But 13 pounds, or even 17 pounds, is a long way from the magic weight of 22 pounds.

That said, Clear Lake is heaven for bass fishermen. It is the largest natural lake in California, with a surface area of 43,000 acres. There are tules everywhere in both ends of the lake, and they surround almost the entire shoreline. There are also hundreds of private and public boat docks, and rock piles throughout the lake. The best fishing will center around these three primary structures, tules, docks and rock piles.

The lake can be divided into two distinct sections, the north and south end. The north end of the lake is a wide, shallow basin that is not much more than 20 feet at its deepest point. The south end is similar to a typical reservoir, it has deep water, with steeper banks and extensive rocky breaks.

The water level fluctuates only about four or five feet during the year, so the only physical feature that changes much on Clear Lake is the denseness of the tules. "Top-water is good around the tules in spring," said Henry Tabor, "but only as they are first coming up and just breaking the water, so you can work a buzzbait around them. When they are a little thicker, go with a spinnerbait. Once they become too thick for a buzzbait or a spinnerbait, go with a worm. Choose a lure that you can work through the tules. When they are real thick, you flip."

The areas of the lake that warm first, attract the early season spawners. Sheltered coves that are protected from wind are good because the water is warmer. Gravel and wood docks absorb the sun's heat and transfer the warmth to the water; this type of structure is a big help in finding early spring bass. The narrows at both ends of the lake are good areas in early spring because they are protected from wind. Another good spring spot is the Clear Lake Oaks Arm; there are channels in this area that have been dredged for private docks, and bass now utilize the area as a primary spawning ground.

"In early spring fish are coming from deeper water up to the shallows," said Henry Tabor, "they'll be on some type of break. But, you have to remember that this is a very shallow lake for its size. In the north end a break might only be six inches to a foot, whereas in the south end you get real breaks that go from 10 to 15 feet, down to 30 feet." Early spring bass hold on breaks in both the deep and shallow ends of the lake, but the difference is that they are somewhat deeper in the south end, and fishermen need to adjust their definition of a break in relation to the maximum depth in a given area.

As the fish move closer to shore, Ken Morrison prefers to flip. He usually uses jig and pigs or Gitzits, in shad and root beer colors. This is not a clear water lake, the visibility is only about five feet. For flipping heavy lures in tules, use lines of 15 to 25 pounds. For smaller, lighter baits, lines of about eight pounds are required for proper presentation.

By summer, bass in the shallow, north end of the lake move away from the shoreline. Bass in the south end move into deeper water, to hold at about 10 or 15 feet. All over the lake, bass seem to orient to wood in summer. They actually

CLEAR LAKE

ELEVATION 1326 FEET ABOVE SEA LEVEL
CONTOUR INTERVALS 6 FEET, & INDICATE DEPTH OF WATER

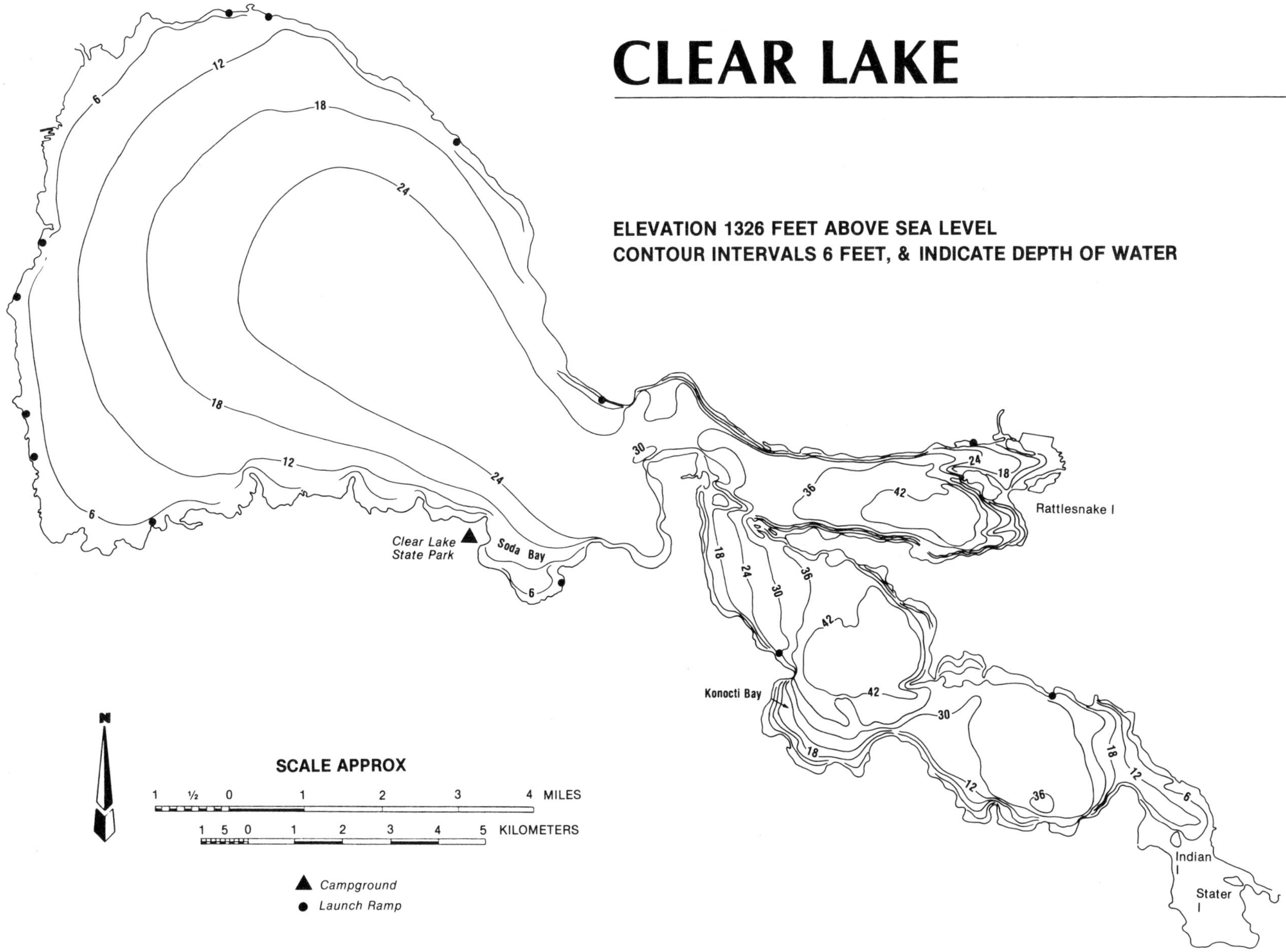

Rattlesnake I

Indian

Stater I

Konocti Bay

Soda Bay

Clear Lake State Park

6 12 18 24 30 36 42

SCALE APPROX

1 ½ 0 1 2 3 4 MILES

1.5 0 1 2 3 4 5 KILOMETERS

▲ Campground
● Launch Ramp

N

Rock piles are a good bet all year. Morning and evening in these areas can produce a fantastic crankbait bite.

stack up on wood structure, a wooden dock that holds one bass, is likely to hold several more. Tabor has pulled 25 fish off of one wooden dock on a summer afternoon. The fish really concentrate in these areas.

"I really like older wood docks," said Hannum, "with both tules and rocks nearby. These are the docks that are about two feet off the water, so they offer shade, and fish can orient around the supports. Don't concentrate on docks that are way off the water, like 10 feet up, because they don't provide good shade; and skip the floating docks, because they won't have any supports in the water. There are enough docks around the lake that you can afford to be selective."

When it comes to summer lures, anything goes. Crankbaits, spinnerbaits, surface plugs, and plastic worms all catch fish. Morrison likes to use crankbaits over the rock piles around Rattlesnake Island. Spinnerbaits and top-water lures are good near tules and in murky areas. Worms are best for fishing right in the tules, primarily because they come through the thicker growth without snags.

Two or three times during the summer, there is a heavy algae bloom. "The algae on the surface gives bass shade," Tabor said, "so the bass will move even shallower. But, fish only where there is a thin layer of algae, so that if you stirred it, the water below would be clear. When it gets to be 1/2 inch to one inch thick, and starts to turn bluish, stay away from it, it's awful. I don't think the bass will stay under an algae canopy that is very thick, but even if they did, it is terrible stuff to fish in."

Even though summer air temperatures get hot on Clear Lake, the fishing doesn't shut down. The bass still bite. It is best to fish on the lake early morning or late evening. In the middle of the day it is usually too hot to enjoy the lake, even if the fish are biting.

Fall is the season for top-water fishing. The bass are shallow and aggressive again, and the algae will have died back enough to allow fishermen to work near the shoreline. As in spring and summer, wooden docks and rocks are good, but also look for deeper water nearby. "You must find the shad in fall," said Morrison, "in order to do well with top-water plugs. Look to see which way the wind is blowing, as it will push the shad in that direction."

Both Hannum and Tabor use a lot of ripping baits in fall. If the fish are at all aggressive, the motion really draws strikes. Hannum also works the deeper water off Jago Bay, where there are rocky flats at 20 to 25 feet. In the deeper water he uses worms and grubs.

By mid-November, the winter pattern sets in. The winter water temperatures drop down to 38 or 39 degrees. The bite slows down considerably. Slow-moving baits hold the only hope of catching fish. Grubs, worms and jigs may do the job if they are worked slow. Slow-rolling spinnerbaits, pulled over the bottom so the blade just barely turns can also be good. Morrison said, "If you think you are fishing slow, slow it down even more."

When it is cold, bass in the shallow end of the lake move a few hundred yards off-shore, to areas with rock structure on the bottom. The fish in the south end head for deeper water on steep banks. "Though it is tougher," Tabor said, "if you work slow, and have confidence in the areas and what you are doing, you can usually pick up fish. They just don't come as quick."

At all times of the year, short-term weather makes a big difference at Clear Lake. The guides speculate that because the lake is shallow, changing weather has a greater impact on the fishing. Whatever the case, the lake may be red hot one day and the next day fishermen might not be able to buy a bite. Hang in there after a front moves in, the lake will be back to normal within a day or two.

The bass population at Clear Lake is holding its own against fishing pressure. This is primarily because the local fishermen have taken the lead in conservation efforts. Since the mid-70s the local bass club has stocked more than 10,000 juvenile bass annually. Now the Lake County Office of Lake Bed Management has taken on the job of stocking fingerlings. And almost every resort and guide practices catch and release.

CLEAR LAKE GUIDES

Dan Hannum (916) 541-8801

P.O. Box 822, 2753 Highway 50, South Lake Tahoe, CA 95705

Dan is a professional full-time guide who owns a tackle shop and guide service in Lake Tahoe. He also guides on Clear Lake and other Northern California bass lakes.

Ken Morrison (707) 998-1503

P.O. Box 1281, Clearlake Oaks, CA 95423

Ken has been a licensed guide for three years. He has lived at and fished on Clear Lake the past 11 years, fishing in tournaments for five. He is able to fish Clear Lake an average of 100 to 150 days a year. He enjoys teaching beginning bass fishermen about the sport.

Henry Tabor (707) 263-3302

2426 Giselman St., Lakeport, CA 95453

Tabor has been a licensed guide for more than six years. He has also fished tournaments for 12 years. He has lived on the lake and fished for bass for the past 15 years, and since he lives on the lake, Tabor is able to go out two or three days a week. Tabor also wants to thank Bob Todd at Ferndale Resort for more than 40 years of conservation efforts to preserve and improve the bass fishery on Clear Lake.

Tules are prime structures at Clear Lake. The best time to fish them is in the spring.

CLEAR LAKE FACILITIES

There are hundreds of resort motels and campgrounds surrounding Clear Lake. However, there are relatively few public access areas for bank fishing. Since most fishermen will use boats on this huge water, that probably doesn't make a lot of difference. There are public launch ramps all around the lake. Following is a short list of places to stay, but there are many more. They range from very nice, to worse than mediocre. Don't bother staying in the second-rate motels (some of them are closer to third-rate), just move on to the next town to find a place with decent accommodations.

State Park: There are 147 campsites in the State Park. None of them have hookups, but there are hot showers, a launch ramp and moorings. The fee is $10 to camp, $2 one time fee to bring a boat in the park. Mooring is $2 per night. Call (707) 279-4293 for information. Reservations are taken through Mistix, (800) 444-7275.

• Ferndale Resort, located on Soda Bay near the State Park, caters to bass fishermen. There are 14 motel units, with kitchenettes. There is also a small grocery store, tackle shop, launch ramp, boat rentals, complete marina, boat repair and sales. There are restaurants in the towns nearby. Owner Bob Todd can put fishermen in touch with the best guides in the area. Call, (707) 279-4866.

• Konocti Harbor Inn, has 250 rooms, ranging in price from $39 to $250 per night. The VIP suite has saunas, hot tub, and a total of five rooms. They have a full marina, boat rentals, two restaurants, bar, health club, four swimming pools, tennis courts and miniature golf. Located at 8727 Soda Bay Rd., Kelseyville, CA 95451. Call (707) 279-4281 or (800) 862-4930.

• Will-O-Point Resort, is located in Lakeport, on 1st and C streets. They offer 125 campsites and 11 cabins. The price for sites with hookups is $17 per night, without is $15. The cabins have kitchenettes and range in price from $57 for a unit that sleeps four, to $70 for units that sleep eight. There is no launch ramp on the property, but right next door there is a public launch. They also have a restaurant, bait and tackle shop, and a gas dock. Other services are available in Lakeport. Call (707) 263-5407.

Lake County Chamber of Commerce, (707) 263-6131.

Lakeport Chamber of Commerce, (707) 263-5092.

Clear Lake Chamber of Commerce, (707) 944-3600.

KEY TO CLEAR LAKE

Best Season: March to June, and September to mid-November. Fish continue to bite well in summer, but it is very hot at midday.

Lures To Use: Almost any lure will work, and the guides use a wide assortment. Choose lures according to the depth and structure to be fished, there is a wide variety on Clear Lake. Be sure to have plenty of jigs, plastics, spinnerbaits and buzzbaits, for working around tule growth. Because of turbidity, lures can be bright colors, in the medium to large sizes. With the possible exception of winter fishing, this is not a finesse lake.

Primary Structure: Tules, rock, wood, and docks. Finding spots with all of these structure types within a small area can be the key to success in finding bass. Fish will move deep or offshore in summer and winter, so look for secondary breaks. Remember that in the shallow section of the lake, a break may be only six inches; in the deep south end, a break would be more in the order of 10 or 15 feet.

Other: This lake holds a phenomenal number of quality bass. Keep moving to find good concentrations of fish.

THE DELTA

The Delta is not a proper lake, it is a waterway. A huge waterway, and all of it is loaded with bass. "The Delta is a maze of channels," Dee Thomas said, "all of it lined with tules and rock. There isn't hardly a bass water in California that I haven't been on, and of all of them the Delta is the best."

To put it simply, the Delta is a very fertile body of water, just this side of bass heaven. There are more than 1900 miles of shoreline, shallow canals and river, winding around low-lying willow covered islands and into the still waters of sloughs. The average depth is about 10 feet. All of it looks like perfect bass habitat. So where do you start fishing? How much of this 1900 miles can hold fish?

Darn near all of it.

"The Delta is easy to fish," Kim Manning said. "It is all shallow, with tules, weed beds and rip-rap. And the water is stained-color, that makes the fish very aggressive and less spooky. There is no need to go with light line, I use 10- to 20-pound test. Because it is a tidal water the fish are extremely aggressive and are ready to take a lure if they have the chance. We don't coax or finesse fish on the Delta."

Flipping baits, spinnerbaits and buzzbaits are the standard fish catchers on the Delta.

The Delta is fed by the San Joaquin and Sacramento rivers. Prime bass water lies roughly between Antioch and Stockton. Largemouth are found throughout the Delta. There is virtually untapped smallmouth fishing in the northern reaches of the waterway, near Sacramento, with large, hard fighting smallmouth that have become strong while living with constant current. The average size of a Delta bass is two to three pounds, and catching limits of these good-sized fish is easy most of the year. Five- and six-pound bass are trophies on the Delta, though bass up to 10 pounds are brought in occasionally.

"This is a tidal water," Don Payne said. "It varies from two to three feet in depth every day. Learning tides is the biggest key to fishing here. In summer I like the incoming tide because it holds more oxygen and makes the fish more aggressive. In fall and winter I prefer the outgoing tide."

The tides don't change all at once on the whole Delta. Because of the size and length of the waterway, there is a time lag, it takes hours for the change in water level to reach areas far from the mouth of the Delta. Suppose, for example, an angler wants to fish the incoming tide. According to Thomas, he would find an area where the tide is coming in and the fish are getting active. But he won't stay there for long. After 20 or 30 minutes on the spot, he would move upriver several hundred yards to similar structure, and fish there until the tide catches up. Thomas said, "You can follow active fish all day long that way, from Antioch to Stockton."

"The seasons are important on any bass water," said Manning. "The fish don't behave any different toward the seasons on the Delta than on other lakes, but you have to know where to look. It isn't a deep to shallow movement." Instead of moving from deep to shallow water in search of food and comfortable water temperatures, the bass on the Delta move in and out of the current. The temperature of the main river channel with its moving water, varies less than the still water sloughs. As a general rule, in summer and winter when temperatures are extreme, look for bass in the moving current.

In spring, the slow water will warm first and that is where bass will be. But, don't look for bass in the very backs of sloughs, where the water is absolutely still, because there isn't enough oxygen in the hot summer months. Stay near areas where current and still water are close to each other, so the bass can move in and out of the current without moving more than a few hundred yards.

"A lot of people have a tough time on the Delta in winter," Payne said. "The fish get off the banks and hold on secondary drop-offs near river channels and the main river channel. A good fish finder is a must. If you can't find those secondary structures you'll have a hard time finding fish."

There is also a temperature difference between the San Joaquin and Sacramento rivers. The San Joaquin runs from south to north, therefore it warms first, maybe several months earlier than the Sacramento. Bass become active and move into a spawning pattern on the San Joaquin as early as March. Though they may not spawn in the waters fed by the Sacramento until June. When considering the seasonal patterns of fish on the Delta, the actual month is less important than the water temperature at the area to be fished. Spring

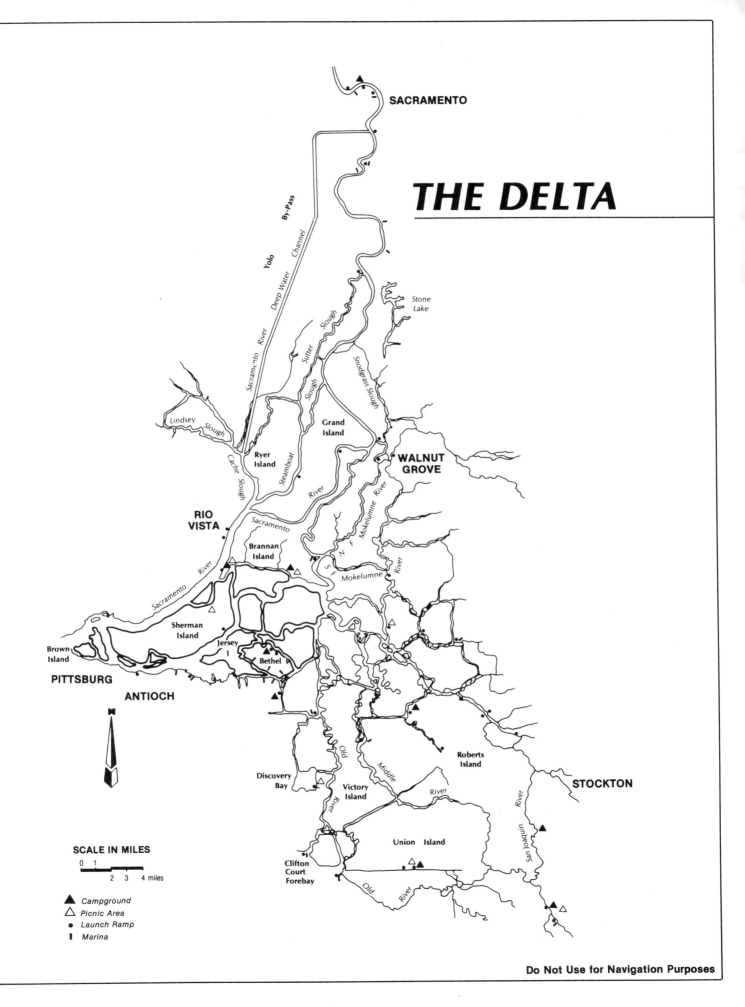

THE DELTA

SACRAMENTO

Yolo By-Pass

Deep Water Channel

Sacramento River

Sutter Slough

Snodgrass Slough

Stone Lake

Lindsey Slough

Grand Island

Cache Slough

Ryer Island

WALNUT GROVE

Steamboat

Sacramento River

Mokelumne River

RIO VISTA

Sacramento

N F Mokelumne River

S F Mokelumne

Brannan Island

Sherman Island

Jersey

Brown Island

Bethel I

PITTSBURG

ANTIOCH

N

Roberts Island

Old River

Middle River

Discovery Bay

Victory Island

STOCKTON

San Joaquin River

Union Island

Clifton Court Forebay

Old River

SCALE IN MILES

0 1
2 3   4 miles

▲ Campground
△ Picnic Area
● Launch Ramp
❘ Marina

Do Not Use for Navigation Purposes

Don Payne, known to locals as Delta Don, landing an average Delta bass.

fishing comes in March on the southern waters and in June on the northern waters.

Once the decision has been make to work the current or the slow water, there are three basic patterns. "Start off with fishing rock and wood," said Payne. "The next step is rock and moss. If that doesn't work, go to spots with rock, tules and moss. Somewhere in there you'll get a pattern that works."

Oxygen is especially important for fish on the Delta. Whereas most impoundment lakes in California have sufficient oxygen in the shallow waters, the Delta is oxygen poor. This is why the backwaters far from any current won't hold bass all the time. But, it also makes a difference as to which kind of structure fishermen should concentrate on.

Moss beds release oxygen in the water on sunny days. The bass like the combination of oxygen and cover. Working the moss beds when the sun is bright can yield one bass after another, all day long. Payne prefers to use buzzbaits on the moss beds, because they come over the vegetation without snagging.

On the other hand, moss absorbs oxygen on cloudy days and at night. The bass will move out of the moss and orient to rock or wood when there is no bright sun. They may stay in an area near moss beds, but they won't hold in the moss itself. A spinnerbait can be dynamite if fished over rock.

Flipping is the essential fishing technique on these waters. Thomas prefers to flip a jig, while Payne likes worms, and Manning thinks a spinnerbait is most consistent. Bass on the Delta are not particularly selective in terms of lures. Fishermen must use a lure they have confidence in, a lure that can cover a lot of water in a short time. With 1900 miles of water to fish, why waste half the day on one point?

Delta bass feed on crawdads and shad; colors and lures that imitate either one of these forage are popular. However, because visibility is poor, the colors should be intense and easy to see, like blacks and browns with a shot of red or chartreuse. The guides use smaller lures when the water is cold, and larger lures, for instance worms up to eight inches long, when the water is warm.

Crankbaits are popular for fishing around rock when the bass are active. "I'll go with a crank in April and May," said Thomas, "and a spinner in June and July. Flipping a jig will always catch some fish."

The Delta is an excellent summer and fall fishery. When other lakes shut down in the heat, the Delta can be at its peak. Fishing near current and the moss beds is a sure fire way to land limits of bass. The fishing on this water is at its toughest in winter, but fish can be caught by concentrating on water that is less than 10 feet deep, and working secondary structure.

"Always carry a map on the Delta," said Manning, "you'll get lost without one. In my opinion, the Delta is the best, bass are everywhere. There is so much cover, every single mile of shoreline is covered with something. It is all good, so don't worry too much about any one area. You could fish the Delta for the next ten years, and not get to know half of it."

DELTA GUIDES

Kim Manning (408) 923-8381

Manning was West Coast Bass Angler of the Year 1986, a title he captured on the Delta. He has 25 years of bass fishing under his belt and has fished tournaments for six years. His sponsors are: Zebco Motorguide, Ranger, and Mercury.

Don Payne (209) 537-4486

In 1984 Payne won every tournament circuit in California. He has been Northern California Bass Federation, Angler of the Year, seven out of twelve years. He is a professional licensed guide. His sponsors are: Berkley Trilene, Berkley Rods, Ranger Boats, Mercury, Eagle, Bob's Marine, Keeper Custom Worms, Brawley Jigs and Spinnerbaits, Keeper Boxes, Pradco products, and Thermo Batteries.

Dee Thomas (415) 634-5669

212 Balfour Rd., Brentwood, CA 94153

Thomas is a tournament fisherman and licensed guide. He has raised five kids and eight grandchildren, and has taught them, along with a lot of other folks, how to fish. His sponsors are: Fenwick, Ranger, Mercury, DuPont Stren, Lowrance, and R&B Tackle.

DELTA FACILITIES

There are dozens of launch ramps, fishing resorts, and hotels on the Delta. It isn't possible to do justice by even providing a partial list here, this is a developed region where life revolves around the Delta waters. Stockton, Sacramento, Antioch, and Rio Vista, all have tackle shops that cater to fishermen and can provide specific information on where to launch, where the fish are biting, and what's hot at the time.

KEY TO DELTA

Best Season: March to October. The Delta is such a large body of water, fed by two different river systems, that the spawn is staggered over three months. The spawn occurs in the southern section in March, and the northern section in June. Summer is the peak, but stay in the current. Fall is more or less a continuation of summer.

Lures To Use: Flipping is the standard technique. Buzzbaits, spinnerbaits, jigs and worms are all good choices, use whatever will come through the structure. The water is usually off-color; use lures with high visibility.

Primary Structure: Everything that bass fishermen could ask for; tules, rock piles, islands, moss beds, and wood. Pay attention to water temperature and current, fish in the current in summer and winter, and just outside of the current where the water is warmer in spring. Look for spots where the current is blocked by structure and forms a still water eddy adjacent to moving water.

Other: This is a tidal water. Fish on the tides, as they move along the Delta waterway. Also, don't bother with light line, 12- to 20-pound test is recommended.

The Delta is a combination of rock, wood and tules. Pick your fishing spots according to water temperature.

DON PEDRO LAKE

Don Payne said, "In the beginning, Don Pedro was a very fertile lake. Anglers took ten-fish stringers in excess of 69 pounds. But that was in the past, the lake is not as fertile anymore. Still it offers an outstanding fishery, year-round. You can catch fish in just about any arm, and since 1985 the smallmouth have really come on. After a lake peaks the smallmouth take off, they like the rocks that are cleared of topsoil. There are spotted bass in the lake now, but very few; in the next few years they'll come on."

Those big fish of the past have made Don Pedro well-known among top bass fishermen. It remains a popular lake for professional tournaments because with almost 13,000 surface acres and 160 miles of shoreline, Don Pedro has enough good fishing spots to accommodate hundreds of boats. Even though 69-pound stringers may be a thing of the past, this is still one of the most productive lakes in the mother lode region.

"This is a canyon-type lake," Payne said. "It drops off rapidly. It's steep with just a few arms that have long sloping areas. Largemouth are back in the river channels with standing timber, like Woods Creek, Jones Bay and Big Creek. We fish standing timber, creek channels, rock piles and points.

While Don Pedro is primarily a plastic worm lake come spring time it often can pay off to be more versatile.

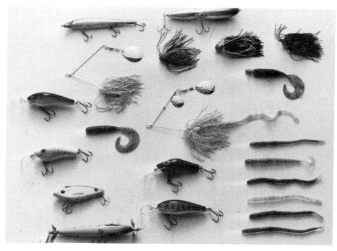

That is just about all the structure in Don Pedro. This is primarily a split-shot lake, 365 days a year — the most dominant baits are plastic worms."

Bass begin to become active toward the end of February on Don Pedro. The smallmouth are up first, in early February, with the largemouth turning on by the end of the month. The largemouth spawn takes place around the first week in May. The water temperature in the winter is slightly warmer than it is at other lakes in the area, because there are fewer snow-fed rivers running into Don Pedro. This makes Don Pedro a slightly better winter fishery, and also allows the spring bite to start about three weeks earlier than on other lakes in the region.

Payne describes Don Pedro as a feast or famine lake. In the spring, almost anyone can catch good quality fish. In recent years, he has had days in spring with close to 40 smallmouth, all of them weighing between one and three pounds, plus some largemouth. The spring bite is great. At other times it is possible to fish Don Pedro hard from dawn to dusk, and hardly get bit.

"The first thing that we use on Don Pedro, starting in about February, is the salt and pepper grub," said Tom Schachten. "That works real well up in Woods Creek, because there is a massive channel cat spawn up there. Salt and pepper grubs are a perfect imitation of channel cat fry. Since cats are one of the last species to spawn in the fall, their fry are only about three inches long in the spring, and it is the first forage fish available to bass as they come up into the shallows. You can also use silver crankbaits up in that area, to imitate the shad that hold in Woods Creek in the winter."

Once spring gets into full swing the main river channel turns on. Schachten thinks that one of the best places to fish prior to the spawn is around the log-jam in the river channel. The log-jam creates a backwash and holds all of the debris that drifts down the river, and it also provides ideal cover for bass. The log-jam moves up and down the mouth of the river channel with the tidal pull, so keep moving along with it throughout the day. Fish this structure by swimming spinnerbaits or grubs along the edge, letting them fall slowly to take advantage of suspended fish.

After the bass have been in the shallows for a few weeks they gravitate to rocky points and rock piles. Schachten thinks they head for the rocky areas prior to the spawn, because there is not a lot of cover in the lake. For fishing around the rock, use jig and pig, soft plastics, or crankbaits.

"In the spawn, fish move into the shallow timber," said Payne, "the water warms up in timber first. Spawning females seek out the warm pockets at the top of the trees. Spinnerbaits and buzzbaits work well right through the spawn. This pattern also works for post-spawn but only in the early morning.

Payne recommends using worms of four inches or less in winter and early spring. When the water hits 50 degrees, switch to worms of 4 1/2 to 5 inches long. Purple is his favorite worm color, he claims it works consistently well on any lake, in almost any water condition.

Schachten on the other hand, feels that the color of plastics matters a lot in a clear water lake like Don Pedro. He starts the day with a standard worm color, like brown with a

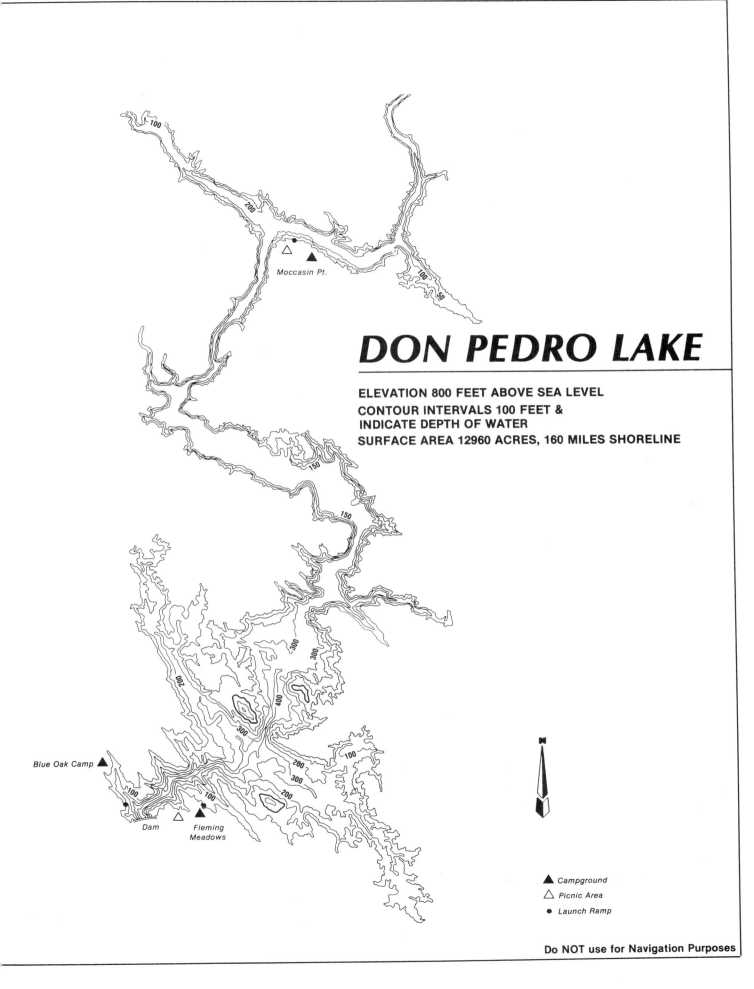

DON PEDRO LAKE

ELEVATION 800 FEET ABOVE SEA LEVEL

**CONTOUR INTERVALS 100 FEET &
INDICATE DEPTH OF WATER**

SURFACE AREA 12960 ACRES, 160 MILES SHORELINE

Moccasin Pt.

Blue Oak Camp

Dam

Fleming
Meadows

▲ Campground
△ Picnic Area
● Launch Ramp

Do NOT use for Navigation Purposes

Standing timber is a primary structure on the lake.

chartreuse tail, or salt and pepper; choose a color that matches the dominant forage. But, as soon as the sun hits the water and the fish go deeper he switches to a worm in the same basic color with a bright flake, for instance brown with red flake. As the sun starts to set he switches to a darker worm without any flake — for a clear silhouette that is easy for the fish to see in low-light conditions. "Normally you find that three different colors of worm work during the day. The sunlight changes, so be ready to change. You need to go out on the water with a set of worms and know the whole set works, then pick the one that works on this particular day. That is what you have to do if you are going to be good."

By late June, bass have moved out of the shallows to deeper water. They'll hold in two kinds of areas, on spots with cover that provides shade or off points with wind blowing onto them. In the heat of the day, bass are going to be below the level of the thermocline, which could be as deep as 25 or 30 feet. Top-water is strictly an early and late in the day proposition.

"Don Pedro gets a lot of water skiers," said Payne. "They form mud lines along the banks. The fish move under the mud lines just like we move into shade on a hot day. After about 10 a.m. in the morning, move up to the mud lines and fish dart heads, split- shot worms and cranks. The mud lines will extend 20 or 30 feet from the bank. The fish will be right under the mud line, often suspended, so sometimes I'll swim a worm rather than work it on the bottom. Swim worms, or crankbaits parallel to the mud line, at the depth you find fishing holding in."

Night fishing is good on moon lit nights in summer. Use as little light as possible on the boat, because a bright light casts shadows that will spook shallow fish. Look for bass from the edge of the banks down to about 10 feet deep; they'll be in as little as one foot of water. Black is the most effective color for night fishing, and black grubs can produce limits of hefty fish in a matter of hours.

Fall is tough on Don Pedro, especially when the water level

is falling, which is most often the case as the lake is drawn down prior to winter rains. In fall the water becomes gin clear and the fish may suspend. Jig and pig works as well as any other lure until October, when the crawdads go into the mud to hibernate. After the crawdad forage is no longer available to bass, switch over to plastic worms for lures. Payne said, "The best fall pattern is to pray a lot."

Concentrate on points with shad balls; find the bait then head for the closest structure. The smallmouth may be in the middle of the lake chasing shad, while the largemouth seek out the wind-blown points. Both species hold in water between 25 and 50 feet deep.

When there is a lot of run-off that clouds up creek channels, the turbid water attracts bass bringing largemouth into the area. Flip jigs into the structure near the deep water access of the creek channel. If there isn't any structure in the area, work a jig down the center of the channel.

Woods Creek offers the most consistent winter bite. Schachten describes the spot as a "giant fish hatchery," and the best spot on any of the region's lakes in winter. "The trouble with winter," Schachten said, "is you can find them, but you cannot make a bass feed. In warmer conditions, you can make them hit, but in the winter, you can do anything you want and if they don't have the urge or the warmth to get up and get a little feed before they go back to their sulking, you are not going to get them."

In winter, bass move down to depths of 55 or 60 feet. Since the bass are deep and lethargic, use lures that work well when fished slowly, grubs and spoons are two of the best choices, because they are effective in deep water and imitate shad, which is the most plentiful forage in winter.

"When you use a spoon," said Payne, "you are sort of hurrying up to slow down. A 3/4-ounce spoon goes like hell to the bottom, it eliminates all of that time from the surface to the depth. Once you locate fish, you can go back to split shot. Until I find fish, I want to get to the bottom as quick as I can."

DON PEDRO GUIDES

Don Payne (209) 537-4486
In 1984, Payne won every tournament circuit in California. He has been Northern California Bass Federation, Angler of the Year, seven out of twelve years. He is a professional licensed guide. His sponsors are: Berkley Trilene, Berkley Rods, Ranger Boats, Mercury, Eagle, Bob's Marine, Keeper Custom Worms, Brawley jigs and spinnerbaits, Keeper Boxes, and Pradco Products.

Tom Schachten (209) 736-4333
Glory Hole Sporting Goods
2892 South Highway 49, Angles Camp, CA 95222
Schachten has been a licensed guide for six years, though he has been fishing the lakes in the region for 28 years. He is the owner of the Glory Hole. He guides for all types of fish including: bass, trout, sturgeon and salmon.

DON PEDRO FACILITIES

There are three county campgrounds at Don Pedro, all with launch ramps. Prices are: $12 a night without hookups, $16 with full hookups, $4 day use fee per vehicle, $5 per day boat fee. None of the campgrounds permit dogs. For information and reservation forms on any of the following camping areas call, (209) 852-2396.
• Fleming Meadows: This campground has 90 full-hookup sites, and 126 sites without hookups. There is a full-service marina and seven-lane launch ramp. Also, bait, tackle, gas, snack bar, and boat rentals.
• Blue Oaks: Open from Memorial Day to Labor Day, 195 sites without hookups. A three lane launch ramp, but no marina or stores.
• Moccasin Point: Fifteen full hookup sites, 65 without hookups. Also a full-service marina with bait, tackle, store, gas and a six lane launch ramp.

Smallmouth bass are becoming dominant in the lake so fish points and rip-rap.

Author Joni Dahlstrom with a nice bass.

KEY TO DON PEDRO

Best Season: Spring, from late February until May. Summer is also pretty good, especially for night fishing. Fall is very tough.

Lures To Use: Four- to six-inch plastic worms, in purple or lighter natural colors. Spinnerbaits and buzzbaits during the spring, also crawdad or shad colored cranks.

Primary Structure: Standing timber, creek channels, rock piles, and points. Log-jams in the river channel, but only in early spring.

Other: A very productive lake, but one where the bite is hot or it's not. Don Pedro can be very tough. June through March expect fish to be deeper than 25 feet.

EL CAPITAN LAKE

Tom Berg said, "El Capitan is a basic lake. As far as tactics and catching fish, out of all the lakes in San Diego, it is probably the most basic lake there is. It has everything, lots of banks and outside structures that hold fish. What it amounts to is, if the fish are not on the banks at El Capitan, they are off. If you don't meter fish in the 25 to 30 foot range, then you can go straight to the two to twelve foot water. It is that simple, you know where the fish are."

El Capitan, like all of the San Diego City Lakes, is famous for producing lots of quality bass. It is popular with local fishermen because of its consistency as well. It is a spot where the bass behave the way all the books say they are supposed to. Bass hit shallow baits in the morning and when the wind is blowing, while they back off to the deeper points in bright sun. Because the water is not super clear, fishermen seldom have to resort to extreme finesse tactics. El Capitan is not only a quality lake, it is a catching lake too.

Better yet, recent changes in the minimum size limits on El Capitan could propel the lake from the good category, to the level of one of the best lakes in the state. The Department of Fish and Game has imposed a 15-inch minimum size limit on

A variety of standard bass gear works on El Capitan.

the lake, with a five fish maximum. On almost every other lake in the state where the size limit was raised from 12 to 15 inches, the catch rates of quality bass improved dramatically within a matter of two to three years.

El Capitan covers nearly 1,600 surface acres. The main arm of the lake, called the Chocolate Arm, is long, narrow and deep by San Diego standards. There is also the Conejos Arm and an arm that extends to the dam. "Conejos is usually a little better than the main lake," said Joe Seale, "especially in summer. This is a narrow, windy lake. There are lot of rocks, points, and when the lake level is up, more brush than you could fish. There is only a little aquatic vegetation in the shallows in summer. On the whole, it is a real consistent lake."

The lake generally opens in late February and closes in September, though the exact dates are always subject to change. It is open only on Fridays, Saturdays and Sundays.

Water temperature is the prime factor governing the depth bass will hold at in the opening weeks. If the water is relatively cool, below 56 degrees, look for fish in 25 to 40 feet of water, on rock piles and major points. Berg said, "Usually the first couple of weeks there is a real good jig and pig bite. It's your basic jig fishing bite, work larger jigs with pork slowly over rocks. There is nothing at all unusual about it."

On the other hand, the lake changes fast, with only slightly warmer temperatures bass move into the shallows almost over night. In fact, Seale thinks that fish are usually fairly shallow in the opener if weather permits, because of the absence of fishing pressure. But, often the fish move down below 25 feet almost immediately when the fishermen arrive, and stay their until they are on a strong pre-spawn pattern.

When the bass move shallow in earnest, and stay up there, concentrate on water from the shoreline down to 12 feet. Seale said, "That is where the bulk of the fish are going to be. They are cruising the shoreline and feeding heavy. Look for the cleaner areas with sparser brush, because these fish are looking for spawning areas."

Since the water is almost always off-colored at El Capitan, there is no need to work with extremely light line. Most of the local fishermen regularly fish eight-pound line, or even line of up to ten pounds. If the water level rises to maximum capacity, the brush will be extremely thick, and then fishermen may even find good flipping on line as heavy as 14 pounds.

El Capitan bass prefer larger lures than fish on other San Diego lakes. One of the most popular spring-time lures is a No. 7 willow leaf spinnerbait, in chartreuse or chartreuse/white. Blades are the number one big fish lure, as Berg points out. He has caught half a dozen big bass from the lake, that weighed-in at more than nine and one-half pounds, and they all came in on spinnerbaits.

"Look for brush to throw the blades around," said Berg. "Brush and rock slides. These are the two types of structure to fish in shallow water. The bass will stay on blades pretty much all day. They'll definitely be on them early in the morning. When the sun breaks through the fish move off and seem to quit feeding as often, then you can fish brown or purple worms in a little deeper water. But, when the wind starts to blow, fish the blades again. The wind almost always starts up by 11 a.m., and keeps on blowing till dark. The canyon that holds the lake is a real wind funnel.''

The bass spawn by late March. Seale points out that it is a staggered spawn, with at least some fish on beds well into June. The spring pattern, of fishing spinnerbaits shallow and worms in slightly deeper water continues through June.

"Pretty much from the beginning of summer on," said Seale, "it is shoreline fishing in the morning, with cranks and spinnerbaits. You want to look for shad up against the shoreline. Then the fish will move off to water from 10 to 20 feet, and you should start fishing Reepers on split-shot, actually Reepers are good from April on. El Capitan is notorious for fish moving back up in the afternoon, then you want to fish the shallows where there is wave action that stirs things up.''

By June, crankbaits are used as widely as spinnerbaits in the shallows. Medium-sized cranks, in shad and crawdad colors, fished around rocky areas produce fish throughout the day. Rather than working standard worms, the three-inch Reepers on small split-shots become the preferred plastics.

For the most part, it is easy to catch lots of fish in the shallows all through the day during the summer months. The problem is most of the bass will be in the 10 to 12 inch range. Berg feels that the better bass start relating to deeper water in the summer, with the larger fish holding on rock piles in 30 feet of water. But when conditions are right, with either wind or low sun, never overlook the shallow waters.

There is a good top-water bite from June until the lake closes in fall, primarily in early morning. Use Zara Spooks

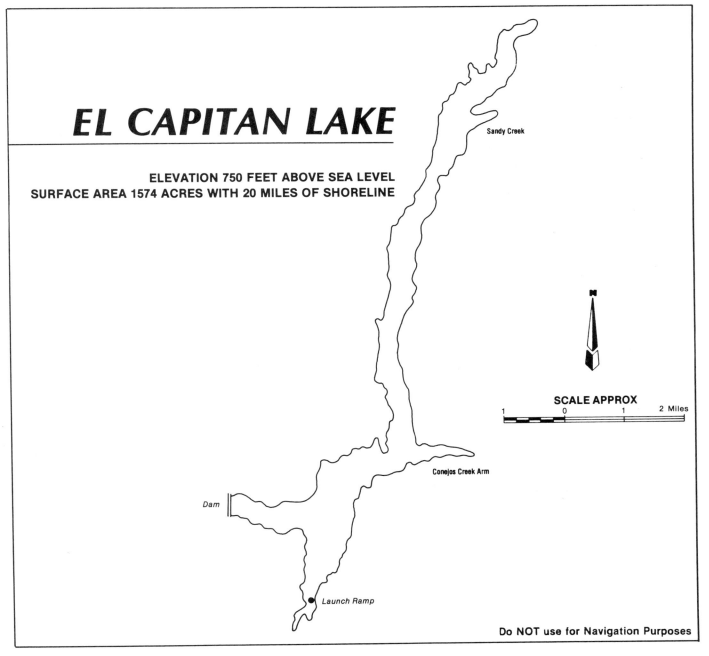

EL CAPITAN LAKE

ELEVATION 750 FEET ABOVE SEA LEVEL
SURFACE AREA 1574 ACRES WITH 20 MILES OF SHORELINE

Sandy Creek

SCALE APPROX

1   0   1   2 Miles

Conejos Creek Arm

Dam

● Launch Ramp

Do NOT use for Navigation Purposes

and Rapalas, in silver and black. These lures will produce bass around areas with thin brush, and in the backs of quiet coves with lots of brush and rock. There must be deep water close to the shoreline.

A few weeks before the lake closes in September, the fish start to school in the deeper, cooler water at 20 to 30 feet. At this time they'll hit spoons and eight-inch worms. This pattern is good when the surface waters have become very warm, forcing the bass into deep, cool holding stations. It is not a long-term pattern, since it usually takes place only in the late summer. If the lake remains open beyond the usual September closing date, deep water spoons and worms could be the key to catching bass right through the fall.

When fishing on El Capitan, wind is always the primary factor. Most fishermen believe that it is the afternoon wind, which hits the lake almost every single day like clockwork, that account for the excellent shallow water fishing on the lake. The wind keeps the water stained, creates mud lines, stimulates feeding activity, and generally brings bass up from deeper water. "Don't fight it," said Berg. "You don't have to enjoy the wind, just learn to use it. Fish those windy banks because the fish are going to be there."

"This is the easiest lake in the county," he added, "as far as catching fish. It is as close to a typical lake as we have got. Establish a pattern, and you'll catch fish every time you go."

EL CAPITAN GUIDES

Tom Berg (619) 562-2275
Tom has fished El Capitan since 1970, and has fished tournaments for the past 15 years. He and his team partner won the San Diego Region of U.S. BASS in 1985, 1986, and 1987, three consecutive years, a feat which had never been accomplished before. Tom provides on the water fishing instruction and is sponsored by Western Plastics.
Joe Seale
Joe has fished the San Diego lakes for about 30 years, at just about every imaginable level. He has fished team tournaments with his son, and they took Team of the Year, three times in a row. He has won more than a few tournaments in the area. He is sponsored by Ranger, Yamaha, Fenwick, and AA Plastic Worms.

Deep diving crankbaits score nice catches.

KEY TO EL CAPITAN

Best Season: From the opening in February until early June, during the spawning season. The bite holds up well through the summer. The lake is usually closed in fall and winter.

Lures To Use: Spinnerbaits are the top producers of large bass whenever the fish are shallow. No. 7 willow leaf in chartreuse or chartreuse/white. After spinnerbaits, four-inch worms are the next best, with three-inch Reepers coming on in about May or June. Crankbaits are good in the early mornings in summer.

Primary Structure: El Capitan has a little bit of everything. When the water level is up there is a lot of brush all around the shoreline. There are extensive rock piles, major points and secondary points. A deeper canyon lake, at least compared to other San Diego lakes. Look for fish on the points and rock piles in 25 to 40 feet, and if they aren't there, hit the shoreline in less than 12 feet of water.

Other: An off-color lake, with water kept stirred up by daily wind. It allows for the use of slightly heavier lines, from eight to ten pounds, rather than the super light stuff. The wind comes up around noon almost every day, and it will bring fish into the shallows, on the wind-swept points and banks. Use the wind, don't fight it.

EL CAPITAN FACILITIES

El Capitan Lake, is open from February until September, on Fridays, Saturdays and Sundays, though these dates can and do change. Call the Lake Hotline at (619) 465-3474, for updated schedules on the San Diego lakes. The cost for fishing on Sand Diego lakes is $3.50 per bass fisherman, $4.00 per trout fisherman, and $4.00 to launch a boat, per day.

Other: There are complete services available in San Diego and the nearby towns. These include motels, restaurants, tackle shops, boat repairs, and gas.

A typical El Capitan bass.

Late evening through morning can be the best time to fish in mid-summer.

FOLSOM LAKE

Folsom Lake is seldom rated as a smallmouth bass hot spot, but maybe it should be. On a good day in spring or fall it is possible to catch between 15 and 50 keeper bass. The lake is positively loaded with smaller bass that are growing at phenomenal rates following three years of drought. All the signs point to a big upswing for the bass fishery in the long-term, making Folsom a lake to watch in the next three to five years.

Folsom is unusual in that it is a deep, clear-water fishery in a lowland valley, only minutes north of Sacramento. The area surrounding the lake is all rolling hills. The lake covers almost 12,000 acres, with better fishing in the two huge arms formed by forks of the American River. The rivers carved deep channels through the rock, creating a canyon-style bass fishery. "Remember, Folsom is a clear-water lake. You have to use light line, subtle baits, and stay far off the fish or you'll spook them," Jon Walton said. "And move a little deeper. Even in spring you should fish all the way down to 20 feet."

"If you use anything heavier than 10-pound line on Folsom, you aren't going to get bit," added Bob Trippe. "These bass are real line conscious. They aren't hook conscious, you could use a 6/0 hook and catch bass, but they won't touch heavy line. Always use six- to eight-pound line."

Light line and subtle baits are the rule on Folsom.

Water fluctuation is also important, especially when fishing for largemouth. When the water is rising it covers grassbeds and willows in the big coves off the arms, and is great for largemouth fishing. When the lake is low there is very little vegetation making largemouth difficult to locate. The smallmouth always relate to rocky points. Even the smallmouth spawning beds won't be more than a couple of hundred yards from rocky structure that extends into the main river channel.

In rising water, look for both largemouth and smallmouth to be in shallower water, facing the bank as they move up. In falling water, they'll want deep water access and face into the main body of the lake; they may hold deeper and suspend off of vertical drop-offs.

"This is an excellent top-water lake," said Walton, "because of the clear water. A Zara is a good big-fish bait, in spring and summer, especially for largemouth. Rebels, Tiny Torpedos and Pop-Rs are good for all fish on the surface. In spring, the top-water bite lasts all day long. In summer, its early morning and late evening." In the clear water bass will come up from 20 foot depths to attack a surface lure.

For largemouth in spring, work over any flats with wood or grassbeds. There aren't a lot of these areas, so the bass concentrate on the little wood there is. The smallmouth flats are going to be close to major points with some type of change that the fish can relate to. It could be as subtle as a change in the rock composition, or brush on an otherwise barren sandstone point. Strata rock, that Walton calls stegosaurus rock, is often good for smallmouth. The key to finding smallmouth spawning beds is to find the points they utilize in winter and summer, then hit the flats that are nearby. Use a thermometer to locate the warmer coves and points for more active bass early in the year.

"In spring, I always start shallow with a spinnerbait," said Trippe. "The water is often a little murkier in spring than at other times of the year, especially if we get a lot of run-off. I start with a chartreuse or white spinnerbait, no matter what time of day I get on the water. Work the spinnerbait down the ledges. Let it fall, don't just use a straight retrieve, spinnerbaits are a lot more versatile than that. A spinnerbait falling down a rock-face is just like a helicopter, with that blade rotating. It annoys the hell out of the fish and they just nail it."

If the fish aren't active enough to hit on top-water or spinnerbaits, switch immediately to a soft plastic. Use the subtle baits, three- to four-inch plastics like: Little Bits, Gitzits and grubs. Shad, crawdad, and purple are popular colors.

There is a spring to summer transition on Folsom, when the bass are active near the headwaters of the forks, while the rest of the lake is in a post-spawn period. At the headwaters the channel is only about six or eight feet deep. To locate fish in this area, start by working in the shallows, and keep moving back off the bank to the deeper breaks. Somewhere between six and twenty feet, there should be good concentrations of fish.

By summer, bass are spending their days in deeper water. Use shallow-running and surface lures early and late in the day, but drop down to 20, or even 60 feet at midday. "They will want deep water access," said Walton, "this is really true at any time of year. By deep, I mean 60 to 100 feet. Not that

FOLSOM LAKE

ELEVATION 466 FEET ABOVE SEA LEVEL
CONTOUR INTERVALS INDICATE DEPTH OF WATER
SURFACE AREA 11,930 ACRES WITH 75 MILES OF SHORELINE

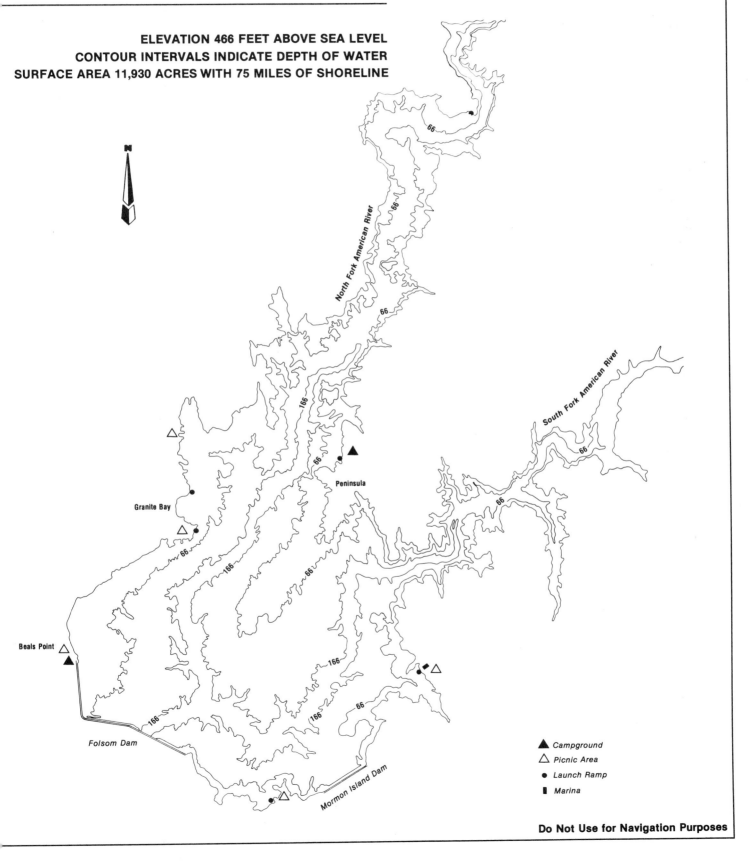

North Fork American River

South Fork American River

66

66

166

66

66

66

166

66

166

166

166

66

Peninsula

Granite Bay

Beals Point

Folsom Dam

Mormon Island Dam

▲ Campground
△ Picnic Area
● Launch Ramp
▐ Marina

Do Not Use for Navigation Purposes

Structure on Folsom is rip-rap with stumps and submerged foundations.

they'll go down that deep, but they want to have it there, especially the quality fish. Fish the shade on breaks."

Trippe adds that smallmouth hold on vertical structure — the steep side of points and breaks — in the heat of summer. The bass slow down as the surface temperature approaches 80 degrees. Use plastic worms, small jigs and spoons. Trippe likes to use Kastmasters, because they give off more flash than most standard bass spoons, "but they have a junky hook. You have to change the hook before you can use them."

In fall, bass become active and move to the shallows for a brief period. This only lasts a few weeks on Folsom, but it can be terrific while it lasts. Trippe uses a pattern that begins with top-water, then moves down with spinnerbaits, cranks, and finally, if there isn't any action, worms.

"Typically, cranks are great in the fall," Trippe said. "Use a stop and start motion. Go five to ten feet first, if you don't get bit, try a deep diver. Or you can rip a fat Gitzit. To rip Gitzits, put them on a 1/8 to 1/16 ounce jighead, and rip them just like a minnow jerkbait. They are deadly."

This fall action is a feast or famine bite. The fish are going to be schooled tight, in only a few areas. It is important to concentrate on spots that look almost perfect, and stick with high percentage baits lyke jigs and worms on these spots. Between the places that look really good, cover the secondary water faster with crankbaits.

After Thanksgiving, the bass go on a winter pattern. There are two ways to fish for them. Trippe likes to go with a deep water vertical pattern, on rocky points off the main lake. The winter pattern is very similar to his summer pattern. The only difference is that it is a midday bite, from 10:00 a.m. until 2:00 p.m. But, the fish don't slow down any, "they'll freight train you. They still fight, even in cold water."

Walton, on the other hand, fishes the shallow-water bite even in winter. He goes for fish that come up into the shallows to actively feed. "You could go and fish the deep-water bass," he said, "but they aren't active. I also find these shallow winter-time fish are all quality fish, I rarely catch any small ones with this pattern. Every bass is two to three pounds at least."

For winter Walton fishes a small jig with a light-wire Aberdeen hook. It must be fished slow. Though these fish are shallow, they will be near vertical structure. Use a temperature gauge to isolate small ledges where the water is just a few degrees warmer, that is all it takes to bring up the active fish.

"Folsom is a fantastic lake," said Trippe, "but people have to take time to learn the spots. The fish aren't everywhere. But when you find one, there are usually a lot more in the area. Usually more than 20 fish a year are taken out of this lake that are better than 10 pounds. It produces a lot of good bass."

FOLSOM GUIDES

Bob Trippe (916) 782-8778
247 Fig St., Roseville, CA 95678
Bob is a licensed guide who likes to teach people how to fish. His sponsors are: R and B Tackle, Hal's Weenie Mania, Joe's Marine.

Jon Walton (415) 782-3932
Walton's Pond Bait and Tackle
23880 Hesperia Blvd., Hayward, CA 94546
Jon has been fishing for over 30 years. For the past 15 years his store, Walton's Pond, has specialized in black bass tackle. He teaches classes on fishing techniques through the shop.

Bob Trippe with a typical Folsom largemouth. Folsom is an up and coming fishery. People think of Folsom as a smallmouth lake, but there are many largemouth to be caught, with several over 10 pounds taken every year.

FOLSOM FACILITIES

There are three State Recreation Campgrounds on Folsom. None of the campgrounds have hookups. The cost per night is $10. For reservations call, Mistix, 1 (800) 444-7275.
• Beals Point has no launch ramp, but boats launch over the hard sloping ground. This is not officially sanctioned by the Park. There are 48 campsites.
• Peninsula has a launch ramp and 100 campsites.
• Negro Bar has a launch ramp and 20 campsites.
The area around Folsom is developed, with suburban cities and small tourist towns near the freeways. There hotels, stores and tackle shops near the main roads. Here are a few, but there are many more.
• Brown's Marina (916) 933-1300: Located in Brown's Ravine on Folsom Lake. This is a full-service marina, with; gas, snack bar, mooring, bait and tackle shop, and a launch ramp. From October to February the marina is usually shut down and the ramp left high and dry by falling water.
• Loomis KOA (916) 652-6737
3945 Taylor Rd., Loomis, CA 95650
This campground is 12 miles from the lake. There are 75 sites, some with full hookups. Also a swimming pool, hot tub ad laundry. The price is: $19.50 for full hookup, $18 with water and electric, $16 for tent sites.
• The Fishin' Hole (916) 791-2248
7120 Douglas Blvd., Roseville, CA 95661
A full service tackle shop located up the street from the Granite Bay Launch Ramp, two miles north of Beals Point State Park.

KEY TO FOLSOM

Best Season: March to June, the spawn is staggered on Folsom, taking place earlier in the main body of the lake than in the headwaters. There is a very good fall bite; October is the peak.

Lures To Use: Top-water lures like Tiny Torpedos, Pop-Rs, and Rebels. Also spinnerbaits in white or chartreuse. Use small plastics: Little Bits, Gitzits, and grubs. Shad, crawdad and purple are the most popular colors. Small jigs with light-wire hooks can be good in winter.

Primary Structure: The arms hold the best fishing on Folsom, not necessarily way back at the headwaters, but just inside the arms above the main body of the lake. The largemouth concentrate on the wood in the arms. The smallmouth hold on points with access to water that is 60 to 100 feet deep. They want shade and deep water nearby, and will congregate around whatever structure is on the point; it could be broken rock, a change in composition of the rock, or a lone tree stump. Smallmouth spawning flats must be close to those points where they hold the rest of the year.

Other: Light line always, don't use anything heavier than eight pounds.

HAVASU LAKE

A few years back, the largemouth bass population of Lake Havasu was declining. Today, the lake seems to be on the rebound and the largemouth are doing well. Fishermen are not going to hook any world record largemouth on Havasu, since the population is strictly northern strain. But, throughout most of the year, fishermen can count on landing a ten-fish limit of bass that average about two pounds. And that's tough to complain about.

Lake Havasu is a fairly typical desert impoundment lake. The primary structure within the 25 mile long lake consists of rocky points and breaks; the only vegetation within the lake are the grass beds that grow in the shallows during summer.

But, Havasu fishermen can't overlook the river. Bass boats can run upriver 65 miles, and that represents hundreds of miles of shoreline and bass water. The river is lined with small bays and there is plenty of shallow water structure. There are almost no trees in the lake, but there are some in the river channel, as well as tules and aquatic plants in the bays and coves. For the most part, river fishing is shallow water fishing, with the deepest spots being less than 15 feet deep.

For lures you have to be versatile, keep in mind that the main food source on the lake is shade.

There are bass throughout the Havasu waterway. The trick to catching them is knowing when to head up the river and when to concentrate on the lake.

"Both the lake and the river hold bass," said Bob Lee, "but it is almost like fishing on two entirely different bodies of water. One of the most important factors is the water level; the river can rise or fall one or two feet in a matter of a day. The river is no good when the water level is falling or when it is low, while the river really turns on when the water is rising. The water level in the lake is maintained at between 440 and 450 feet; because of the hydroelectric plant, rainfall has no effect on water levels. This helps the fishing in the lake to stay more consistent. Concentrate on fishing in the lake if the water level in the river is falling."

From March until May, concentrate on the bays and coves, at depths from two to twenty feet, in both the lake and river. The lake warms about a month before the river; for the early spawners, target the coves within the main lake, and then later in the year head for shallows and bays in the river. Sam Manning said, "You're going to find pre-spawn and spawning fish around Black Rock, Steamboat Cove, and within four or five miles to each side of Blankenship Bend. Another spring spot is at the north end of Devil's Elbow, back in the cattails."

"The key in early spring is water temperature," said Okie Vaughn. "One bay may be four or five degrees warmer than one that looks just like it. Even one side of a bay may be two or three degrees warmer. Look for the warmer water and areas with sand or gravel, rather than mud bottom. You don't need deep water, it is more important to have a lot of light, and tules or brush nearby."

At this time of year, Vaughn doesn't fish an area unless he has seen bass; polarized glasses are a necessity. Since not all areas will hold fish, Vaughn eliminates fishing dead water by casting only to fish that he knows are there. A boat coming into the clear, shallow water may spook these bass, but if fishermen leave and return quietly a little later, there is a good chance of landing the fish.

Havasu bass aren't terribly selective during spring, most shallow running lures can catch fish. Vaughn recommends working Gitzits, spinnerbaits and cranks, fished close to the bottom at slow to medium speeds.

The shad in Havasu are numerous, even in late winter. There is more than enough shad for the bass and stripers to feed on. Often the problem for fishermen isn't so much to locate bass, since the shad provide an excellent clue, the hard part is to get a bass to take a lure when it is already stuffed with shad.

"Lures with a spot of red somewhere on them are the hottest things going right now," Bob Lee said. "Almost all your shad colored baits work well, but they work better when they have a red belly or a spot of red around the eye. That little patch of tomato color might make the lure look like a wounded fish. When the bass are looking at a thousand shad, that small difference in the one that is your lure can be enough to trigger a bite." Another popular color is pumpkin with green flake, that imitates bluegill, which is the other primary forage fish on Havasu, especially in the river.

As a general rule, bass move to deeper, cooler water in

LAKE HAVASU

ELEVATION 450 FEET ABOVE SEA LEVEL

CONTOUR INTERVAL 10 FEET, AND INDICATES DEPTH OF WATER

SURFACE AREA 19300 ACRES

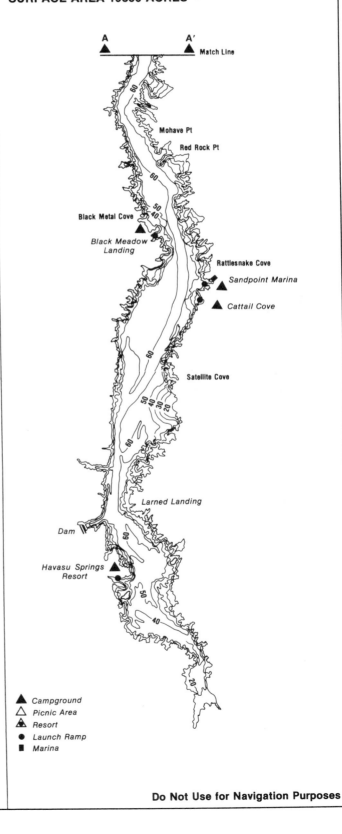

A   A'
Match Line

Mohave Pt

Red Rock Pt

Black Metal Cove

Black Meadow Landing

Rattlesnake Cove

Sandpoint Marina

Cattail Cove

Satellite Cove

Larned Landing

Dam

Havasu Springs Resort

Havasu Landing Resort

Windsor Beach

Crazy Horse

LONDON BRIDGE

Lake Havasu Travel Trailer Park

Lake Havasu Marina

Nautical Inn Resort

Thompson Bay

Grass Island

Contact Point

Copper Canyon Bay

Teal Point

Friendly Island

The Narrows

Pilot Rocks

Havasu Palms

Whipple Bay

Steamboat Cove

Beaver Point

SCALE APPROX

0   ½ MILES

A   A'
Match Line

▲ *Campground*
△ *Picnic Area*
🔺 *Resort*
● *Launch Ramp*
■ *Marina*

Do Not Use for Navigation Purposes

summer. There are two options for summer fishing on Havasu. One pattern holds for the lake and the other for the river.

In the lake the fish move a little deeper and hold off of points near shallow, shaded breaks. "On an open water impoundment like this, we are fishing on rock structures and rocky points," said Bob Lee. "Look for gravel points, barren rock holds nothing. Look for porous rock because that can hold food particles. I look for a shallow point with an abrupt drop-off. There is very little timber or vegetation, so look for areas where the roots of manzanita and mesquite are covered by water, or even better, where brush hangs into the water. Since there isn't a lot of this, what there is almost always holds fish. That's where the food is and that is where the bass are."

Even though the river doesn't have cool, deep water areas for fish to retreat down to, the constant current flow keeps the main river channel relatively cool. Bass move out of the bays that have become too warm and hold off of outside points in the channel current. Vaughn suggests flipping tules in the main river channel, in two to five feet of water, because the tules also help to keep the water temperatures down. A third way to fish the river is to drift with plastic worms. "It is almost like drift fishing for trout," Lee added. "Concentrate on the slower pockets of water and drag the worm slowly over the bottom, as the boat drifts downstream."

The London Bridge on Lake Havasu.

With such a variety of structure and depths that can hold bass in summer, there is no single lure that is going to do it all. Locals flip large spinnerbaits, grubs, jig and pig, Gitzits, and saltcraws. Plastic worms are popular in almost all areas, with darker colors preferred for muddy water, and light, natural colors in clear water. "Cranking will help you locate fish," said Lee, "and when I get a hit I switch to jigs and worms. An area that is good for one fish, is usually good for more. If I miss with a crank, I toss a smaller lighter worm. Throw a slower bait, and they'll hit it."

Very early morning, before the sun comes up, the top-water bite is great. Vaughn prefers a floating lure with propellers or rattles to make noise, like a Devil's Horse. Fish these over and next to grassbeds, in areas where there is a deep water break nearby.

Havasu is bright and hot so the fish will often be in the shady side of points and islands.

The desert weather is scorching in summer. For the most part, good fishing is in the early morning hours. Guide trips often begin at three or four in the morning, in order to get off the water by nine or ten. In addition to the heat, there is also heavy boat traffic on the lake by mid-morning. The skiers and other water tourists tend to restrict themselves to the lake. For those who want to find a little solitude, the river is the place to be.

September to November is premiere largemouth season. The air and water temperatures are a little cooler and the summer crowds drop-off considerably. The top-water bite is excellent through fall. White buzzbaits fished over grassbeds in the lake work well. "I've seen this bite last all day long," said Vaughn, "even when it's 100 degrees at noon, they'll eat a buzzbait."

The bays and coves where bass were found in spring are good areas to look for bass in fall, as long as there is deep water nearby. In November, fish move out of the bays and onto outside points, as the shallows become cold. The top-water bite will continue for a few more weeks in the river channel, before it too becomes chilly.

Winter is tough. A good graph is essential. Look for fish off of steep rocky points, in deep water. There is almost no timber in the lake, points are it. Use the standard, slower winter lures, jigs, spoons, and worms.

"After three or four days of warm sunny weather, fish may come up into the shallows, especially in the river bays," Lee said. "Try looking for fish in the shallow back bays that get sunlight all day, near tules or large boulders that help to absorb heat from the sun and transfer it to the water. This isn't the way to catch limits of fish on one spot, but each bay may hold a few aggressive bass. These large, hungry fish come shallow when a bay gets warm, even if it is a short-term fluctuation.

This is also a great lake for striped bass. In August and September, stripers hit lures as fast as fishermen can throw them. One hundred fish per day is not unusual. This is fast top-water action, on any bright, flashy lure. The stripers will bite all year long, though they are going to be below 30 feet deep in winter. For the most part the fishing strategy consists of following shad and using lures that work at the depth bait balls are found in.

HAVASU GUIDES

Bob Lee (602) 855-6744
Bob Lee's Professional Tackle Shop
40 Capri Blvd., (inside True-Value Hardware) Lake Havasu City, AZ 86403
  Bob owns his own tackle shop and has been a licensed guide on Havasu since 1972. He teaches fishermen while he guides, and tries to give them all the knowledge they want. He is comfortable guiding for black bass, stripers, catfish — whatever the customer prefers.
  Sam Manning (602) 855-FISH
Fishermen's Bait and Tackle
1509 El Camino, Lake Havasua City, AZ 86403
  Sam's tackle shop runs a guide service. Sam has been a licensed guide on Havasu only since 1986, but he has lived and fished for black bass on the lake since 1979.
  Okie Vaughn (602) 855-1544
  Okie is a pro tournament fisherman. He won back to back Western Bass Tournaments on Havasu in 1981. He qualified for the Red Man Regionals three years in a row, and he has qualified for seven Tournaments of Champions. He is a Touring Pro for Ranger Boats.

HAVASU FACILITIES

  Havasu is the home of the London Bridge. The bridge isn't worth a darn for fishing, so who cares, right? The point is, the bridge has spawned a whole mess of businesses that cater to visitors. There are dozens of restaurants, shops, motels and RV parks. There is plenty for non-fishing members of the family to do, while the fishermen hit the lake.
  For more information call:
  Lake Havasu Chamber of Commerce, (602) 855-4115.
  Lake Havasu Tourist Bureau, (602) 453-3444.
• Boat Ramps: There are public launch ramps at Windsor Beach, Nautical Inn Marina, Island Marina, and Sandpoint Marina. There are quite a few others as well. The average fee is about $3.
• Camping: There are a number of RV parks around Lake Havasu, including one on the island by the bridge. These are fine for RVs, but because of hot summer weather, there aren't any real tent campgrounds, at least there aren't any with sites shaded by oak trees, this is desert after all. For information on RV parks, call the Tourist Bureau or the Chamber of Commerce, listed above.
• Bob Lee's Professional Tackle: Bob carries a complete line of fishing tackle, and runs guide trips on the lake. Located inside True-Value Hardware at 40 Capri Blvd., Lake Havasu City, AZ. Call (602) 855-6744 and ask for the tackle shop.
• Fishermen's Bait and Tackle: Sam's tackle shop carries complete fishing tackle, and can provide guides for fishing on the lake. Located at 1509 El Camino, Lake Havasu City, AZ. Call, (602) 855-FISH.
• Lakeview Motel, offers rooms and boat storage. Singles go for $24 Sunday through Thursday, and $26.95 on the weekends. Doubles are $34.95. Located on 440 London Bridge Rd., Lake Havasu City, AZ. Call (602) 855-3605.

Bob Lee with a three-pound largemouth. This lake was on the decline but that seems to have turned around.

KEY TO HAVASU

  Best Season: March to May is the spawning season. September to November may be the very best season for largemouth, with fine weather, few people on the water, and hungry shallow bass. Summer is good, prior to sunrise.
  Lures To Use: Four- to six-inch worms and Gitzits. Crankbaits, spinnerbaits, and buzzbaits, as well as top-water plugs. As far as color, any shad imitation will be good, especially if it has a patch of tomato color in it. Bluegill imitations are good up in the river.
  Primary Structure: Think of Havasu as two separate bodies of water, the river and the lake. The river is good when the water is rising and the temperatures or boat traffic are excessive on the main lake. When the water level is falling, fish in the lake. On the lake look for points, drop-offs, any kind of break near deep and shallow water that can provide shade and fast access to deep water. Concentrate on porous or broken rock, also manzanita roots or brush hanging into the water. In the river, fish the bays and coves in spring and fall, when the water temperature is appropriate for bass. When it is too warm or cold in the coves, move into the river current where the temperature is moderated.
  Other: Clear water, use light lines less than eight-pound test.

HENSLEY LAKE

Hensley is a good northern-strain bass lake. Wait a second, at times Hensley just plain busts loose. As Jim Van Tassel said, "Last February Rob and I were up there split-shotting Green Weenies and we caught 99 bass. We were fishing over flat, bare, nothing ground, from 10 to 15 feet deep. You don't run into that everyday, but that was fun."

Hensley is located a few miles east of Madera. It is a lowland bass lake, at an elevation of only 540 feet. The lake covers about 1600 acres when full. It is fed primarily by rainwater run-off, and the water tends to be murky.

On Hensley, a car full of the newest, hottest lures won't bring in more fish than a coffee can filled with spinnerbaits, jigs and worms, in one or two colors. The Van Tassels, they're cousins, not brothers, have honed it down to the point where they use spinnerbaits of only one color, black. When it comes to jigs, they like the option of choosing between black and brown. As for the soft plastics, they know that brown with a dark flake will catch fish, all year long.

Honing in on the right type of structure is almost as easy. Rock piles are the number one structure. In the spring, there is newly submerged vegetation on the flats, and of course it is necessary to follow the fish from shallow to deep, but for the most part, find rocks and they'll hold bass.

Big, noisy and traditional lures catch fish on this lake.

Now basics doesn't necessarily imply easy fishing, what Hensley offers is a fairly consistent pattern. There aren't a whole lot of different types of structure for the bass to hold on in the first place, and there aren't several arms with different environments. Therefore, what works at one end of the lake, will work at the other. And the Van Tassels have more or less pared the whole fishing process down to the five or six patterns that work.

By February, bass come shallow in the pre-spawn movement. The fish won't spawn until March on this lake. From February until May is prime time for fishing on Hensley. Fish are aggressive, shallow, and easy to locate in the newly submerged vegetation on the banks and flats. Basically, where there are flats, fish will be on them, and there are flats all over the lake.

"In the springtime, we throw spinnerbaits back up into the shallow water," said Jim. "We use black spinnerbaits with a single blade, usually a Colorado, but it doesn't matter a lot. Sometimes I'll put a black pork trailer on the spinnerbait. It helps the lure float so you can slow down and reel a little slower. If we don't do real good on spinnerbaits, we move off a bit and fish brown and black grubs, or Green Weenies, in 10 to 20 feet."

In spring concentrate on the main lake flats. Rob Van Tassel said, "Just fish the long flat points in the main lake, the eastern side of the lake produces better. You can also fish the flats up towards the river, these are flat nothing banks, with hardly any rocks at all. Lots of guys fish the trees and the structure, 'cause they think that's what you need to find bass. But, hard-pan holds fish and doesn't get hit. Fish hold in those little breaks and not too many fishermen come and pull them off."

Flipping the trees in the river can be good, but only bother with it if there aren't a lot of other fishermen already on the pattern. If there is a lot of traffic on the lake, head to the spots that nobody else would fish on, like nothing banks or rock piles.

By summer, the bass move deeper and are associating with rock. Jim likes to use jig and pig, Gitzits, or grubs, in brown colors. "We use a 1/4 ounce leadhead on the Gitzits and grubs, mostly around rocks," said Jim. "Split-shotting Green Weenies is really good too, down at about 20 or 30 feet. All the baits we use are smaller, in the three- to four-inch range."

Hensley doesn't hold any shad, and that might be part of the reason why the bass don't move into super-deep water or suspend, as a rule. It also makes brown and black lures more effective, because that is a better imitation of the main forage base. Hensley bass eat crawdads, bluegill and rockfish. Rockfish look like brown bluegill, but they have a mouth that is shaped like that of a bass.

During the day in summer, fish over submerged rock piles that top out at 15 feet and then fall off steeply to between 25 and 40 feet deep. To fish this steep structure, hold the boat in the deeper water, cast up to the shallows, and work the bait all the way down. Rob points out that rockfish associate with these steep rocks, and they could be holding anywhere from shallow, to deep, and everywhere in between; so the feeding bass can be at almost any depth around these big rocks. To cover the whole area thoroughly means working

HENSLEY LAKE

ELEVATION 540 FEET ABOVE SEA LEVEL
CONTOUR INTERVALS INDICATE DEPTH OF WATER
SURFACE AREA 1570 ACRES WITH 24 MILES OF SHORELINE

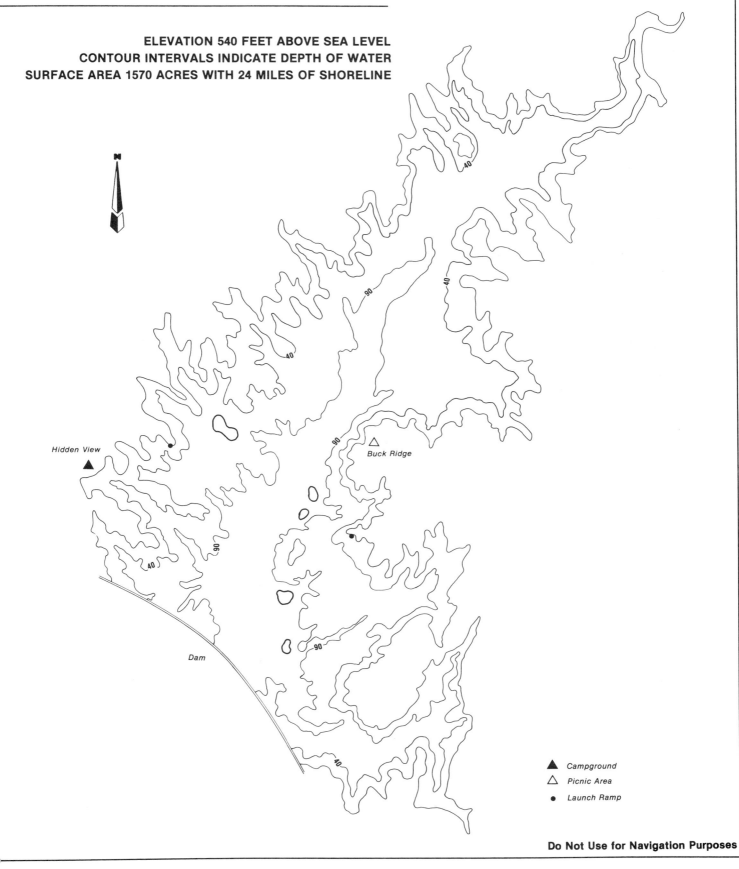

Hidden View

Buck Ridge

Dam

▲ Campground
△ Picnic Area
● Launch Ramp

At one end of the lake you fish trees; the other is all rocks and drop-offs.

Rob Van Tassel battles a nice Hensley largemouth.

the rocks not just from side to side, but also from the top to the very bottom.

"There is lots of moss on the lake in summer," said Rob. "It's sticky stuff that forms on the surface. But, you'll find bass underneath it. Throw ring-worms and jigs in there."

Jim added that there is a good top-water bite early and late in the day during summer. He uses buzzbaits, Pop-Rs, and Zara Spooks. Work a top-water bite anywhere that bass have quick access from deep to shallow water.

Night fishing is very good on Hensley all through the spring and on into fall, but it is at its peak in summer. Fish that move deep during hot summer days, come up into the shallows at night to feed. At night, throw black spinnerbaits with pork trailers, buzzbaits, or dark-colored worms. Cast right onto the bank and work out to water about 10 or 15 feet deep. Rob said, "I'd take night fishing over anything else. As long as you can take the cold, you can get a fish. And nighttime is when you're going to catch your big fish."

By the middle of September, the bass are on a fall pattern. The key to catching them is to work slow and deep. Work rock piles in the main lake, anywhere from 20 to 30 feet deep with Gitzits and jigs. "You can also crank a real deep diver on the steep wall, like a 20+ diver," said Rob. "Park in open water, and crank along the banks. You have to make a long

cast and just bring it back in at 20 to 25 feet. But, if cranks don't produce pretty quick, you have to go do something else, 'cause those deep divers will wear you out."

"In winter, it slows way down," said Jim. "What happens is the lake is down at minimum pool, and then it starts to rise a little and that shuts the fish off. When it is rising the lake will come up over a foot a day. Until it stabilizes, the fish won't bite well."

During winter use black jigs with black pork and head for the dam. Work water from 20 to 40 feet deep, on rock piles or steep ledges. "Also in winter, if the river gets to running good, the trout will move in there," said Rob. "You can go and catch bass back in there, right in the running water 'cause they are feeding on trout. Throw black or chartreuse spinnerbaits, into the eddies. The bass get into the dead water, behind or against a tree, and if something comes by, they'll hammer it."

Winter fishing lasts only from December to January. By February, it's back into pre-spawn.

Rob displays a good bass.

HENSLEY GUIDES

Jim Van Tassel
26385 Ave. 26, Chowchilla, CA 93610
Jim fishes with his cousin Rob, in team tournaments in their area, and they have done well on their local lakes. Jim has been fishing seriously for bass for the past five years, though he has fished since he was a kid. He lives within minutes of the lake, and gets out on the water frequently. He is sponsored by Super Lures in Madera.
Rob Van Tassel
26707 Ave. 26, Chowchilla, CA 93610
Rob has fished for bass for the past seven years, and lives right by the lake. He was Angler of the Year twice with the Fresno Bass Club, and has won many pro tournaments in the Central Valley. He is sponsored by Ewing's 76 in Chowchilla and Super Lures out of Madera.

HENSLEY LAKE FACILITIES

Hensley Lake Recreation Area, has a 52 site campground, with rest rooms and hot showers. There are two launch ramps, at Hidden View Campground and Buck-Ridge day use area. There is no launch fee. The camping fee is $8 a night, from March 1 to September 30. There is no fee the rest of the year. A group campsite is available by reservation at $25. Other than the group site, there are no reservations accepted. For more information, call, (209) 673-5151.

Other: There are motels, restaurants, and tackle shops in Madera and Chowchilla, within a few minutes of the lake.

Good sized crappie are always an alternative when bassing is slow.

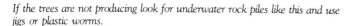

If the trees are not producing look for underwater rock piles like this and use jigs or plastic worms.

KEY TO HENSLEY

Best Season: Spring and summer. From February to April or May, terrific fishing for quality northern-strain largemouth. In summer, good top-water in the morning, but the real ticket is to fish at night.

Lures To Use: Black spinnerbaits, through the spawn and summer. Also jig and pig, Gitzits, and grubs, all in browns or blacks. Four-inch worms, in browns and Green Weenie colors, for split shotting.

Primary Structure: Newly submerged vegetation in spring, and, and rock piles year-round. There are only a few trees up in the river. When there is a lot of pressure on the lake they get pounded; better to go for the nothing banks that don't attract fishermen. Also, fish through the moss that covers the surface in summer.

Other: On a murky lake, go with eight- to twelve-pound line.

HODGES LAKE

Lake Hodges, in San Diego, is famous for big fish. The average size bass caught from the lake ranges from three to five pounds. Those who fish Hodges regularly can bring in nine or ten fish of 10 pounds or better each year. The lake is very rich in nutrients, producing enough bass to provide initial stockings for many other lakes in the San Diego area. Hodges was the first of the California lakes to be stocked with the fast-growing Florida-strain largemouth.

The bad news is; Hodges isn't the place to head for peace, quiet, or solitude. In fact, it is probably the most consistently crowded lake in California. Fishermen literally wait in line all night to get on the lake in time for the early morning bite. And once on the lake, an isolated fishing spot is impossible to come by.

But, the crowds shouldn't get in the way of the fact that Hodges is one of the top contenders for the next world record bass. In spite of pressure, the fishery is not declining. It should remain excellent for many years to come.

Hodges is not open every day of the week, or all year long, so before planning a trip check with San Diego City Lakes for the current schedule. The lake usually closes in September and opens sometime in March.

This can be a tough lake so be versatile. Work lures that enable you to fish through the water column and experiment with different sizes and colors.

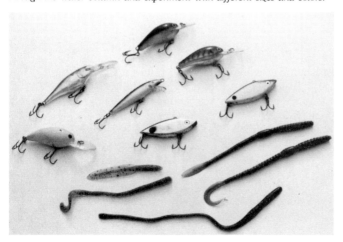

Hodges covers 1,234 surface acres and has 12 miles of shoreline. Since it is relatively small, this is a spot lake, rather than a pattern lake. Most of the areas likely to hold fish can be covered in a single day. Look for fish near the flats, especially flats with stick-up, and along migration routes formed by structure. Both sides of the dam are good, as well as the Narrows and the area known as the Beehive. The Bernardo Arm is great when the water is up, but terrible in low water years. When the water is low, there are no tules or timber areas for bass to use for cover.

Hodges bass go through standard yearly migrations, seeking out spawning flats in spring, slightly cooler water off points and breaks in summer, and holding off steeper banks near shallow water in fall. Fishermen will find that Hodges bass don't move a lot, they tend to hold in the same general areas. Look for breaks with deep and shallow water nearby, and cover as well. The best fishing depth varies little; eight to twenty feet is the most consistent range on this lake, no matter what the season. This is partly because when the bass move deep in winter, the lake is closed.

When working any pattern, keep in mind that fishing pressure affects the bass. "The lake gets hit so hard, the fish don't do what they should do sometimes," said Rowan Stone. "There are a lot of coasters, a lot of suspended fish. There are eight or nine areas where the bass pull off of structure that is being fished heavily. You might say that we fish in spots where the shoreline fishermen almost drive the bass to us."

Frank Pierce added, "The lake opens at daylight, and everybody runs for the same spot. The fish just go. So I head for the outside of those shoreline areas that get nailed and fish for bass that are moving out to deeper, safer water. Usually we jig vertically with spoons, sometimes we'll use worms."

In spring, when the lake opens, the bite is excellent. Any experienced bass fisherman can plan on catching nine or ten shallow bass in the morning. Later in the season, the bite becomes tougher and remains fairly slow through summer. In summer, bass aren't going to be deeper than 20 feet on this lake, but they will be in thick cover, or on the outside of points for most of the day. "The fish really like the tules at Hodges," Stone said. "If they can't get in the tules because of low water, they'll stack up off the points in slightly cooler water."

Pierce and Ray Koetter favor plastic worm fishing throughout the year on Hodges. Koetter likes worms with some blue in them, in fact he likes a little blue in all of his Hodges lures. Cinnamon-blue is one of the most popular colors on the lake. Pierce uses watermelon, black, "Otay brown" and purple, depending on the clarity of the water. The worms are generally four to six inches long, sometimes eight or twelve inches, and the way they are rigged is a matter of personal preference.

"We also use Reepers down here," said Pierce. "The Reeper is a staple. Whenever the bite is tough, at any time of year, put on a Reeper." Use the three-inch Reepers, fished super slow, on a size one or two hook. The pressure bite can be light on these small slow lures, so set the hook at the slightest change in line motion.

On the other hand, Stone likes to use spinnerbaits during

LAKE HODGES

ELEVATION 320 FEET ABOVE SEA LEVEL
CONTOUR INTERVALS 10 FEET, & INDICATE DEPTH OF WATER

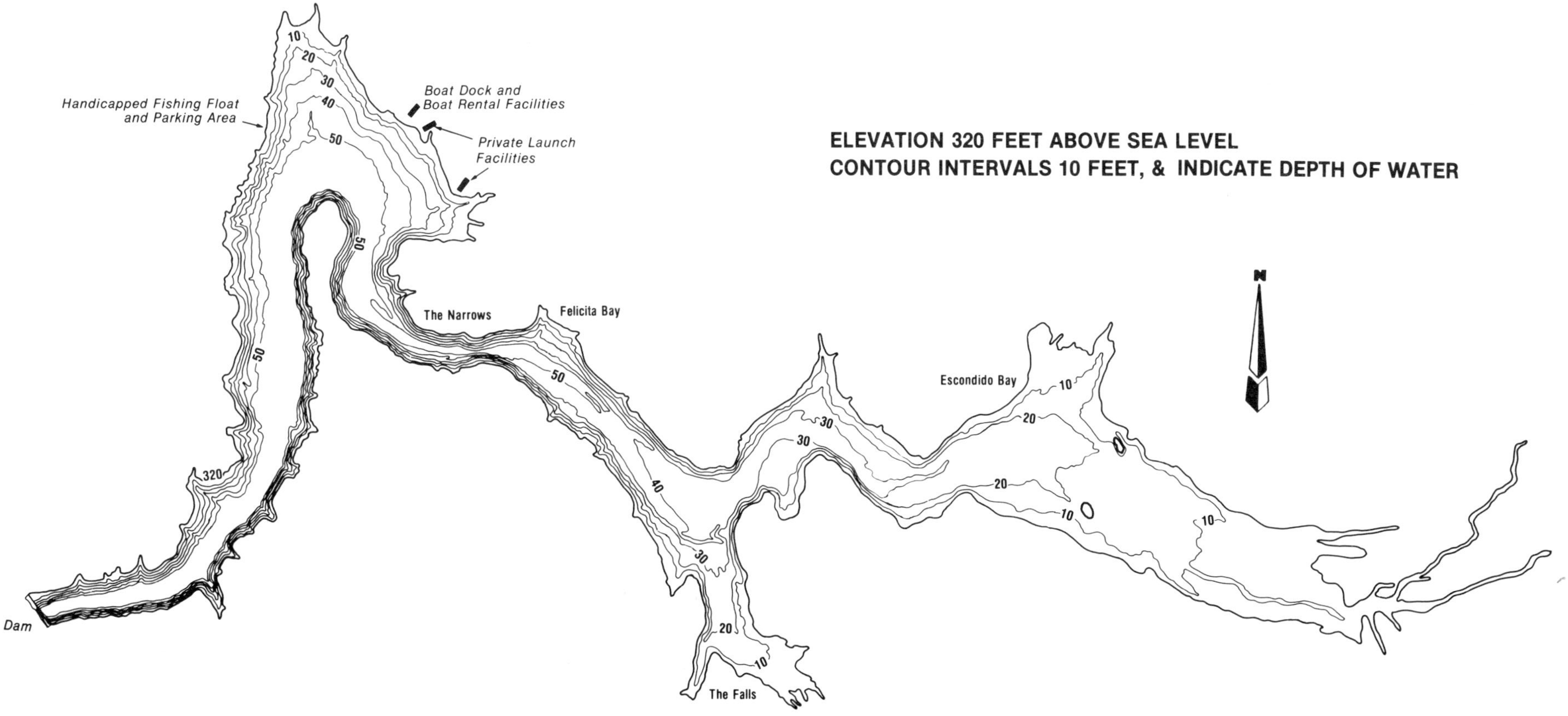

Escondido Bay

The Falls

Felicita Bay

The Narrows

Boat Dock and
Boat Rental Facilities

Private Launch
Facilities

Handicapped Fishing Float
and Parking Area

Dam

10

0

10

20

20

30

30

10

20

30

40

50

10

20

30

40

50

50

50

320

spring. He'll fish them on the flats and shallow breaks; also try flipping into the tules or casting parallel to the tules. He also uses a lot of jigs for fish that are in 10 to 20 feet of water and waiting to move up onto the flats for the spawn.

The top-water bite is excellent in fall, when there are fewer fishermen on the lake to put the fish down. Use Spooks, Rapalas and Pop-Rs, wherever there are shad busting the surface. The bite often lasts all day long, even in bright sunny conditions. "It's the movement of the bait that is important," said Pierce. "If the bait stays up, the top-water bite will stay on all day."

But, the real tactic on Hodges, is to go after fish that are moving off the primary structure, as it is pounded by other fishermen. Look for the migration channels, where fish can move off of the shoreline structure to a secondary off-shore spot. These fish may suspend well off the bottom, moving in a lateral line, rather than heading down to very deep water. For example, the bass may move at a constant depth of 10 feet, while the bottom drops down to 30 feet or more. Spinnerbaits will catch the shallower fish, and spoons jigged vertically are good for the deeper fish. Stay beyond the casting range of the shore fishermen and there is a good chance of finding fish.

Ray Koetter shows why people like to fish Hodges.

Fish near outlets.

Windy days in summer and fall can be great. Koetter said, "I throw cranks a lot when it is windy. I look for straight, long ledges and drop-offs where I can work parallel to the banks. Most guys throw into the wind, but I work with the wind so I can get longer casts. Use a lipless crank and count down, keep the lure on the bottom, so it bumps and kicks up a little dirt as it works."

While fishermen on most lakes head to points where the wind will create feeding action, Stone moves to the flats at the far end of the lake. It is just another example of choosing an area that on many lakes would be considered secondary, because the obvious primary areas are always hammered by

other fishermen. "All the fishermen are going to the points when the wind blows," Stone said. "So I head for the open flats. You have to cast into the wind, 'cause that is the way the fish are facing. It's a pain to hold there and cast into the wind, but it can be very productive."

It isn't surprising that the fish at Hodges can be very selective. Simply having the right lure and the right spot isn't always going to do the job. In some years, the fish have refused to hit any lure that is moving, in other years the only way to make a fish bite is by shaking a worm like mad. Sometimes a stop and start technique is the only way to get a bite. Be resourceful. Check with the locals and find out what retrieves and methods have been producing recently.

In a normal year, the lake will close before the fish move deep in a late fall pattern. However, if the lake stays open late, and it is unusually cold with water temperatures below the mid-50s, try working the steep drop-offs with jigs and spoons.

For big fish, Koetter suggests going into deeper water. He'll graph in 12 to 25 feet until he finds a large fish. Now these big guys can be pretty spooky and it is likely that the boat coming into the area will scare them off. So once Koetter finds a spot he sits and waits quietly, it may be as long as a few hours; but that fish will come back. When the fish does return, Koetter tries to get the big bass on an eight- or twelve- inch worm or a jig and pig, worked slow and quiet.

Of course, the best way to catch a hog is to use Koetter's method to find fish, and then drop a crawdad or shiner over the side. Shiners are legal in San Diego and bait is readily available in almost every tackle store.

There are big fish in this lake, and plenty of them. For those willing to adjust their tactics Hodges will offer a fine day of fishing as well as the chance for some spectacular bass.

HODGES GUIDES

Ray Koetter

Ray has fished the San Diego lakes for the past five years. He is active in the San Diego bass clubs, and has been to several Tournaments of Champions, in addition to taking Club Champion one year. He works very hard to put his non-boaters onto fish.

Frank Pierce, R.P.Guide Service (619) 944-7834

7916 Avenida Diestro, La Costa, CA 92009

Pierce has been a licensed guide for four years, and has fished the San Diego Lakes for 12 years. He was California State Champion and California Angler of the Year twice, with Military BASS.

Rowan Stone (619) 698-8826

2425 Massachusetts Ave., Lemon Grove, CA 92045

Rowan has been a licensed guide for eight years and he has been fishing these lakes for 20 years. He has been Hidden Valley Bassmasters, Angler of the Year and has finished in the top ten of U.S. Bass a few times.

Structure includes points, rock, and some tules.

HODGES FACILITIES

Hodges is controlled by the San Diego City Lake Department. There is no camping on the lake, but there are plenty of hotels, motels, campgrounds, stores for bait and tackle and everything else, and other services in San Diego. There is a lake fishing fee of $3.50 per bass fishermen, or $4.00 per trout fishermen. There is also a $4 launch fee. The lake is not open all year. The tentative schedule opens the lake in March and closes it in September. Hodges is open only on Wednesday, Thursday, Saturday and Sunday. Call the Fishing Hotline for current information, (619) 465-3474.

Dusk is usually a good time to fish for bass.

KEY TO HODGES

Best Season: Spring and fall. The lake opens in March, and is very good for the first few weeks. Then fishing pressure makes it tough until late August or September — when the weather cools off a bit, the fish come shallow again, and the crowds stay home.

Lures To Use: Eight- to twelve-inch worms for big fish. Four-inch worms and three-inch Reepers for more bites. Spinnerbaits and other swimming lures that can be used in the tules, or for suspended fish off the flats. Also top-water plugs that imitate shad and crankbaits for windy days.

Primary Structure: Fish don't move real deep, at least not while the lake is open to fishing. Concentrate on water of less than 20 feet. That might be in an area off the flats where fish are suspended over 30 feet of water, but they will have moved offshore in a lateral line to somewhat deeper water, without moving all the way down to the bottom. Tules, flats, shallow breaks, and points, are all good for bass. When the bite is tough, work in the thick cover, or on offshore migration routes and rock piles.

Other: Eight to twenty feet is the most consistent fishing depth. Use lines of six to twelve pounds.

ISABELLA LAKE

Isabella is a quality largemouth lake. The current lake record is 18 pounds, 13 ounces, caught in February 1989. Even though Isabella has produced some large fish, it doesn't seem to have peaked yet, in all likelihood the lake record will be broken again within the next few years.

Isabella is ideally suited for producing trophy bass. It is located in the foothills above Bakersfield, at 2600 feet. The moderate elevation provides these fish with an almost year-round growing season, much like the famed San Diego Lakes and Lake Casitas. But, Isabella is much larger than any of these waters, with more than 11,400 surface acres. It is a heavily fished lake, but compared to other big fish lakes in California, Isabella doesn't come under extreme fishing pressure. With 38 miles of shoreline and a variety of structure types, bass have a fighting chance to reach wall-mount size.

Don't get the idea that this is a lake with only a few monster-sized bass in it, guides on the lake can practically guarantee a 10 pound or better bass in March and April. On the other hand, they can also virtually guarantee a limit of bass. This is a quality over quantity lake, but there is a strong population of largemouth in the three to four pound class that keeps the action going.

This lake can be tough. The guides recommend starting the day with a top-water bait and working the water column until you get into fish.

There are two primary factors that affect bass movement on Isabella. The first is seasonal migrations which follow a classic pattern for shad lakes, with bass holding shallow in spring and fall, and deep in winter and summer. The other important factor to consider, especially in recent years, is water fluctuation. In rising water, the bass move into the newly submerged vegetation in the shallows. In falling water they suspend.

It is easy to get into a rut, and stay on a fishing pattern that produced bass in rising water. But, this spells disaster on a lake with extreme water level fluctuations. "Last year, everybody went and fished the same old spots," said Steve Merlot. "These were fine when the water was high, but the fish had moved. Most guys weren't catching anything. I went out and approached each day as if I had never seen the lake before."

"The first thing I did each day was locate bait. I'd go right to the middle of the lake, in deep water and mark it with a float. Then I made circles around the float, getting wider with each pass, until I located a big school of bait, which I would fish for a while. Then I took note of the depth and searched until I found the nearest structure at that depth, and I would fish there, too. This seems like it takes a long time and a lot of guys thought I was crazy, driving around in circles in the middle of the lake, but there were plenty of times that I caught limits of bass and nobody else was catching anything. The fish just weren't holding in the usual spots."

With rising water, finding fish is a good deal easier. Look for fish in the two main arms of the lake, and near submerged cover. When the water holds steady, the bass follow standard seasonal patterns.

In early spring, the pre-spawn bass move up the long points and rock structure that is near deep water. Look for fish on the migration routes to the spawning flats. "There is a lot of light and sun in the northwest coves," Jerry Corlew said. "These are the first areas to warm, and they are good in March and April. Always have a top-water lure and a crankbait ready to go, they are excellent during the pre-spawn. Actually, they are good all year, except in winter."

As the spawn gets fully underway, bass hold in all of the shallow warm coves, in less than 10 feet of water.

This is a crankbait and top-water lake; these are the first baits to try on any of the spawning flats. If they don't produce, split-shot four-inch worms over the warm flats and around cover. Green worms work well on Isabella, try any of the mossy green colors, as well as Green Weenies, and also any worm with some brown in it.

Cloudy days are a good sign, since the lack of bright sun keeps the fish on a shallow, top-water pattern through the day. But, the lake really turns on in the wind. Corlew said, "The harder it blows, the better the fishing gets."

Fish the points that the wind is blowing onto, where there is wave action and muddy water. This may require anchoring, since it is often the only way to hold a boat right in the wind where the fish are biting. It is practically impossible to work a worm in these conditions, so stick with crankbaits and top-water lures, the wind will bring the fish up. There are warning lights and a siren, on Isabella, that indicate dangerous winds. Conditions can change in about 15 minutes, if the siren goes off or the warning lights turn to yellow, get off the lake immediately. Fifty mph winds are not unusual in spring.

By summer, the bass hold in deeper water, but they still hit top-water early in the day. "Start out with a top-water lure, like a Zara Spook, a Devils Horse, or a buzzbait," said Corlew. "It can last all day long, even on a bright sunny day and you want to stay with the pattern as long as it works. The bass may be in only six inches of water; don't ever overlook the shallows, throw on the bank and drag the lure off. The best summer areas are in the main lake at the big points, they are tremendous."

When the top-water action isn't on, work finesse baits in 18 to 25 feet of water. Four-inch split-shot worms are the lure to rely on, whenever crankbaits and top-water aren't working well. The action of the lure can be important in the summer, experiment with shaking and doodling to attract a strike.

There are a lot of submerged trees along the North Fork river channel that hold bass in late summer, especially when the water is low. Flip the trees and the break along the river channel with jigs rigged with plastic trailers. When the water is high and the trees are too deep, flip the rocks in the North Fork.

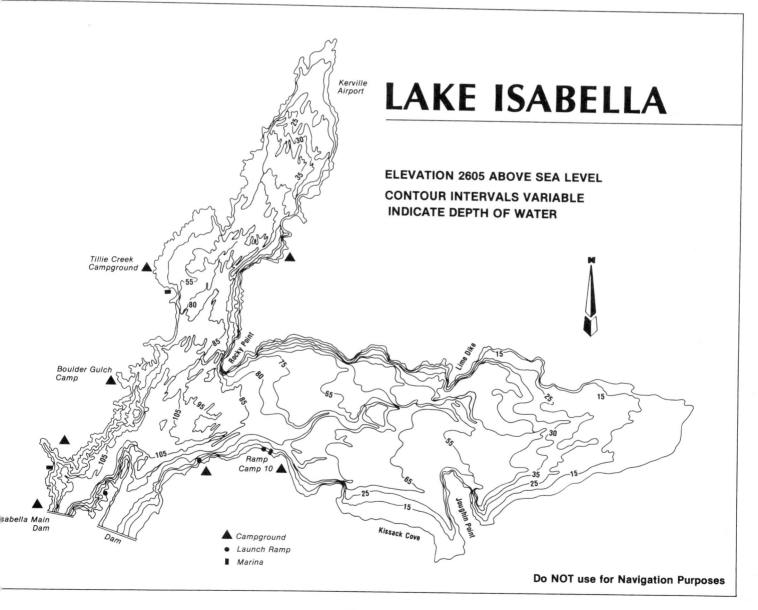

LAKE ISABELLA

ELEVATION 2605 ABOVE SEA LEVEL

CONTOUR INTERVALS VARIABLE
INDICATE DEPTH OF WATER

Kerville Airport

Tillie Creek Campground

Boulder Gulch Camp

Rocky Point

Lime Dike

Ramp
Camp 10

Isabella Main Dam

Dam

Kissack Cove

Joughin Point

▲ Campground
● Launch Ramp
■ Marina

Do NOT use for Navigation Purposes

"In October and November, there is a real feeding binge. The fish bite all over the lake," said Merlot. "There will be bass on Rocky Point, Engineer Point, and Pine Point, pretty much the same areas where you can always find them in summer, and still at about the same depth. But, they are more active. It is a good time to go fishing."

Finding shad is critical in fall. The bass are having their final feed before the cold of winter, and they are going to be wherever shad is readily available. But, the shad are on the move, as they migrate to winter waters. The shad may have moved deeper or they may migrate to the backs of coves, off the river channels. The trouble with fall is that the bass could be anywhere in those parameters, at depths from five to forty feet.

Jerry Corlew sticks a fish on a ripping bait. When you do this the same pattern will hold up until there is a change in conditions.

Think of fall as a transition period. A good graph, like a Lowrance X16, is the best tool for finding shad and bass in fall. Use it to find the depth the bait-balls are at. If they are shallow, stick with top-water, if they are below 20 feet, use jigs and worms. When shad are busting in the backs of coves, the top-water fishing is great with any lure that imitates shad.

Winter is a different ball game altogether. Whereas during the rest of the year, there is always a good chance of catching active bass on top-water and fast crankbaits, winter is the time to slow way down and move deep.

Jig and pig, and split-shot are the consistent winter baits. Super deep diving crankbaits can work, if they are fished slow enough and deep enough. In winter the bass hold anywhere from 20 to 60 feet. They won't be shallow, unless the weather has been warm for several days, and there is very deep water nearby. As in fall, a graph is essential.

The bass often hold on the same areas as in summer, off of the steep rocky points in the main lake. If the water is high, they may also hold on the submerged trees and the breaks in the river channel, in both the South and North Fork. Use vertical jigging techniques around the trees and on the breaks, where the bass suspend.

In summer and winter, fishing walls and points in the main part of the lake can be effective.

"By February, fish may already be moving shallow. If the water is rising, the bass can be around the newly submerged cover," Merlot said. Concentrate on the sunny banks, late in the day, where the water is warmest. The bass are still lethargic, go with slow finesse baits, like worms and jigs.

"Keep an open mind year-round," Corlew added. "On this lake, patterns vary widely from day to day. The fishing is good all year-round, but you can go from a 30 fish day, to a no fish day, like that. Don't get locked into a pattern. Always keep your top-water handy, but be ready to change. At any time, you could catch a wall-hanger."

In spring, fish the newly submerged vegetation.

ISABELLA GUIDES

Steve Merlot (805) 832-9644

Steve has been fishing Isabella and other lakes in the area for many years. He fishes tournaments and does well in them. He is not a licensed guide, but will provide on the water instruction.

Jerry Corlew (619) 379-3500 or (800) 832-5873.
Anglers Pro Specialties
3833 Lake Isabella Blvd., P.O.B. AE
Lake Isabella, CA

Jerry is President of APS, a lure company. He has designed a full line of finesse baits for tough to catch fish. His line is best known for the Shakin' Shad. He is not a licensed guide, but provides on the water fishing instruction. He also speaks at seminars and has been featured in video productions on Lake Isabella.

ISABELLA FACILITIES

U.S. Army Corps of Engineers, operate five launch ramps and three marinas that sell bait and tackle on Isabella. There is no fee to launch at any of these public ramps.
• They also operate 10 campgrounds on or near the lake. Not all of the campgrounds charge fees, those that do all charge $8 a night, from March 1 to September 30. Call (619) 379-2742 for information, reservations are not accepted, except for group camps. Following is a summary of the campgrounds:

Main Dam, 82 sites. There is no fee.
Pioneer, 78 sites, a marina, showers, and a playground.
Boulder Gulch, 79 sites and showers.
Hungry Gulch, 78 sites, with showers.
Live Oak North, is near Wofford; 60 sites and showers.
Live Oak South, 90 sites and showers.
Tillie Creek, 159 sites, showers, marina and store.
Eastside, 109 sites, rest room, boat ramp, no fee for camping. Popular with fishermen.
Paradise Cove, 138 sites, and a restaurant across the street.
Auxiliary Dam Recreation, camping-at-large (the sites are not numbered), there is a marina nearby. No fee is charged.
French Gulch Boat Permit Station: Boat permits are required for Isabella; the fee is $10. They are obtained at the Station, which is open dawn to dusk, seven days a week. Call (619) 379-2806.
• Lake Shore Motel: This is the only motel on the lake. They have 10 units at $35 and $40 a night, depending on if there is a kitchen in the unit. There is also a double-wide mobile home, with two bedrooms, two bathrooms, a kitchen, living room and bar, for $75 a night. The motel is open year-round. They do not have a launch ramp, but the Tillie Creek Ramp is only one mile away. (619) 376-2898.
• Lake Isabella Motel, is 1/4 mile from the lake. There are 17 units ranging in price from $30 to $40. There is a boat parking area, swimming pool, TV and coffee. Located at the junction of Highway 155 and 178. (619) 379-2800.

Other: The nearby towns have stores, restaurants, and motels. There is no shortage of services in the area.

Bass can give you quite a fight.

KEY TO ISABELLA

Best Season: March and April, for big fish as well as numbers. October and November are good too. In summer, fish top-water early and late in the day.

Lure To Use: Crankbaits and top-water, are the first lures to try at any time when there is a chance feeding fish might be shallow. Four inch split-shot worms are the lure to rely on when the faster moving baits don't produce. Jig and pig, or jigs with plastic trailers are good for deep-water, and flipping into the trees, especially when there is current.

Primary Structure: Early in the year, fish back in newly submerged vegetation if the water is rising. Also go for the spawning flats in the northwest coves and the migration routes leading to them. The submerged trees in the North Fork may hold bass in summer, and the main lake points are good too. In fall, look for bait and fish on all the main lake points. In winter fish steep, rocky points on the main body of the lake, at 20 to 60 feet. Points with wind blowing onto them are good most of the time, fish to the bait action, rather than mud lines.

Other: A boat permit is required for all boats on Isabella. The fee is $10, permits are available at French Gulch Boat Permit Station, see Facility Section. Wind is a big factor, and a big problem on this lake. Especially in winter and spring, the winds on the lake can be greater than 50 mph. There are warning lights and sirens on the lake, when the light changes to yellow, get off the lake. That is tougher to do than it sounds, since wind often turns the fish on.

JENKINSON LAKE

Dan Hannum said, "The smallmouth in Jenkinson get up to four pounds. It is such a good fishery that they pull smallies out to stock other lakes. It is almost like a natural hatchery."

Jenkinson is hardly a household word among bass fishermen. It is one of those out of the way, unexpected bass fisheries. At an elevation of 3,500 feet, 45 minutes west of Tahoe on Highway 50, this small lake has gained renown as a trout and mackinaw hot spot. But, the smallmouth fishery has remained untapped.

The steep, red, mud banks and cool, clear water are ideal for smallmouth. The lake, surrounded by pine-covered mountains, covers only 640 surface acres. This small size keeps large tournaments off the lake. At the same time it makes Jenkinson an ideal spot for a family fishing vacation; it is possible to fish all the good-looking spots in a single day.

As far as the size of the bass goes, Jenkinson isn't exactly a trophy smallmouth lake. This could have to do as much with over-population of bass, as with the shorter growing season a high elevation lake affords. The smallies get up to four pounds, but the average size is closer to two pounds.

Jenkinson Lake is a great smallmouth lake. But experiment with your lures, if they want plastic they won't take anything else.

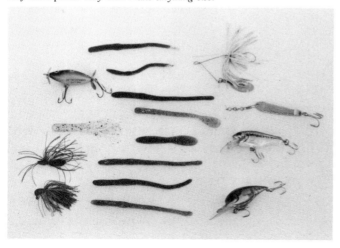

Since Jenkinson has clear water, light lines and smaller baits are the rule, six- to eight-pound test is standard. The primary forage is crawdad and shad, so crawdad colored baits are excellent. Salt and pepper, silver and black, and other light-colored shad imitations are also good.

"I have had my best luck with crankbaits in the rocky areas," said Don Wilbanks, "where there is small broken rock covering a bank. I also catch fish in the weeds and stuff too, but cranks seem to be best around the rocks. When a crank doesn't produce, I go with four- to six-inch worms, in lighter crawdad colors. Gitzits are real good on this lake. I have even caught mackinaw on Gitzits — one was 21 inches long. The salt and pepper colored Gitzits make a good shad imitation, so all the fish in the lake that eat shad will hit Gitzits. The brown Gitzits are good for imitating crawdads."

The water starts to warm on Jenkinson in late March or April. The smallmouth are into pre-spawn pattern by April; they'll spawn in May. "Early in the year, the place to look for bass is in the areas where sun warms the water, mostly along the northwest shore," said Hannum. "I'll cast parallel along steep vertical banks. The smallies tend to move more than largemouth; you have to keep moving with them. They may come up from forty to five feet of water in less than an hour."

In early spring, the best time of day to fish on a high elevation lake like Jenkinson is in the early afternoon, when the water is at its warmest and the fish are most active. As the water temperature nears 60 degrees, the morning bite improves. However, unlike many lakes, the midday through afternoon bite is always decent at Jenkinson.

Slow-moving worm tactics produce bass the entire year and during the spawn is no exception. Basically, any lure that can be worked slowly over the bottom is going to catch fish. "Sometimes when they are spawning, I'll throw right on the bank and then drag the lure into the water real slow," said Wilbanks. "That seems to bother them as much as a lure worked through the water; when it comes off the bank it really gets to them. A lot of their food comes right from the banks."

In summer, the smallmouth may be in shallow water early in the morning before the sun hits the water. However, as soon as the sun is up, they'll move down and into shade cast by points and steep walls.

"In the heat of the day, get the graph turned on," said Hannum. "Work slower. Graph fish on those steep walls, then bring them up with a Tiny Torpedo. Cast right against the wall, and barely move it, they'll come up from the deeper water and hit it. Sometimes you'll even get two fish coming for it at once. A friend of mine even got two fish on one lure. There's a lot of fish in this lake, and they are real aggressive at times."

At this elevation, the water cools off fast in fall. The smallmouth may go through a short feeding binge, but it is brief and hardly worth relying on. After October, the bass concentrate off the major points, seeking a suitable temperature range and food. On Jenkinson, the fish are getting hit with double trouble in fall; as the water cools, the lake is also drawn down. These bass have to cope with a major change in the water level, just at the time when their metabolism is slowing. It makes the fishing tough. "When the water starts cooling down in October," said Wilbanks, "I kind of look at it as the dog days of bass fishing."

In a sense, winter offers better fishing than fall. At least it is more predictable. At this elevation it is obviously cold, but after a few warm days in a row, feeding bass come into shallow water.

The lake partially ices over in winter, though it won't freeze solid. In winter, fishermen are pretty much restricted to bank fishing with plastics and jigs. For this reason, the winter fishing is still shallow, for fish that come close to the shore to feed. Even though most of the bass may hold off-shore in deeper water, they aren't within fishing range without a boat. So fish from the bank near deep water, in areas where the sun shines all morning long.

"I caught a 2 1/2 pounder, with snow all over the banks," said Wilbanks. "It was great, I was out there all by myself and could see the snow-caps on Tahoe. There were deer and mallard ducks, and then I caught a fish too. As long as it is warm enough for you to stand it, you can catch fish on this lake."

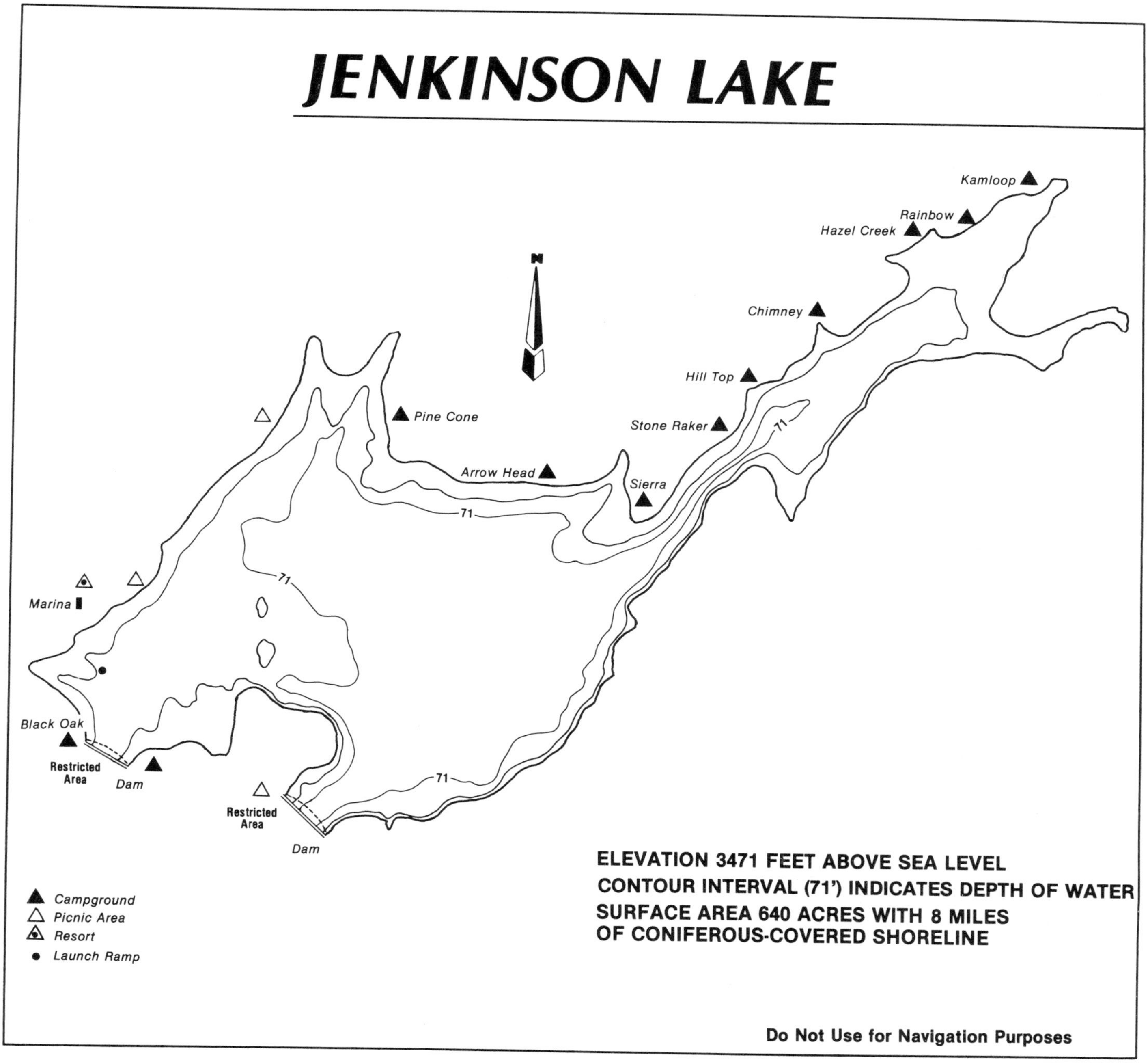

JENKINSON LAKE

Kamloop
Rainbow
Hazel Creek
Chimney
Hill Top
Pine Cone
Stone Raker
Arrow Head
Sierra
71
71
Marina
71
Black Oak
Restricted Area
Dam
Restricted Area
Dam
71

▲ Campground
△ Picnic Area
⊿ Resort
● Launch Ramp

ELEVATION 3471 FEET ABOVE SEA LEVEL
CONTOUR INTERVAL (71') INDICATES DEPTH OF WATER
SURFACE AREA 640 ACRES WITH 8 MILES
OF CONIFEROUS-COVERED SHORELINE

Do Not Use for Navigation Purposes

For lots of hard fighting smallmouth this mountain lake is hard to beat.

JENKINSON GUIDES

Dan Hannum (916) 541-8801
P.O. Box 822, South Lake Tahoe, CA 95705
Hannum has been a licensed guide for the past five years, after a lifetime of fishing. He guides on Tahoe and Jenkinson. Hannum is a field tester for DuPont/Stren.

Don Wilbanks (916) 644-2413
Pine Lodge Club
6231 Pony Express Trail, Pollock Pines, CA 95726
Don has been fishing for bass on Jenkinson Lake since moving to Pollock Pines 11 years ago. He knows the lake as well as anybody around. Since it is right behind his house, he is able to get out and have a few casts several times a week.

JENKINSON LAKE FACILITIES

Sly Park Campground: launch ramp, 182 campsites, without hookups, on a first-come/first-serve basis. $9 per night, call (916) 644-2545.

Sly Park Resort: Directly across the road from the campground and lake. There is a general store with gas, bait and tackle, bar and grill. Call (916) 644-1113.

Pine Lodge Club: This tavern is located at 6231 Pony Express Trail, Pollock Pines, just across highway 50. The bar serves drinks and snacks, and is open year-round.

KEY TO JENKINSON

Best Season: April through September. Spring fishing starts later at this elevation than on lowland lakes and fall comes early and hits hard. But the fishing is good all summer, even on top-water.

Lures To Use: Shad colored Gitzits, crawdad colored worms and jigs. Tiny Torpedos for top-water.

Primary Structure: There is very little vegetation in the lake. Stick to the red clay banks, covered with broken rock. The lake is small enough to cover all of the good looking water in a single day. The main river channel arm is closed to skiing making it a good spot to head on a busy summer weekend.

Other: Clear water, use four- to eight-pound line. Jenkinson may partially ice over in winter.

Dan Hannum landing another nice bass.

Dan holding a typical Jenkinson Lake bass.

This lake does have a fair amount of stick-up but it does not seem to hold fish nearly as well as the rocky banks.

KAWEAH LAKE

L ake Kaweah is a decent bass fishing lake. It may not produce the biggest bass in the world or the most fish, but that isn't to say it isn't worth a visit. During spring and fall, and at night in summer, it isn't much trouble for the average fisherman to land a limit of keeper bass within a few hours. Quite a few of those bass will be in the two to three pound range.

Kaweah covers 2,000 surface acres when full, though it fluctuates drastically, and is dropped to minimum pool through fall and winter each year. When the lake is down, the deepest water is about 50 feet deep, when full about 150 feet deep. The contours of the lake are made up of steep, rocky walls, with boulders, creek channels and cuts as the primary structure. When the water rises after April 1, mustard, willows, and grass provide excellent cover.

In the past Kaweah produced quality northern-strain bass that hit consistently from spring through early fall. Recently the lake was poisoned with rotenone, to remove white bass. There were fears that the white bass would escape from the lake into the Delta and destroy the salmon and striper fisheries. Kaweah was treated in fall of 1987 and restocked with Florida-strain largemouth and spotted bass brood stock.

Lure selection for Kaweah.

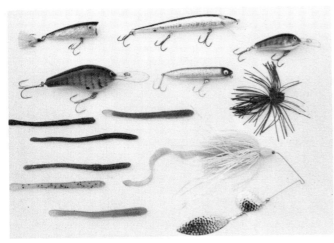

So far, the impact of the lake's treatment on the bass fishery has been positive. Fishermen are catching limits of decent-size bass, and occasional lunkers up to 12 pounds that were part of the initial brood stock. In addition to the rotenone treatment, the Department of Fish and Game, in conjunction with local fishermen, implemented a number of measures to improve Kaweah's bass fishery.

The first step was the creation of a spawning pond, located above Greasy Creek. Each spring, fishermen take five pairs of spawning stock and place them in the pond. These bass spawn slightly earlier than those in the main lake because of warmer water temperatures, and their spawn is not endangered by the water level fluctuations that always take place in the main lake. After they spawn, the adult bass are removed from the pond, to allow the fry to grow to fingerling size without predation. As the lake level rises in spring, the spawning pond is flooded, and the juveniles are released into the main lake.

Fishing clubs also planted willows around the edge of the lake and placed plum trees in Horse Creek, along with brush piles and Christmas trees to provide sanctuaries for fry. Given a few years of normal rain and snow fall, all of this work should pay off in an excellent fishery.

Pre-spawn fishing usually gets underway by late February, when the fish become active and begin to move into water of 15 to 25 feet. The best early season baits are four-inch plastic worms, spider jigs, and three-inch grubs. Look for long sloping points and migration routes. The lake level doesn't rise much until April, when it is filled by snow-melt; prior to April 1st, even if it rains, the water level is dropped by the Army Corps of Engineers to insure adequate storage capacity for snow melt.

By March, the water temperature is usually up to 55 or 60 degrees, and the bass are feeding in less than 15 feet of water. The key for spring fishing is to concentrate on the newly submerged vegetation. Fish to the rising water because bass come up from the deep main lake looking for food, warmth and spawning flats. The most extensive flats are in Horse Creek and Greasy Cove.

"The lake will back up into Horse Creek," said Terry Hamlin, "and the bass are venturing into those cockleburs, willows, weeds, and mustard. You can pick them up on spinnerbaits. I usually fish a willow leaf, with a two-inch blade. You can work spinnerbaits over the top of the mustard. Or try twitching a Rapala or a Rattlin' Rogue in there. There is a pretty good top-water bite over the weed beds in spring."

This pattern of concentrating on brush and the high water line lasts until the end of May. By this time the majority of the bass have completed the spawn. Hamlin points out that because the lake is still high, fish are dispersed throughout a larger body of water than is available in the fall and winter. The number of fish per acre of water is lower in summer when the lake level is high. The difference in spring is that the fish aggregate along the rising water line, and they are more aggressive in the optimum water temperature. The wide dispersal of bass, combined with overly warm temperatures during the day, makes fishing in summer pretty tough.

The basic pattern for daytime fishing from June to August,

LAKE KAWEAH

ELEVATION 694 FEET ABOVE SEA LEVEL

**CONTOUR INVERVALS 40 FEET &
INDICATE DEPTH OF WATER
SURFACE AREA 1945 ACRES**

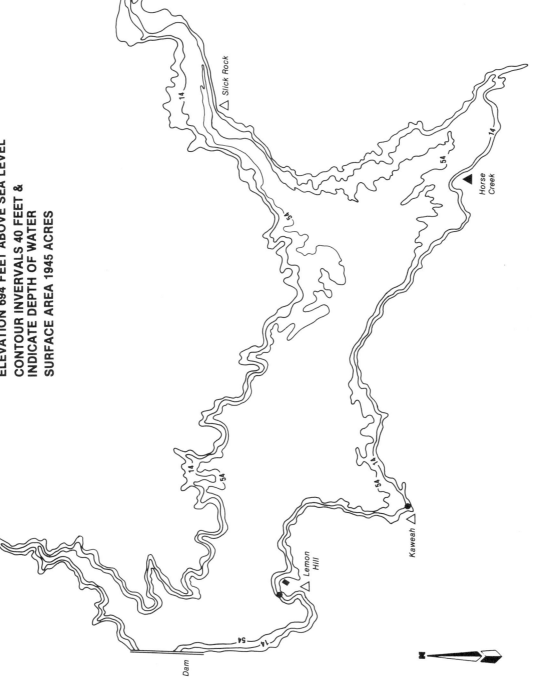

Dam

Lemon
Hill

Kaweah

Slick Rock

Horse
Creek

▲ Campground
△ Picnic Area
● Launch Ramp
■ Marina

Enjoy the scenery at Kaweah Lake.

consists of working water from 15 to 30 feet deep with split-shot worms. Look for bass on cuts, breaks and ledges, with a drop of three feet or better, near deep, cool water. Early in the morning and late in the evening, top-water lures and spinnerbaits will catch fish at depths of six to eight feet, as long as these baits are fished fairly close to deeper water.

Bill Bibbler gets around the tough fishing during the day in the summertime by fishing at night. He said, "I like the night fishing in summer. It always seems you get more action. Fish that are at 30 feet during the day will come up shallow at night. I use a regular light, rather than a black light on the boat, because it attracts the insects, and the insects attract the little fish and that brings in the bass. When I am working depths from five to fifteen feet, I use a six inch or longer black, plastic worm, Texas-rigged. To fish shallower, I go with a spinnerbait or spider jig. Throw them right to the edge of the bank and work it back, the closer the lure gets to the bank, the better."

By August, the lake level is dropping. It will approach minimum pool by the middle of September. Hamlin feels that the fish tend to suspend as the water falls, but he copes with it by moving with the falling water. He works the bridges at the mouth of Horse Creek, when the water falls to the level where the top of the bridge is about 20 feet deep. Also look for little drops and rock structure, in 15 to 30 feet of water.

As the lake gets down to minimum pool, Hamlin feels the fishing improves for about two months in September and October, though Bibbler thinks that fall is the toughest time of year. They disagree on one primary point, while Bibbler thinks the fishing is good throughout the year, with the exception of periods of falling water; Hamlin feels that high water is the toughest condition. Perhaps their disagreement is more a matter of personal fishing styles working better at one time of year, than an indication of a big difference in the quality of the fishing.

"In fall, the lake is getting down into minimum pool and the temperature starts cooling down," said Hamlin. "The bass come up and concentrate in water from six to twelve feet deep, or sometimes out to fifteen. Find breaks with 12 to 15 feet of water on top, and then you'll find the fish lying right on top of those breaks. They are real aggressive at this time of year."

For fall lures, Hamlin recommends six-inch worms, jig and pig, and spinnerbaits. Also, crawdad-colored crankbaits have been very productive since the rotenone treatment of Kaweah. The rotenone killed the shad, but it didn't affect the crawdads, which went through a major population explosion. Panfish were restocked along with the bass. Now the primary forage species in the lake are crawdads, panfish, and catfish fry. Both guides suggest that brown, green, and reddish lures, typical imitations of crawdads, are likely to be even more effective than they were in the past, when shad imitations were also popular.

There is a decent top-water bite during September and October, in the morning and early evening. Fish the points and banks with medium-size Pop-Rs. Use top-water lures when the sun is low.

By mid-November, start fishing the winter pattern. In December and January, the water temperature is down to about 45 degrees. The bass hold in the areas of the lake where the bottom is 35 to 50 feet down. The only water that is 50 feet deep in Kaweah, when it is at minimum pool, is in a few holes near the dam. The deepest water in most of the lake is only 35 feet.

In any case, the fish are fairly dormant, holding in water as deep as they can find. Slow down and fish finesse baits. Small plastic worms on split shot, or jig and pig, are the best winter lures.

"I like winter for a couple of reasons," said Bibbler. "In the first place, you have almost the whole lake to yourself. And I love worm fishing. It is a real super, super slow bite; when you think you are fishing slow, slow down about half that again. Find the steep cuts and breaks, use a super-light split shot, and light tackle; fish it slow, and it will make all the difference. If you have confidence that there are fish in a spot, keep working it and make them bite."

KAWEAH GUIDES

Bill Bibbler (209) 594-5922
Sierra Sporting Goods
21695 Hwy 198, Exeter, CA
Bill owns Sierra Sporting Goods and has fished on Lake Kaweah for about 25 years. He has fished for bass very seriously for the past 11 years, following the pro circuit and local club tournaments. He is on the pro-staffs of Ande fishing line, Mister Twister, Tru-Turn hooks, and C.O. Custom Worms.

Terry Hamlin
448 Pomegranate, Woodlake, CA 93286
Terry has fished on Kaweah, ever since the lake was built and fished the river before the dam went in. He has lived in this area his entire life and now lives within seven miles of the lake.

Terry Hamlin with a really healthy looking 4 pound bass.

FACILITIES AT KAWEAH

Lake Kaweah Recreation Facility, has two launch ramps operated by the Army Corps of Engineers, there is no fee for launching. They also have 80 campsites, at $8 a night from March 1 to September 31; in the off-season there is no charge. There is a full-service marina at the Kaweah launch ramp, with bait and tackle, boat rentals, and gas. Call, (209) 597-2526.

Other: There are motels, stores, and restaurants in nearby Visalia and Tulare.

Kaweah is full of rock piles.

KEY TO KAWEAH

Best Season: Spring, after April 1st when the water is rising. The lake is good for night fishing in summer. It is also good from the time water gets down to minimum pool in fall, until the lake turns over — there is a period in November with really tough fishing.

Lures To Use: Spinnerbaits, with a single large willow leaf blade. Also spider jigs, in spring put a twin-tail trailer on them for more action. Three- to four-inch plastics are always good in spring, six-inch plastics for fall. Shad imitations used to be very popular, but now that the shad have been removed, it seems that crawdad and panfish imitations work better.

Primary Structure: When the water is down, points, rocks, ledges, cuts and creek channels, all of these are contour-type structure. When the water is high, fish in the newly submerged, mustard, cockleburs, willows, and grass. There is very little wood in the lake, though plum trees have been added in Horse Creek, these are only used by bass when the water is up.

Other: White bass were killed off in fall of 1987 with rotenone treatment. The lake was restocked with Floridas and spotted bass. Both species seem to be doing very well in the post-treatment period, this lake could become very good in the next few years.

LOPEZ LAKE

Phil Whittemore said, "Lopez is a great lake that few people fish seriously. It is a real sleeper. You can catch five- and six-pound bass with consistency and land a limit easily in spring." Though Lopez is small, with only 950 surface acres, the lake is slowly earning a reputation as a quality bass fishery. The largemouth average better than two pounds, with enough larger fish to keep things interesting. It is hard to give a realistic average size for the smallmouth, since they tend to sort themselves by size. One spot will hold either a whole lot of dinks or a few two- to three-pound fish. In addition the lake holds crappie up to three pounds.

Lopez is a consistent fishery. No matter what the season, a fisherman can always expect to catch bass on this lake. The number of fish may not be quite as high in winter, but that is made up for by a larger average size, with almost no small fish caught. And even on a day to day basis, the lake remains predictable. Lopez fish don't go into a feeding frenzy one day, then shut down the next. If bass were biting in a particular area yesterday, the odds are they will be on the same spot today, and taking the same lures. Nothing is guaranteed in fishing, but Lopez comes pretty close.

Most of the fishing area is in the two main arms of the lake. These arms are former creek channels, with steep-sided canyon walls and sharply defined points. When the lake is full,

Plastic worms catch fish reliably all year on Lopez. The lake is known to be a good spinnerbait lake. Jigs and gitzits work well in the winter.

oak trees grow down to the water's edge. A lot of wood was left standing below the water line when the dam was constructed, providing excellent structure. Grass and moss cover the bottom and the shallows from late-spring until the onset of winter creating additional cover, especially for the largemouth.

The lake has fairly clear water, most of the year. The only exceptions are: during rains when run-off causes the water to become murky, during the algae bloom, and during turnover. The guides recommend using light lines of about six to eight pounds. They also prefer to use smaller lures that imitate the small shad and crawdads that are the predominant bass forage in Lopez.

"Spring fishing starts about a month late, in comparison to other Southern California lakes," said Dan Frazier. "The spawn will kick in around late March or April when the water temperature hits 62 to 64 degrees. In early spring I like to use crankbaits and spinnerbaits. The fishing is best late in the day when the water temperature is warmer."

Jim Hale recommends combining a faster reaction bait pattern, with slow-moving worms and jigs. He divides a bank into 50 to 100 yard sections and fishes each section first with a reaction bait, and then returns and covers the same water with a small jig. He always works the same area a second time, even if he has caught fish on spinnerbaits or crankbaits, to be sure that he doesn't miss less aggressive fish.

While the overall water temperature is cool, look for largemouth in the warmer sheltered coves. Smallmouth will stage their spawns in slightly deeper water, on gravel banks. For both species, once the spawn begins, the males remain on the beds and the larger females move offshore and suspend.

Summer water temperatures are not as extreme on Lopez, as on many lakes farther inland. The bass will keep right on biting. The smallmouth move a little bit deeper and hold off of the main points, but the largemouth feed in the shallows early and late in the day.

"Summer is my favorite season on Lopez," said Phil Whittemore, "because the grasses make it easy to find fish. I don't even use a graph in summer, I go right after the grass beds. I use a lot of Rat-L-Traps and spinners in summer. And I'll flip the grasses with a gator-tail worm. A gator-tail is a fat six- or seven-inch worm, with a serrated tail. I fish it on a 5/0 Weapon hook with 20-pound line. This is a great lure for catching fish that are holding right in the thick of the grass."

Frazier prefers to move off of the deep main points, ledges, and the bends in the river channel. He feels that where he finds bait near structure, there will be bass. He uses a variety of lures, but on a tough bite he turns to 2-inch grubs and 4 1/2- inch worms. Worms and grubs should be fished with split-shot to allow the worm to float up and out of the moss that covers the bottom in summer.

"Top-water buzzbaits are really good," said Whittemore, "especially when it is dark. One of the nice things about this lake is they let you get on the water before light — and this is a morning lake. If you get out before daybreak and throw a buzzbait around the grass, you'll get a limit before the sun comes up."

Hale adds that the top-water bite is real good in the evening too. He often fishes for only an hour or two after work

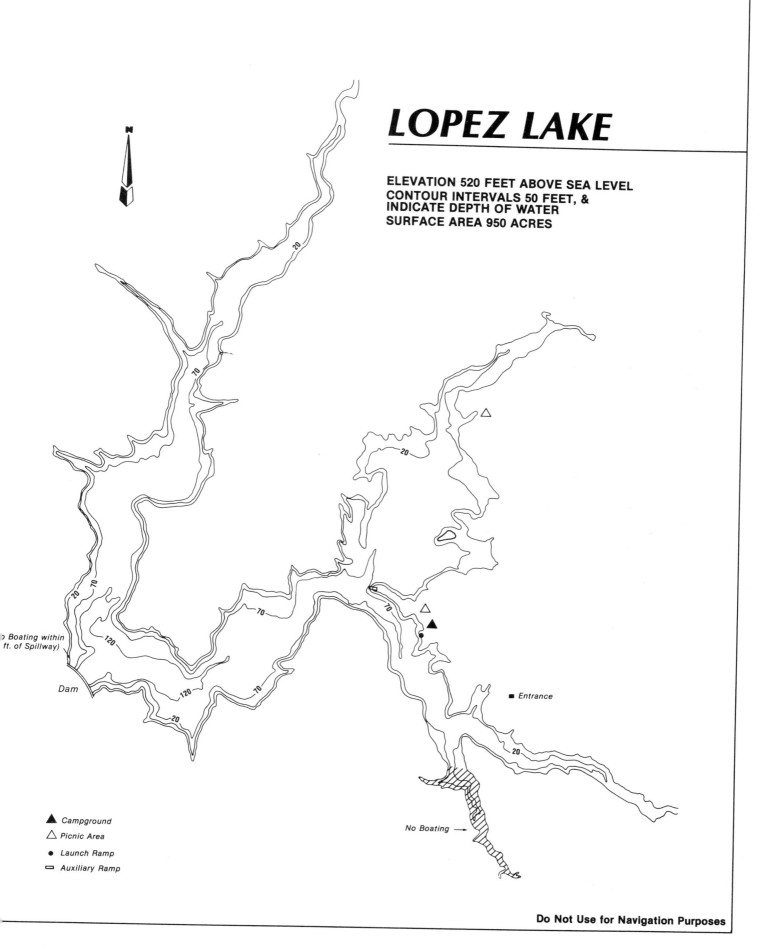

LOPEZ LAKE

ELEVATION 520 FEET ABOVE SEA LEVEL
CONTOUR INTERVALS 50 FEET, &
INDICATE DEPTH OF WATER
SURFACE AREA 950 ACRES

20

70

20

70

70

70

120

120

20

70

20

□ Boating within
ft. of Spillway)

Dam

■ Entrance

20

No Boating →

▲ Campground
△ Picnic Area
● Launch Ramp
▭ Auxiliary Ramp

Do Not Use for Navigation Purposes

Fish at Lopez hold to rip-rap, rock and trees.

during the summer, and catches plenty of bass in a short time.

To some extent, fall is a continuation of the summer pattern. The bass seem to congregate more, where one or two bass may have held off a particular point in summer, there may be five bass in fall. The bass begin to slowly move deeper, but it isn't a sudden shift, just a slow trend over the months. Whittemore continues to concentrate on the largemouth in the grassbeds as long as the vegetation lasts. There is usually some grass until the end of November. Frazier keeps working the points, fishing deeper as the weeks go by.

"I'll go fish the chunk-rock banks," said Hale. "Chunk rock is where the rocks are about as big as a fish. These are steep banks, mostly on the west-side of the Lopez Arm of the lake. But, I start by working a jig through areas I think hold fish. If I don't get bit, I'll go back and try to draw a strike with a crank. Rat-L-Traps work good in fall. To find the depth the fish are holding at, I start fishing parallel to the bank in water about 10 feet deep and keep moving out, to 20, 25, 30 and so on. Once I find the depth the smallmouth are holding at, I work sections of bank at that depth. The fish will hold at about the same depth, all around the lake."

"Winter hits all of a sudden on Lopez," said Frazier, "it happens in a week, like a buzzer going off. Winter is my favorite season to fish at Lopez, because you know where the fish are. You can spend a dollar in gas and fish all day, because you aren't going anywhere. The fish are on the five or six major points. That's it. There is no searching."

The bass are going to hold on the major points, at a spot with structure. A graph helps to locate fish, but don't be fooled by the crappie, they look like hundreds of suspended bass on a graph. The bass are the fish that are holding near structure, and they aren't in such large groups.

The dam is a great place for smallmouth, but because of the large rocks it is difficult to see fish that are holding tight. A graph isn't much use in this area of the lake, except for locating bait. The best system to target schools of smallmouth is to use Hale's technique of working vertically, parallel to the dam and at a shallow depth, then gradually move deeper until you find fish. The larger smallmouth are usually grouped into only two or three areas near the dam, so mark the spots where they bite, and keep working them. The fish are most likely to be at about 50 feet, but that varies 20 feet in either direction, depending on the severity of the winter.

Small jigs, worms, and spoons are good for winter on Lopez. The key is to use a lure that is easy to maintain contact with, when fished deep and slow.

Hale uses a jig and spoon combination in winter. "The spoon is a little faster," he said, "you can cover a little more water. I often start out with a spoon, jigging it around steep rocky areas. If I don't get bit, I switch to the jig and fish it slow, real slow. I might drop the jig down on the bottom and let it sit. Just leave it there. It doesn't seem like you're doing much, nothing is happening. Then you lift the rod up, and there is a fish on. That is how light the bite is, and how slow you have to go. I consistently catch my better fish from November to February. You don't catch a lot, but almost every fish is over two pounds."

Lopez is a popular spot for local bass clubs to hold their winter tournaments, primarily because stringers of more than 15 pounds are not at all unusual. Most tournaments of only 20 or 30 recreational anglers, will see the top three places weigh in more than 15 pounds of bass. They may not always get limits, but the fish that are caught are heavy.

The only catch is that in winter the fish are localized, grouped up in only a few spots on the lake. The guys who are fishing the wrong areas will rarely score. Stick to the main points, use a graph, and it should pay off in good winter bass fishing.

LOPEZ GUIDES

Dan Frazier (805)481-7539
388 Chaparral Ln., Arroyo Grande, CA 93420
Dan has been a licensed guide for five years, he guides not only on Lopez, but on many Central California lakes. He has won many first place awards in tournaments on these same lakes.

Jim Hale (805) 349-0399
1054 Red Bark Rd., Santa Maria, CA 93454
Jim has fished Lopez since 1975 an average of several times a month. He has fished many tournaments on the lake, and as yet, has always placed in the top three. He is a smallmouth fiend, and has had two articles published on smallmouth fishing. He manufactures Skinny Bear jigs.

Phil Whittemore (409) 597-6343
174 Pine Ridge Ln., Montgomery, TX 77356
Phil was a bass guide for many years in the Santa Barbara area. He has now moved to Texas to try his luck at the pro circuit, where he has been doing well.

Dan Fraizer lands a black bass.

LOPEZ LAKE FACILITIES

Lopez Park, has camping, launch ramp, lake store with bait and tackle. It is popular for wind surfing and water skiing, there is one arm of the lake that is reserved for fishermen only. There are 349 campsites. Sites with full hookups are $16 per night, electricity only $14, no hookups are $10 per night. Day use is $3 per day. Boats entry is $3.50. Reservations are taken six months to fourteen days in advance at (805) 489-8019. A taped recording with current weather and other pertinent information can be heard by calling, (805) 489-1006.

Other: There are grocery stores and restaurants in nearby Arroyo Grande. Motels are in Pismo and San Luis Obispo.

KEY TO LOPEZ

Best Season: The spawn gets underway by late March or April. The fishing stays good until the lake turns over in fall. This can occur any time from the end of October to early January. Good in winter.

Lures To Use: Four-inch worms and jigs. For all lures, stick with smaller sizes that imitate the small shad and crawdads in the lake. Big gator-tail worms are good in the grass.

Primary Structure: Grass beds, wood, main points in the lake. Lots of shallow bays for spring fishing, stick with those on the north side of the arms. Deep vertical walls and the dam area in winter.

Other: A sleeper lake with quality bass. The water is clear, stick with six- to eight-pound line.

Submerged trees are always good spots to fish.

MARTINEZ LAKE

Bass fishermen don't have to travel farther than Martinez Lake on the lower Colorado to find classic, southern-style bass fishing. Jim Waits described Martinez Lake as, "aggressive western bass fishing, on a shallow-water tule lake.

Unlike most reservoirs in California, Martinez was never clear-cut or dredged. The native mesquite trees were left in place and provide excellent structure for bass. Tules grow everywhere and bass thrive. Though the number of bass caught and released in a day is good, this isn't a "dink lake." There are a few eight and nine pounders caught each season and in 1988 the Lower Colorado River record was broken with a largemouth that topped 12 pounds, taken out of Martinez.

But, this is a difficult water for most California fishermen, primarily because it is large and unlike anywhere else in the state. Martinez Lake should really be described as a landing on the Lower Colorado. From Martinez, there is boating access to more than 90 miles of river, and almost 120 small lakes, called potholes by the locals.

The big question is, where in this vast waterway will the fish be biting?

Before fishermen can even begin to answer that, they need

The main lure choice for Martinez has to be either worms or jigs which can be used for flipping.

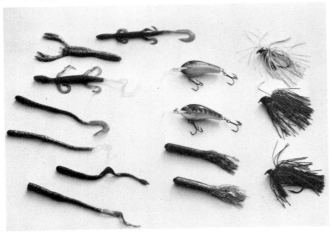

to get a mental picture of four distinct fishing areas: one, the river above the landing; two, the small lakes and bays that are for the most part above Martinez; three, the river-channel adjoining Martinez Lake; and four, Martinez Lake itself. The quality of fishing in each of these areas varies with the season and water-level fluctuation. First, we'll cover each of these areas and when to fish them, then describe techniques and lures that work in the region.

Martinez Lake itself is a large and relatively shallow body of water, surrounded by tules. According to Waits, the lake is the best place to fish on the entire waterway. The reason being that 40 or 50 tournaments a year weigh-in at Martinez Lake. A single tournament may release 300 fish into this area, so it is constantly stocked with large fish. "You see it all the time," Waits said, "guys drive for miles to catch fish and the tournament is won with fish caught right in the lake."

The river-channel from the lake down to the dam has to be considered separately, primarily because the water temperature of the river-channel can vary from that of the lake by as much as 20 degrees. In summer, the lake becomes too warm for active bass, while the flowing river seldom rises above 75 degrees. The river-channel may hold fish throughout the year, but as Bob Kinley said, "Summer is the best because fish move out of the lake and the river really turns on.

"We fish the river by 'back-sliding'. This is a drift fishing technique. We drag a worm on the bottom, using the trolling motor to slow the boat down. We also flip the tules on the banks as we drift, hitting spots that look good as we slide downriver."

The miles of river above Martinez also offer excellent fishing. (Consider it separately from the river next to and below Martinez Lake, because the water level fluctuation is much greater above Martinez.) There are seven major bends upriver forming the primary fishing areas. These spots offer ideal bass habitat with deep, slow water, tules, rock, and timber.

There is one particular segment of river that flows east to west, with bays on the north side. Fish in these northern bays will move into pre-spawn and spawn a full month before they do anywhere else in the region. This is the place to be in early spring.

Other areas that hold fish on the river are on straight runs, that Ed Legan said, "don't look like they offer any type of cover for bass." These are areas with dead-fall and trees hanging into the water; fish in the slow still water just below the obstructions.

Now, for those 120 lakes mentioned earlier. These smaller lakes and hundred of bays can be reached from the river by boat, but many of them are inaccessible in low water. The lakes are best from late fall through spring and in high-water conditions, in summer the tiny lakes become too warm for bass.

These small lakes are great for fishing from float tubes, many can be reached by car and a short walk. In addition to the lakes on the river, there are also 30 totally land-locked lakes that are seldom fished. The landlocked lakes are virtually untouched, and can be great spots to fish from the bank or from float tubes.

The key non-seasonal factor in deciding which of these

MARTINEZ LAKE

Including the All Pocket Lakes.

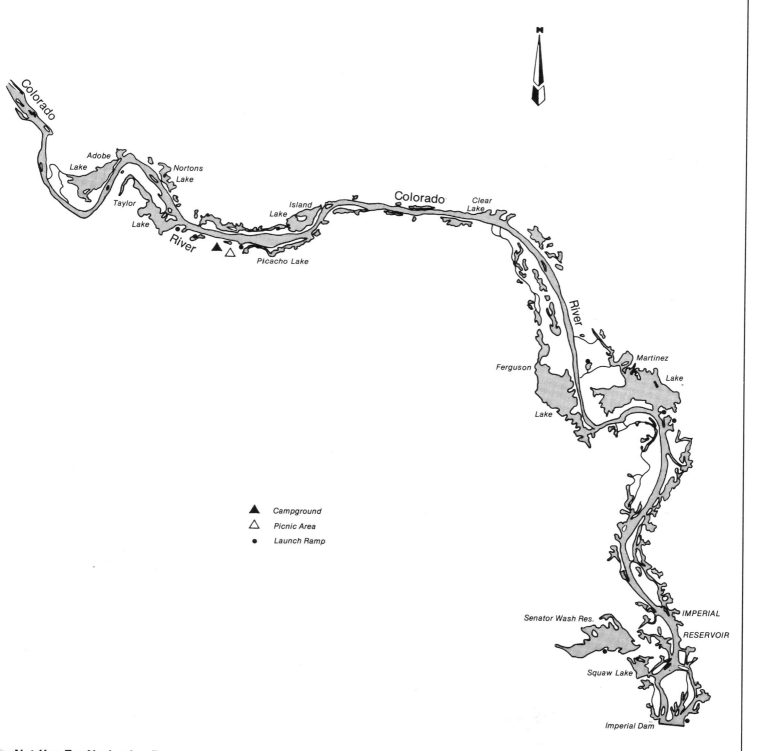

Campground

Picnic Area

Launch Ramp

four types of water to fish on, is the water level. "The first thing I want to know when fishing at Martinez," guide Ed Legan said, "is how much water is being released from the dams upstream? I figure if the water flow is below 5000 FPS, the fishing will be marginal upriver. You can find out the amount of water being released at local tackle shops or the local office of the Bureau of Reclamation."

The basic rule is: in falling or low water, stay in Martinez Lake and in the river downstream of the lake. Don't bother heading upriver in low or falling water.

Once settled on the general area where one plans to fish, the water-level can help to pinpoint the best spots. In high water, especially if the water breaks the brush, fish the backs of bays, around tules or newly submerged grasses. "With falling water," Bob Kinley said, "I move off-shore, 10 or 12 feet from the banks and fish the secondary structure."

One clue that this is not the average California bass water is that none of the locals use depth-finders or graphs on the lake. There is no deep water anywhere in the waterway; the maximum depth is about 10 feet. Actually there are two or three deep holes, of about 40 feet, but none of the guides have ever caught bass at these spots. For the most part, feeding fish are in three to four feet of water. Sharp eyes are as useful as any graph.

Throughout the year, fish on breaks where tules and rocks meet, or if that pattern fails, fish right in the timber. There are subtle variations; in spring, the bass tend to associate more with broken rocks and gravel, but tules nearby are still a good sign. In early spring and summer, the bass are more likely to be off rocky points, with deeper water nearby. Yet, all three guides said that 90 percent of the fish are caught in shallow water around the tules — year-around.

Fishing is good all year long. Unlike deep water reservoirs, there isn't any season when Martinez bass shut down. There is always relatively cool water in the river that keeps the summer bite going, and the bass can't escape to deep water in winter.

Since the same structure and depth are fished all year long, a good lure in winter is probably a good lure in summer. Waits added, "Fish aren't picky here."

Jigs and worms are the standard lures throughout the year. The area looks like heaven for flipping a spinnerbait, but the local pros and guides all prefer to flip plastic crawdads. Soft plastics are Texas-rigged or worked on lead-head jigs, with a twin-tease skirt, rigged weedless for fishing in the tules.

Worms are good for fishing in the river or around rocks, always Texas-rigged, sometimes with the sinker pegged. The standard length for worms is about six inches, in black, chartreuse, smoke sparkle or motor oil colors. Smoke sparkle is most popular, outselling every other color in local tackle shops by 30:1. Go with light weights for shallow slow waters, but have plenty of 3/8 to 1/2 ounce weights and jigheads for fishing in the river current.

Jig and pig is considered the best choice for winter fishing. "When it is cold, you can still pick them up on plastics," said Legan, "but jig and pig is better. These are usually at least 3/8-ounce jigs, with blue/black, brown/chartreuse, or brown/orange skirts.

There can be a fantastic top-water bite, especially over submerged grass and near the banks. Buzzbaits, spooks, and Lucky 13s, are all popular. "I like a noisy bait," said Waits, "since this is a dirty water lake." Give top-water at least a half an hour in the morning, but remember, it can stay good all day; if the fish keep biting stick with the pattern.

Crankbaits are popular as well, though they work best when the fish move away from the tules, on to rocks or points. The two best crankbaits on this water are the Fat Rap in shad or crawdad color, and the Fatso, in moss green.

This is a murky water lake, fishing is for the most part around tules, so forget about using light line. For flipping, go with 20- to 25-pound line. Ten pound is the absolute minimum and is only used for worming in areas where fish won't break off on structure.

When on the river, keep an eye out for sandbars, shallow water, and timber just beneath the surface. Legan, Waits, and Kinley, see boats damaged every year, usually by fishermen who didn't pay attention. The deepest water is not in the center of the river channel, but on the edges close to the tules; stay on the outside edge on the bends.

Boats launching for a days fishing on Martinez Lake.

As pro-fisherman Ed Legan shows, a top-water lure worked parallel to the tules can do the job. This might not be the most productive way to catch fish at Martinez, but it is exciting.

$200. There is also a launch ramp, boat repair, snack and tackle shop, docks, gas, restaurant, and bar with live entertainment on the weekends. Call, (602) 783-9589.

Other Camping: Primitive camping is permitted along most of the river. On the California side there are primitive state campsites at Picacho and Taylor Lake. There are no ramps, but a car can be driven to these areas over a dirt road. Bring the boat up the river to the campsite, and tie it off for the night. Other campsites on paved roads (there is a lot of pavement, it is like camping in a parking lot) with facilities like bathrooms, showers, and launch ramps, are located at Squaw Lake.

KEY TO MARTINEZ LAKE

Best Season: Spring and fall; roughly March to June, and September to December. The lake can be pretty unbearable in summer when the heat pounds down.

Lures To Use: Soft plastics and jigs. Big jigs with salt craws are great for flipping in the tules. Other than that, Texas-rigged, six-inch worms, in salt and pepper are the top selling color. This isn't really a finesse lake, the water is murky and there is a lot of structure, go with bigger lures. Carry 3/8 oz., to 1/2 oz. bullet-head weights for fishing in the current.

Primary Structure: Tules, wood, rock piles — this lake has it all. None of it is deep. Look for the optimum water temperature, and keep moving to similar spots with the same temperature. When the water is rising, fish right in the newly inundated brush and tules. When it is falling, move offshore a good 10 feet at least, and fish secondary structure. When the lakes and bays are too warm or cold, move to the river current.

Other: Watch for obstructions. Submerged rocks and wood can eat props when the water is falling.

MARTINEZ LAKE GUIDES

Bob Kinley 602/783-3577
P.O. Box 72294, Martinez Lake, AZ 85365
Bob is a licensed guide who has been working on the lake for five years. He has been fishing tournaments for seven years, took 4th in the U.S. Bass World Teams, 9th in the WON Bass teams, and 17th in Red Man National.

Ed Legan 602/726-7273
2425 27th Ave., Yuma, AZ 85364
A licensed guide for eight years, Ed likes to teach his clients how to fish. He is currently the Tournament Director for WON Bass and has lived on the river for 20 years.

Jim Waits
Jim lives on the lake and grew up fishing these waters. He has been fishing pro tournaments for five years, and has won tournaments on the Red Man and WON Bass circuits.

MARTINEZ LAKE FACILITIES

Martinez Lake Resort is a full-service fisherman's resort. There are motel cabins, $40; trailers with kitchens and air conditioning, $60; and large waterfront houses, $150 or

This area looks to a fisherman more like the deep south. Martinez is miles of wood and tules connected to the Colorado River.

MILLERTON LAKE

Bob Perry said, "Millerton has been on the decline for a few years, but we have a lot of habitat programs going on. The lake has all the things it takes for a good lake, it just needs a little help, like habitat, shad, and a constant water level."

The Fresno Bass Club and the Department of Fish and Game, through the Adopt a Lake program have been hard at work to give Millerton the boost it needs. They are placing trees and brush in the lake, to provide critical dense habitat for juvenile bass. R.J. Villoria said, "We are doing a lot of work on the lake. It will get better, but not right away."

Millerton covers 5,000 acres. Partly because of its large size, it is a popular tournament lake. The water is very clear, with better than 15 foot visibility most of the year. Like most California reservoirs, this lake was clear-cut when the dam was built, which puts the bass at a disadvantage, especially against a strong striper population. Along with the bass, shad, bluegill, and crappie have declined in recent years, possibly because of striper predation. In any case, the only cure is shoreline habitat and that is what the Adopt a Lake program hopes to provide. Right now, the only shoreline vegetation is sparse grass and willows that are covered by rising water. Other than that, this is a rock and "nothing bank" lake.

A red-hot day on Millerton will result in about 15 keeper

Lure selection for Millerton Lake.

fish. When the fishing is bad, even the best bass fishermen can expect to blank half the time. This lake can be frustrating. But, fishing Millerton is considered a true test of skill, which is the other reason for its popularity with the tournaments.

"The funny thing about Millerton," said Villoria, "is that you can catch fish between five and fifteen feet, just about all year long. There are times when you have to fish 45 to 50 feet deep, but overall I have my best luck shallow. You need to approach this lake with the understanding that 95% of the tournaments are won in the main lake. That's the place to fish. The only reason to go upriver, is when the bite is really bad, and you are just looking for something else to do. For the most part, the main lake is it."

"There are a lot of flats around the lake," said Perry, "the secret is finding the migration routes up through the channels. They may be only three to four feet, but you have to work those little breaks to find bass." Millerton is a lake where minor differences in location and presentation, make the difference between success and failure. When even the best fishermen must work to catch a limit, there isn't any margin of error for sloppy fishing tactics.

In the spring, Perry suggests looking for submerged cockleburs. Top-water works well over this vegetation early in the morning, or split shot a worm through it, on six- to eight- pound line. The only trouble is, a hooked bass must be kept up out of the stick-up, if it turns and gets back down into the thick of the cockleburs, only good luck is going to bring it back out again.

Also in the early mornings of spring, spinnerbaits and larger jigs worked in five to ten feet of water can produce largemouth bass. Villoria likes to fish quick during the first light of the day, because he believes if the fish are up, they'll be aggressive. They'll bite right away, or they won't, and if they don't he can move on to try another spot. If the bigger baits don't produce, he switches over to a worm in shad or cinnamon color and uses the same tactics, moving quick and covering water until the sun comes up.

The majority of the largemouth spawning areas are between Squaw Cove and Winchells Cove, with a number of fishable flats and points in-between. This area consists of rolling flats interspersed with broken shale and rock.

Farther up the lake, closer to the mouth of the river, there are sandy ledges and nothing banks where spotted bass spawn. Spots spawn a month or so earlier than the largemouth, and in water between five and twenty feet deep, rather than in the super shallow water. Because spots turn on earlier than the largemouth, fishermen may be surprised to find them in eight to ten feet of water, as early as February, when the largemouth are just beginning to move up.

"Look for spotted bass on banks with submerged cuts — long straight banks where the bass can migrate in and out of coves," said Villoria. When it is available they like cocklebur and sand too. Or they will hang off the channels that go into coves leading to flats with cocklebur or sand. The best way to fish for spots is to look for banks that don't look that good, where there may only be a few isolated rocks. Then work along the bank. Once you catch one fish, check the depth, and keep working parallel to the bank at the same depth."

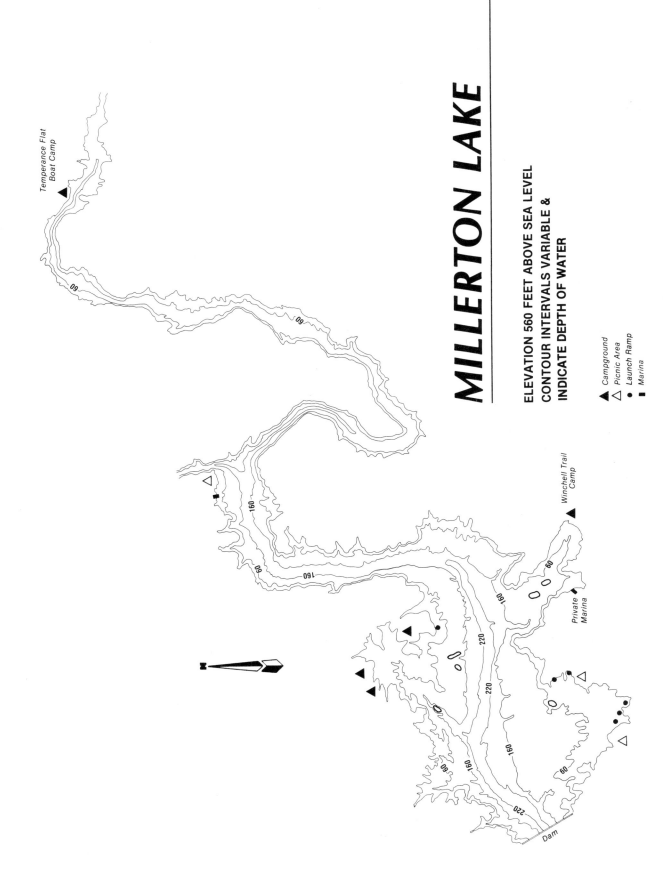

MILLERTON LAKE

**ELEVATION 560 FEET ABOVE SEA LEVEL
CONTOUR INTERVALS VARIABLE &
INDICATE DEPTH OF WATER**

▲ Campground
△ Picnic Area
● Launch Ramp
■ Marina

Temperance Flat
Boat Camp

Winchell Trail
Camp

Private
Marina

Dam

Spotted bass like smaller lures. Use four- to five-inch worms on split shot or 1/8-ounce jigheads. Also smaller jig and pig, in brown on brown, then fish slow. Villoria said, "When I'm out there, I ask myself, how slow can I go? And that keeps me in line."

Summer is tougher than spring. The average size of the bass is smaller, and bites are hard to come by in the heat of the day. The bright side is an excellent top-water bite in the evenings. "Look for a shaded wall," said Perry, "then throw right next to the wall with small stickbaits. The bass'll come right up to get it."

During the day, try doodling off the steeper walls, at 30 to 40 feet. Look for deep shaded structure in the main lake where the water temperature is slightly cooler. Night fishing is not allowed from boats, this closes off the best possible summer pattern to serious fishermen.

"In fall, the fishing tapers off," said Perry. "It's the pits in September. Then it begins to pick up and peak around October, when fish start relating to structure again."

For winter fishing, work structure from 30 to 60 feet deep. Spoons are good for the deeper structure, as well as jigs and doodling worms. Also, any two-inch soft plastics, like Gitzits or grubs on split shot, have a good chance of bringing in fish in winter. Just work it slow, whatever the bait. Especially for spotted bass, they'll keep on biting in winter, but they prefer the bait to be almost still, rather than moving.

"In winter the bass hold in the deep water off the channels," said Perry. "I won't fish for them unless I graph three or four fish in an area. Then they seem to compete for the bait. I actually apply this rule year-round, whenever the fish are in deeper water. The winter bite starts getting decent by December, and the average size really picks up by the end of January. Our big fish months up here are January and February. The best season to fish is from December to June."

Up river there are lots of rocky cliffs and points; water temperature is the key.

MILLERTON GUIDES

Bob Perry (209) 431-5449
3210 E. Shields, Fresno, CA 93726
Bob is a licensed guide, who has fished tournaments in this area since 1972. He provides on the water instruction strictly for bass fishing.

R. J. Villoria
R. J. has been active in Fresno tournament fishing for many years, and he has won many local tournaments.

Top water baits early in the mornings will help you to catch the better quality fish at Millerton.

Locals add structure to Millerton. Areas of sunken Christmas trees like these are great fish attractors.

MILLERTON LAKE FACILITIES

Millerton Lake Recreation Area has 130 campsites, though they plan to expand that number within the next year. There are no hookups, but there are hot showers, which is also a recent improvement. The camping fee is $10 per night, day use is $4. Reservations are available through Mistix, at (800) 444-PARK.

The park has three launch ramps. One is on the Madera side, at the campground. The other two are on the Fresno side of the lake. The fee for launching is $2, plus $4 for day use in the parks. The boat ramp on the Fresno side has a marina, with boat rentals, gas, bait and tackle, and food.

Other: Full services are available in Fresno, and towns in the valley.

KEY TO MILLERTON

Best Season: Big fish months are January and February. The best fishing is December to June. Fall is the pits.

Lures To Use: For the largemouth, plastics of four to five inches. Also, spinnerbaits and top-water in the spring. Small plastics in the two-inch range during winter. For spotted bass, go with smaller jigs and plastics, in sizes that are often used for smallmouth.

Primary Structure: The largemouth concentrate off Squaw and Winchells coves. In that area there are a lot of largemouth spawning flats. Up at the top end of the lake, there are spotted bass on the long "nothing" banks, and in the cuts and migration routes. The river doesn't hold a lot of good fish. There is very little wood, most of the structure is rock or cuts. When the water is up, there are submerged grasses and cockleburs, which will hold bass in seasons when the fish are shallow.

Other: The fishing has been declining for quite a while. Now extensive habitat improvement has turned the bass fishery around. Also, the spotted bass are thriving with the lake as it is. This could become a dynamite spotted bass fishery in the next few years.

LAKE MIRAMAR

Lake Miramar is a tiny, San Diego City Lake, of only 162 acres with four miles of shoreline. For the most part, this guide book has avoided covering such small lakes for two reasons; one, the lake usually can't take added pressure; two, a small lake can be fished from end to end in a single day. The point is, no matter what this book says about depth and where to fish, on a 162-acre lake most anglers are going to cover every inch of water three or four times in one day of fishing.

But, Miramar is something of a dark legend. It demands its own chapter. This is the lake that produced two of the biggest largemouth bass ever recorded. One fish tipped the scales at 20 pounds, 15 ounces, and put San Diego on the map of bassing hot spots. The other fish came in at 19 pounds, 1 ounce.

Both fish became the epicenter of a tangled web of controversy. In the eyes of many bass fishermen these bass were tainted. The big fish have left Miramar more infamous than famous. This will always be the lake where "you know who, caught you know what."

Miramar earned its spot on the map that counts, in 1973, when Dave Zimmerlee caught a 20 pound, 15 ounce largemouth. At the time, this was the second largest bass in

Purple is the popular color for Miramar; use a salt and pepper reaper for the tough days.

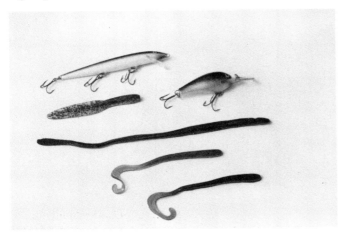

history, and the largest ever from California. The trouble was, other fishermen on the lake claimed they had seen the fish floating on the surface earlier in the day. The whole incident quickly became a scandal, and in the end Zimmerlee's fish only received the California State Record. He did not file with either the International Game Fish Association or the Freshwater Fishing Hall of Fame.

Then in 1988, Sandy DeFresco caught a bass that weighed in at 21 pounds, 10 ounces. There was only one problem, the bass had a lead diving weight in its stomach. In the end, only the Freshwater Fishing Hall of Fame recognized the catch, after docking the weight of the weight. This brought the fish in at 19 pounds, 1 ounce, for a 15-pound line class world record.

The stories about the two huge bass continue and will probably always leave DeFresco and Zimmerlee as the notorious duo. In Zimmerlee's defense, how many fishermen would drive past a 20-pound floater? Wouldn't they have gone and fished it out, if only to take it back to the dock and honestly describe how they found it? It's just something fishermen don't pass by.

In DeFresco's case, the story got incredibly complicated. If there are five pounds of trout in a fish's belly, this counts toward the total weight of the fish. Rocks count toward the total weight. But, fish don't eat diving weights, so it looked like something dishonest had occurred. On the other hand, the stomach and contents of record fish are supposed to be preserved by the taxidermist, but they disappeared, or got lost, or something. Some say, the missing stomach lining proved the weight had been in the bass for a long time, which would at least clear DeFresco of the slur. Others still hold that somebody loaded the fish with weight after it was caught.

Neither case can be proven. But, for those who aren't involved, it makes good gossip.

Anyway, on to the fishing.

Miramar is a very clear-water, structure-poor lake. The only structure consists of tule banks that ring the entire lake, and barrels and boats that were sunk for structure by fishermen.

The spawn gets underway in about March, and lasts into May, or sometimes even into the first two weeks of June. While the bass are spawning, the best pattern is to concentrate on the beds in front of the tules, and throw black or purple worms. For fishing around beds, use Texas-rig. The rest of the year, fish the worms on split shot. Zimmerlee said, "San Diego lakes have a layer of grass and slime on the bottom. Split shotting keeps the worms visible all the time, because it can float up above the grass."

When the water gets up to 62 degrees, use a Rapala 11S, early and late in the day. A No. 5 Fat Rap is good at midday in water six to eight feet deep.

In summer, it is difficult to fish the tules, because the bass move deep into the cover and are practically impossible to reach. Instead of getting wrapped up in a frustrating battle to flip into the growth, look for bass that are cruising in search of shad. The main cues will be boils on the surface. Fishermen can also work the water in front of the tules for aggressive fish.

By June, the shad are busting on the surface. "You can nail

the bass all day,'' said Zimmerlee. ''Just chase the shad. Throw the Rapala at the boils and twitch it. Or sometimes you can use a salt and pepper grub on a 1/8-ounce scrounger hook and fish it near the surface. Throw the grub over the boil and bring it back at a depth of about six to twelve inches. This pattern lasts through August. When the shad are busting, fish top-water, if there is no activity, go with worms on the bottom.''

By fall, the fishing gets tough. The only worthwhile tactic is to work the points at 20 to 30 feet with worms. In fall, it is important to work the worm uphill. Put the boat on the bank, cast out and retrieve uphill; this brings the worm in front of the fish that are facing out into deeper water as they migrate to their winter sanctuaries.

In winter, the bass can be anywhere from 20 to 60 feet deep. They hold on the sunken structure. Use spoons, black jigs, and worms, depending on the depth of the fish. Zimmerlee thinks fishermen will do almost as well by drift fishing the lake with a do-nothing technique. The lake is so small it is possible to cover all the water, rather than having to concentrate on a few hot spots.

That's fishing on Miramar. It is real straight-forward. This is not a quantity lake, it is a trophy spot. The fishing is tough, but there are big trout-fed bass in Miramar's super-clear water. In spite of loads of controversy, this tiny lake has to rank as one of the top big fish producers in the country.

Anglers experiencing the fine fishing Miramar offers.

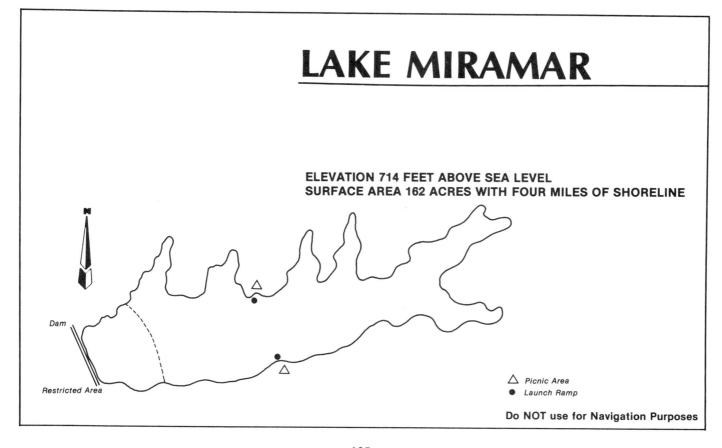

LAKE MIRAMAR

ELEVATION 714 FEET ABOVE SEA LEVEL
SURFACE AREA 162 ACRES WITH FOUR MILES OF SHORELINE

Dam

Restricted Area

△ Picnic Area
● Launch Ramp

Do NOT use for Navigation Purposes

Dave Zimmerlee with the California state record Florida bass. June 2, 1973

LAKE MIRAMAR GUIDES

Dave Zimmerlee (619) 271-8726
8957 Helen James, San Diego, CA 92126
Dave caught the third largest bass ever officially recorded, on Lake Miramar. He now lives in San Diego and is active in tournament bass fishing.

MIRAMAR FACILITIES

Miramar is a San Diego City Lake. As on all of the city owned lakes, there is a $4 launching fee, plus a fee of $4 for every bass fisherman in the boat. The lake is open Saturday through Tuesday all year long, with the exception of a three week period in October.

Motels, restaurants, and bait and tackle shops, are all avialable in the San Diego area. Fishermen will have no problem finding services. There is no camping at the lake.

KEY TO MIRAMAR

Best Season: March through May. Summer is fairly good. Winter and fall are tough.

Lures To Use: Purple or black plastic worms, on split shot; during the spawning season use Texas-rig. Also crankbaits and top-water Rapalas.

Primary Structure: Tules are the only natural structure in the lake. Fishermen sank empty barrels and boats at five or six different spots on the lake.

Other: A very clear water lake, use light lines, six- to eight-pound test.

Dave Zimmerlee hooks a nice fish at dusk.

Fish the tules.

MORENA LAKE

Bobby Sandberg says, "Acre for acre, Morena is the best lake in the U.S.; you can have 50 fish days on some spots." Coming from a pro who lives near and fishes all of the famous San Diego City Lakes, that is no small statement.

One thousand acre Morena Lake was formerly considered a "dink" lake. A mere 45 minute drive from San Diego, at an elevation of 3000 feet in the Cleveland National Forest it was always known as a pretty spot, surrounded by trees with good camping facilities, but the fish didn't have any size. "We used to have to go through 30 or 40 bass to find one keeper," said Ray Koetter. "Now there are so many good fish, you get tired of catching them."

Morena now pumps out lots of quality seven and eight pound fish, with a good number of 19 pounders. Besides excellent action and big fish, this little lake is uncrowded by Southern California standards, a rare find on a lake so close to a major city.

Morena is one of the few bass lakes in the state in which shad is not a principle forage fish. The bass feed on bluegill, crappie, minnows, and crawdads. "These forage species will be wherever the cover is, they don't school in the open

Plastic worms are very reliable on the lake. There is a surprisingly good crankbait bite in pre-spawn and winter.

water," said Frank Pierce. "So you can key on the brush and rock, and catch fish every day of the year."

The Morena largemouth behave the way all the books say bass are supposed to, they associate with shallow water structure. On this lake, bass are almost never found far from the banks or secondary structure, and they are seldom found in water deeper than 30 feet. In fact, they can almost always be caught in less than 10 feet of water at some time during the day, even in the dead of winter.

The relatively high elevation is another factor that changes the fishing picture. The spawning season tends to lag behind the other San Diego Lakes by at least a month, as it takes longer for the mountain waters to warm. Fish won't start pre-spawn until well into March. Winter-style fishing, on jig and pigs worked slowly starts about November. And then there is the occasional winter snow storm that might be rough on fishermen, but won't stop the bass from biting.

The guides describe this as a "brushy, rocky" lake, with lots of flats, good points and ledges, and steep rip rap near the dam. The flats behind Goat Island are loaded with brush piles that hold lots of bass, especially during the spawn. The dam is the primary winter fishing spot, with lots of crawdads hiding in the broken rock. The lake is fairly clear, except during the algae bloom in summer or in periods of high winds. It is a small enough lake that fishermen can easily cover all of the fishable water in a single morning, making the task of finding active bass that much easier.

For spring fishing, look for bass in 12 to 15 feet of water, on the ledges near flats and brush. In early spring work the shallow end of the lake, where the water warms up first. As the lake warms, the fishing turns on near the brush on flats all around the lake.

"On Morena, the best bait all year-round is a plastic worm," said Sandberg. All three guides recommend using plastics in spring, of about four to six inches long. Worms can be jigged or drifted slow, but a lot of folks like to give the worm extra action by shaking the rod tip fast. Think of this as a fast doodling technique. Motor oil is one of the top colors, but Pierce likes green and red worms too, his favorites are watermelon and cinnamon green.

"This is a good top-water lake, from post spawn through summer," said Pierce. "We'll use No. 11 or 13 Rapalas, Bang-a-Lures, Zaras, and Pop-Rs. The key is to twitch it, shake it, try to make the lure look nervous on the surface. We get big fish during summer this way; we almost always get a six- to eight-pound fish on Rapalas in the morning."

The top-water action is an early morning bite, lasting only through the first two hours of the morning. Later in the day the guides switch to worms and grubs, and concentrate on the secondary brush piles that are just offshore. Small crankbaits can also be good in these secondary brush piles and rocks. But when the bass are biting, they'll hit a worm just as easily as any other lure, and the worm will come right through the brush better than most other lures. The midday bite is still a shallow- water pattern; the best fishing is in less than 20 feet of water.

By October or November, the fish are on a fall pattern. "Jigs become good, and fish will be deeper," said Sandberg, "but you can almost always get bit shaking a worm or doodling."

Pierce would look for fish around the rocks of the dam, with a jig and pig as a crawdad imitator. He doesn't ever use a jig of more than 3/8 or 5/16 of an ounce. The best color combos are black with brown, or black with blue. He fishes the jigs down to 30 feet through the winter. If he graphs bass, he might work isolated wood or rock structure in the deep waters of the lake by vertically jigging a spoon. But, this pattern is only worthwhile when fish show up on the graph first, and most of the guides don't turn to deep water unless the shallow water patterns simply fail to produce.

The winter fishing is largely a continuation of the fall fishing pattern. Pierce feels that this lake offers the best winter fishing around. It may be because the forage fish the bass rely on, which are all panfish since there are no shad in the lake, don't move out to super deep water — this lack of shad keeps the feeding bass up in the shallows.

A standard fall/winter pattern would be to start shallow in the broken rocks, then move out to the cuts. If that doesn't pay off move to the rock piles in less than 25 feet of water. Go deep if the fish won't bite anywhere else.

Sandberg adds that if there is a snowstorm, or any type of weather front moving through, look for fish right off the banks in super shallow water. The bass will get active, no matter how cold it is for fishermen.

To take these winter bass, work jig and pigs slow, in less than 30 feet of water. If it doesn't pay off, try to graph fish and use any lure that is effective at the fish's depth.

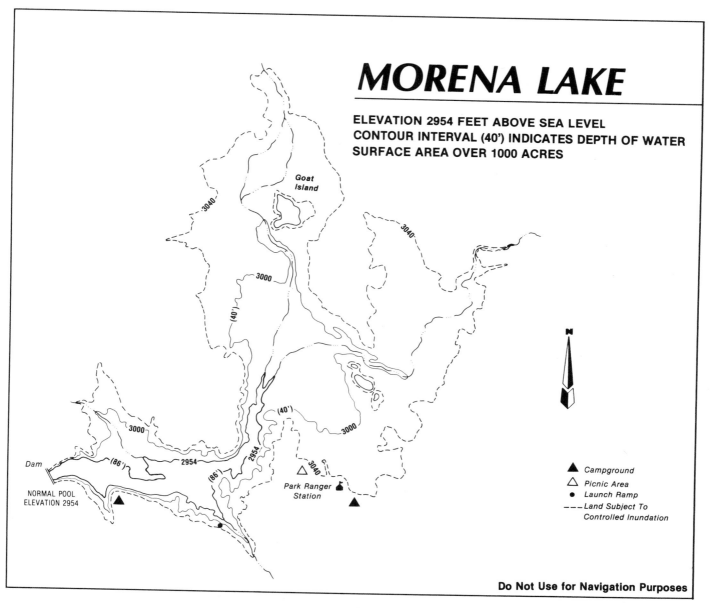

MORENA LAKE

ELEVATION 2954 FEET ABOVE SEA LEVEL
CONTOUR INTERVAL (40') INDICATES DEPTH OF WATER
SURFACE AREA OVER 1000 ACRES

Goat Island

Dam
NORMAL POOL
ELEVATION 2954

Park Ranger Station

▲ Campground
△ Picnic Area
● Launch Ramp
--- Land Subject To Controlled Inundation

Do Not Use for Navigation Purposes

Frank Pierce lands a bass.

Frank Pierce with typical Morena Lake bass.

This is a light line lake, the guides seldom use anything over 10-pound test for fishing at Morena. Other than that, it is all standard tackle. Koetter pointed out, "When the fish are on, you can throw almost any lure in your tackle box and get one fish right after the next."

Unlike the other San Diego City Lakes, Morena is open seven days a week throughout the year. It is also the only lake in the area that has camping facilities. This lake is not under the jurisdiction of the City Lake Department. With the recent drought, a good deal of water has been drained from the lake. When the lake is very low, it can be impossible to launch a boat, so check with a local tackle shop before heading to the lake. However, there is a minimum pool of over 900 surface acres that will continue to maintain a quality bass fishery in the future, even if fishing access is a problem in the short run.

As one guide said, "This lake is worth the drive. The fishing is great."

MORENA GUIDES

Ray Koetter

Ray has been fishing the San Diego City Lakes for five years. He has been Club Champion and qualified for the Tournament of Champions for San Diego County, earning both credits twice. In his first year as a tournament boater, in seven out of twelve tournaments his partners caught fish, and five of those times they were in the money. Ray likes to see other guys catch fish almost as much as he likes to catch them himself. He is currently Vice President of the San Diego Council of Bass Clubs.

Frank Pierce, R.P.Guide Service, (619) 944-7834
7916 Avenida Diestro, La Costa, CA 92009.

Frank has been fishing the San Diego City Lakes for 12 years, and has been a professional licensed guide for four years. He is a member of the San Diego Bass Council. Frank was California State Champion and California Angler of the Year twice, for Military BASS.

Bobby Sandberg (619)226-2805
7878 Chatsworth Blvd., San Diego, CA 92107

Bobby has been fishing for bass since he was 10, and has been a pro tournament fisherman since 1971. He is now a licensed guide and fishes eight to fifteen days a month. Bobby has attended the National Tournament of Champions 13 times. He is a touring pro for Yamaha, Ranger, and Kunnan fishing rods.

Structure on the lake is brush and rock.

MORENA FACILITIES

Morena Lake County Park has a campground, day use area, boat rental, and launch ramp. There are 86 campsites; 58 have water and electric hookups, at $12 a night; the rest are tent sites, at $10 a night. Day use fee is $2 per car. The launch fee is $4. Fishing fees are; $3.50 per adult per day,

juniors from eight to fifteen years old can fish for $2. There is a senior citizen and disabled discount, $2 during the week. Call (619) 565-3600 for information. Reservations can be made at this number during regular business hours, on the weekends a taped information message is played.

Lake Morena Trailer Resort: Located on Lake Morena Road, on the way to the lake, has 42 sites. All spaces have electric and water, about half have sewer hookups. The fee is $16 per night. Call (619) 478-5677.

Other: The Oaks Malt Shop and Express Gas sell fishing tackle. Both are located in Morena Village on Lake Morena Road.

Fish the stick-ups and rocky area.

KEY TO MORENA LAKE

Best Season: A very good winter lake. The fish bite consistently all year long. The spawn lags about a month behind San Diego City Lakes, fish won't be on pre-spawn until mid-March, and it is winter fishing patterns by November. Post-spawn through summer, fish top-water in the morning.

Lures To Use: Plastic worms, of four to six inches. Motor oil, green and red, are both good colors. No. 11 and 13 Rapalas, Bang-a-lures, Zara Spooks, and Pop-Rs. For cranks, go with the small sizes, in crawdad and perch colors.

Primary Structure: Fish in less than 20 feet of water, all year long. If the shallows don't produce, move deeper and look for fish with a graph. But, overall, Morena is a shallow fishing lake. Look for brush and aquatic vegetation along the shoreline and secondary brush piles off-shore, as well as shallow broken rocks, points, and timber. A fairly small lake, Morena can be covered thoroughly in a single day.

Other: Morena is one of the few lakes in the area that does not have shad. Therefore, the bass feed on bluegill, crappie, minnows, and crawdads. These forage species concentrate in the cover; they don't make huge migrations like shad do, so the bass tend to stay up in the shallows, near the food source, at least that is where the hungry bass are going to be. A clear water lake, except during the algae bloom.

NEW MELONES LAKE

New Melones holds a quality northern-strain largemouth fishery. But, it isn't going to be easy to land those six- to eight-pound bass. The reason is — trees.

"The water is gin clear," said Jon Walton, "but the bottom of the lake is a forest of trees. You take your chances fishing with light line, but you go to heavy line and you'll drastically decrease bites. This is a lake of deep, rolling river gorges in the extended arms, that open up into flats in the main body of the lake. There are few spots without trees."

The first problem for bass fishermen is that trees make it tough to hook and hold onto fish. The other problem it presents is that many California fishermen are used to fishing structure-poor lakes, where a few stumps act as fish attractors. On Melones, trees don't mean much, they're everywhere. The bass like them, but it isn't as if fish congregate on the one wooded area in the lake. Fishermen need to adjust their fish-finding tactics on Melones, to look for other cues besides wooded structure. In addition successful fishing tactics must draw the bass out of the wood and brush, whenever possible.

This is a mother lode lake, located on the Stanislaus River, near the town of Angels Camp. The lake lies at an elevation of 1,100 feet, just high enough to escape the blazing heat of

A wide variety of lures work well on New Melones. Lure selection should be made to fit the type of structure that you are fishing.

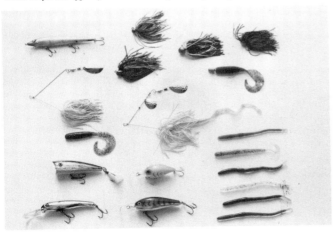

the central valley, but low enough to be a reasonable winter fishery. The lake covers 12,500 surface acres, and the water level fluctuates drastically.

The Stanislaus River, the main river that fills the lake, is rocky and snow-fed. This has a fundamental effect on the bass fishery. First of all, the water coming out of the river is not extremely rich in nutrients or food, so it doesn't have any attraction for bass from the food angle. Second, through the spring, snow-melt keeps the river arm of the lake cool for at least a month longer than the main body of the lake. Cold, nutrient poor water, for all intents and purposes, repels bass, especially in spring when they are seeking the warmest water available. Finally, in a lake with drastic water level fluctuations, the larger bass seldom migrate far up the river arms, because they would simply have to turn around and move back out again.

All this places the best spring fishing down in the southern end of the lake. "In the first part of spring, around February, those fish are from 20 to 40 feet," said Tom Schachten. "They go back and forth a lot, moving up the creek channels because that is where the rain water starts coming in. The rain water is warmer and that helps to bring them in. Then as the lake water starts to warm up, they start moving to brushy and rocky points. Then they move real shallow, and into all types of areas to find food."

The forage foods that are immediately available to bass as they move up are crawdads and baby channel cats. The channel cats are available first. This is one of the last species to spawn in fall, so when early spring rolls around, the channel cats are only about three inches long. Schachten points out that they look just like salt and pepper grubs. This is probably why grubs work so well on almost every lake. The channel cats are in the backs of bays around creek channels — use grubs with weedless jig-heads, but work them slow.

The crawdads come up, out of red-clay mud, where the rocks and trees are sparse. Schachten adds that you would expect the bass to be back near the brush, but they will fan out over empty banks that don't look like they would hold anything. The bass are there to feed on the crawdads as they come up out of the mud. To catch these bass use a jig and pig, again worked very slowly while the water is still cool.

Later, as the water warms and the fish become more aggressive, a spinnerbait works well. Cast the spinnerbait alongside the brush and let it helicopter down. The lake is usually murky after the spring rains making a large lure with big blades easier for the bass to locate. "That works very well for a short time, and catches way bigger fish," said Schachten, "because the bass that are feeding on bigger bluegill are usually three to eight pounds or so at Melones, and that is the size fish you get on a spinnerbait."

Spinnerbaits are also good for slow rolling through the cuts. Find a spot near brushy structure, with a little rocky channel running down to it, where the bottom of the cut is in about 15 to 25 feet of water. Work the spinnerbait very slow, just like a worm, right on the bottom. "This method works well on any lake," Schachten added, "because the larger fish stay in those cuts for quite a while before they move into the shallow water."

Crankbaits are good from April until late June when fish move deeper. Brush and trees prevent fishing the crank right

NEW MELONES LAKE

ELEVATION 1,080 FEET ABOVE SEA LEVEL
CONTOUR INTERVALS VARIABLE
AND INDICATE DEPTH OF WATER

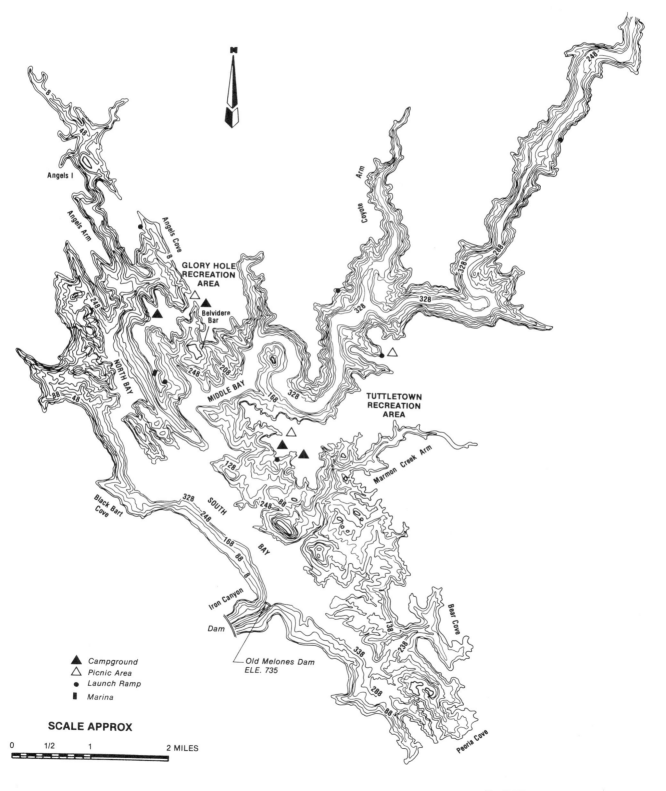

▲ Campground
△ Picnic Area
● Launch Ramp
▮ Marina

SCALE APPROX

0   1/2   1   2 MILES

along the bottom. Instead, use a lure that dives to a depth just above the brush line. When fishing cranks around brush, work them very slowly — to give fish time to see the lure and come out of the brush to hit it. In areas of sparser brush, move crankbaits faster, because the fish can see them from farther away.

There is a fantastic top-water bite on New Melones. It lasts all day during the spawning season, but in late spring through summer bass hit top-water whenever the sun is low or the moon is bright. "As the fish are spawning, a top-water lure really bothers them a lot; we do twitching over the nest," Schachten said. "We get a silver Rattling Rogue or a five-inch Rapala and keep casting along the shoreline and letting it sit very quiet. Just the presence of it hanging there bothers them, they'll attack it before you even move it. Twitch it three or four times, then cast again."

From April through June the fish are very active, they'll hit just about anything. The standard spring pattern is to spend the first hour of the day with top-water, then switch to jig and pig or plastics fished on the bottom. The fish move back down to about 12 feet during the day in spring. In late afternoon cranks work well, because as the sun warms the water through the day the fish become more active. In the last two hours of the day go back to surface lures.

Tom Schachten with a 6.5-pound bass caught on a crank. Crankbaits work well for big fish from April until late June. Use a bait that will dive to just above the brush and tree line that covers the bottom of the lake.

Thick brush often will cover the bottom of the lake. A salt and pepper grub on a darter head retrieved just above the brush can work well.

By summer the water has cleared up and the bass move out to water about 30 feet deep. The two methods that work best are top-water and plastic worms. Fish the top-water over trees and brush in deeper water, but move it slow to give bass time to come up and hit it.

"Shaking and doodling works pretty good in summer and fall on this lake," said Walton. "Look for fish in the trees in 30 or even 60 feet of water, they'll generally be on the deeper side of the structure. Free-spool a plastic straight down, next to the trunk, right through all the tangles. Then shake it and work it up, doodling as you go. As on any clear lake, always look to the shady side of points and structure."

Night fishing is the way to go in the hot summer months. New Melones gets good by May, but becomes even more productive after June. "We go out in the full moon," said Schachten, "using very little light. Since these bass are holding in one foot of water, they are very spooky. The best thing to use at night is a dark grub with a fat body, so it is easy for the fish to see. Cast it into the bank and work it off real slow, you will get fish almost every other cast. Usually you can catch hundreds of bass in a night."

Fall is the slow season on Melones. Top-water no longer works well. Plastics and spoons are the only effective lures. The trouble is the bass start to bunch up in tight groups, in 30 or 40 feet of water. They'll be over the tops of taller trees and on rocky points. Once they are into the trees, it is tough to get them out.

"This is a good winter lake," said Walton. "In general, wood holds heat, and there are a lot of northwest bays on the lake that will warm up after a few sunny days. But, the fishing isn't that great on any of the lakes in the area in winter. Use a large, heavy, white spinnerbait with a single blade and work it through the trees. Go slow and it can pay off in some quality fish."

The lake can turn on in winter, after one to three days of good hard rain. As in early spring, the fish will move up in the creek channels where the warmer water runs in. This lasts for only a couple of days after the rain, so it is important to get on the water fast. After this short-term bite shuts down the lake is tough.

Small, rocky areas like this are often passed up on this lake because people become so involved fishing the trees.

NEW MELONES GUIDES

Tom Schachten (209) 736-4333
Glory Hole Sporting Goods
2892 South Highway 49
Angel's Camp, CA 95222
Schachten has been a licensed guide for six years, though he has been fishing lakes in the region for 28 years. He is the owner of the Glory Hole and guides for all types of fish: bass, trout, sturgeon, salmon, you name it.

Jon Walton
Walton's Pond Bait and Tackle
23880 Hesperia Blvd., Hayward, CA 94546
Walton has been fishing for 30 years and is the owner of Walton's Pond. He does not guide himself, but through his shop he can provide referrals. He also teaches bass fishing classes through the store.

KEY TO MELONES

Best Season: Spring, from March to June. Summer, good for top-water and plastics during day, but night fishing is better. Fall and winter are real slow.

Lures To Use: From April to June anything will catch fish. The rest of the time match the forage, but use lures that will come through the trees. Salt and pepper grubs, Green Weenie worms, and jigs are good early in the year and when it is tough. Shad or crawdad colored spinnerbaits and buzzbaits produce large fish. Shallow-running cranks score well when skimmed over submerged brush.

Primary Structure: Trees and brush are all over the place. Also red clay banks covered with broken rock and vertical rock banks. Look for combinations such as a break in the brush adjacent to a creek channel. Trees or brush alone aren't enough to be sure of bass on this lake, combinations have to be there.

Other: A very clear-water lake. Use lighter lines, as light as possible considering the amount of brush. The lake can really turn on after spring rains, stay away from the main river channel early in the year and after rains. Instead, fish the turbid water in the backs of coves where rain water runs in.

NEW MELONES FACILITIES

U.S. Bureau of Reclamation Campgrounds: The bureau runs two new campgrounds on Melones. They do not have hookups, but there are rest rooms, showers, and launch ramps. Both of the campgrounds charge $7 per night, though there is no charge for day use or launching. Tuttletown Campground has 90 sites, and Glory Hole has 144. There is a full-service marina at Glory Hole, with boat rentals, gas, groceries, and bait and tackle. Reservations are not accepted. Call (209) 984-5248 for more information.

Glory Hole Sporting Goods: Offers complete bait and tackle as well as other sporting goods. Located at 2892 South Highway 49, Angels Camp, CA 95222, just before the turn off to the Glory Hole Campground. Call (209) 736-4333.

Other: There are additional services in nearby Angels Camp including grocery stores, small hotels, and restaurants.

LAKE OROVILLE

Lake Oroville is formed by the world's highest dam, built at the junction of the four branches of the Feather River. The dam was constructed in 1962 as part of the State Water Project and it towers more than 770 feet above the city of Oroville. The lake covers more than 15,500 surface acres, with 167 miles of shoreline that is for the most part steep-sided canyon walls.

Oroville has four species of black bass: northern-strain largemouth, smallmouth, spotted, and redeye. Largemouth over eight pounds are rare, though not unheard of. But, the spotted bass are already approaching record sizes even though they were introduced only a few years ago. The lake has produced six and seven pound spotties. The spotted bass are gradually becoming the dominant species, because they spawn in deeper water and earlier in the season than largemouth, therefore they are less vulnerable to water level fluctuations.

Though Oroville is not known for producing exceptionally large bass, it holds lots of quality fish that range from three to four pounds. There is a slot limit on the lake; all fish between 12 and 15 inches must be released, and five fish over or under the slot limit may be kept. Oroville was the first lake in California to experiment with a slot limit, by all accounts it

Lake Oroville has been on an upswing in recent years. In spring just about any lure will work. Fish cranks fast or spinnerbaits in pre-spawn. Later in the year spend more time with plastics.

has been very successful. Most of the local fishermen feel that the slot limit is responsible for the large numbers of quality bass this lake produces.

"Spring is the best time to fish on Oroville," said Dave Rush. "Key in on the major coves that have real deep water access. You want coves with sandy banks, good spawning banks of clay and grass mixed together, or sand with big boulders, and also tree stumps. The largemouth will be in five to fifteen feet of water. Smallmouth and spots will be a little deeper."

On Oroville, fishermen can count on catching spawning fish through at least four months and possibly even five months, from March to July. There are two reasons. First, each bass species spawns at a slightly different temperature. Smallmouth and spotted bass start spawning when the water hits 50 to 55 degrees, the largemouth don't spawn until the water reaches about 63 degrees. Second, Oroville is made up of four separate arms and they don't reach a suitable temperature for spawning at the same time. The variations in temperature stagger the spawn among the four arms of the lake.

"The South Fork is the first place to warm up," said Bud Sipes. "It is not as narrow as the other arms of the lake, and because of this it gets more sun and warms up faster. It also has the most spawning flats, especially for largemouth." Look for spawning bass early in March in the South Fork, then in a month or so move to the northern arms as they become warm.

As far as structure goes, all four arms of the lake are similar. This isn't a matter of one arm holding the ideal wood structure and another arm consisting exclusively of gravel banks. There is wood and gravel in all of the arms — perhaps a bit more wood in the South Fork, but not enough to make a significant difference to the bass. Temperature should be the primary guide as to which arm to concentrate on. Target specific structure that is going to attract the bass species that are most active in that water temperature.

Pre-spawn and spawning fish are aggressive. Rush recommends using crankbaits and spinnerbaits before the spawn and plastics while fish are on the beds. "These fish aren't that picky when it comes to lures," said Sipes, "you just have to choose a lure to match the depth and warmth of the water where fish are holding. Fish the fish, and fish the weather and you'll do fine."

Oroville has very clear water, the guides recommend light lines and smaller lures. They seldom use line weights greater than 10-pound test.

"By summer, the fish start traveling out of the shallows," said Rush. "They stop on secondary points off the major coves." Early on bass are anywhere from 10 to 20 feet deep. As the surface waters get too warm they move farther and farther out into the main lake and they go deeper. Sipes added that in summer the bass relate to the river, holding in the cooler moving water.

"In summer, I always start with top-water until the sun gets on the water," said Steve Klein. "The first thing to do is find major points, and fish them with Pop-Rs, Spooks and Rapalas. Later in the day switch to plastics; you are still working the same fish that you were onto earlier in the day, you just have to work on them a little harder. Hop the worms off the bottom fairly fast in the summer, the fish will be a lot more aggressive."

Look for bait. Key in on the points and structure near bait, because bass will hold next to bait or just below it. If the day is sweltering hot, look for quick access to deep water. A ledge that drops from five feet down to thirty feet is perfect.

By mid-summer, fishing during the day is miserable because of the heat. Switch to fishing early in the morning and late in the evening, or fish at night. With the surface temperatures approaching 90 degrees, large bass switch to night feeding patterns.

The primary baitfish in Oroville are pond smelt and shad. The smelt are two to three inches long and look like pencil-thin shad. Over time these baitfish species have become the dominant forage for bass, and the preferred lure colors have gone from crawdad imitations to shad imitations. Crawdad colors remain popular for deep winter fishing, but crawdad/browns are no longer the killer colors they once were.

Another color combination that Rush suggests during the spawn is bluegill, which could be described as green with pumpkin flakes or green-blues. Bluegill prey on bass fry.

LAKE OROVILLE

ELEVATION 800 FEET ABOVE SEA LEVEL
SURFACE AREA 15500 ACRES WITH
167 MILES OF SHORELINE

West Branch Feather

North Branch Feather

French Creek

Lime Saddle Marina

Goat Ranch

Bloomer Primitive Camp Area

Middle Branch Feather

Foreman Creek

South Fork Feather

Craig Saddle

▲ Campground
△ Picnic Area
⏢ Boat in Campground
■ Marina
✧ Moorings
◉ Cartop Launch Ramp
• Launch Ramp
■ Visitor Center

Dam

Bidwell Canyon Marina

Loafer Creek

Do NOT use for Navigation Purposes

Dave Rush with a three-pound largemouth. Oroville is a lake where suspended fish can be caught. Don't always work the bottom, cast out and let the lure sweep back at different depths.

While the adult bass are concerned with defending their nest, they will hit anything within striking range that looks remotely like a bluegill. Imitations of these panfish incite an almost sure-fire defensive strike.

When the weather starts to cool off, the bass again move shallow. They won't be found in the same concentrations as in spring, but they are caught in the same areas. Klein finds that the fish migrate up the creek channels, where they can move from deep to shallow water. Look for a good break that really drops off, with a well-defined creek bed, in five to fifteen feet of water.

"In fall you'll catch bass on plastic worms and jigs," Klein said. "I like to use crankbaits bumped real slow around rocks. Keep 'em on the bottom, you have to keep contact. When you are fishing a crank you want to keep it bumping into stuff. That lure shouldn't be any good at the end of the day. If you knock all the paint off, you're doing what you should do."

The top-water bite is good during the day in October and November. Look for coves where shad are busting on the surface. Rush points out that the baitfish head to the major coves with still water, because in these areas they won't have to expend energy fighting the river current during winter. As the baitfish concentrate in the back of the coves, the bass follow and have a final feeding binge before winter sets in.

As the water drops below 50 degrees, the fishing pattern roughly parallels that of summer, with bass holding in deeper water. The main difference is that the bass are far more lethargic and will only hit slower moving lures. "Bites are few and far between," Sipes added.

"In winter the reservoirs are dropping," said Klein. "The fish suspend in the trees and on vertical walls, because of the fluctuation." Use a graph to locate suspended fish; where there is one bass, there is often a school. The bass generally hold at 30 to 40 feet, but they may be much deeper. Doodling with Don Iovino's method, or working jigs and spoons very slow are the best bets for taking bass in winter. January is the toughest month on Oroville.

The lake is not crowded with fishermen at any time of year, though there are a lot of water-skiers on holiday weekends and in summer. During the spring and fall when the weather is perfect and the fishing is great, there are few boats on the lake.

OROVILLE GUIDES

Steve Klein (916) 533-8381
11 Rosita Way, Oroville, CA 95965
Klein has fished on Oroville his whole life, and is now a licensed guide. He has several tournament wins to his credit, including a first in the Won Bass Tournament on Oroville in 1989.

David Rush (916) 534-6598
2544 Palermo Rd., Palermo CA 95968
Rush has been a licensed guide for four years and has 10 years of experience on the lake. He has fished tournaments professionally for eight years, consistently placing in the top ten. His sponsors are: Tournament Lures, Kalin Co., Fish Formula, and Berkley Trilene.

Bud Sipes (916) 533-5548
6368 Lincoln Blvd. #28, Oroville, CA 95966
Sipes is a licensed and insured guide. He has been a tournament fisherman in the past, but now he devotes his time to guiding others. He specializes on Oroville, Trinity, Shasta, and Ruth lakes.

Rocky points with deep water access are the main structures on the lake.

OROVILLE FACILITIES

Oroville State Recreation Area: the State Parks Department operates five launch ramps. Two are regular launch ramps for boats on trailers. They are: the spillway ramp near the dam; and Lime Saddle Marina, with a launch ramp and full-service marina. The fee at these two launch ramps is $6. The other three launch ramps are all car-top launches, with no fee.

There are two State Park campgrounds, both with launch ramps. There is a $6 day use and launch fee. Bidwell Canyon has 75 sites with RV hookups, hot showers, a marina, bait and tackle, boat rentals, and gas; the camping fee is $16 per night and it is open year-round. Loafer Creek has 137 tent sites and hot showers. It is open only from April 1 to October 1, the fee is $10. For information call, (916) 536-2200. Reservations are taken through Mistix (800) 444-7275.

Other: There are motels, stores and restaurants in nearby Oroville.

KEY TO OROVILLE

Best Season: Spring, from March to July. The spawn is staggered on the lake, starting in March on the South Fork, but it is not over with until June or July on the cooler arms. Fall is good too.

Lures To Use: During the spawn, just about anything will catch fish. Use faster baits like cranks and spinners early in the season and plastics while fish are on the beds. For plastics, use three- to four-inch grubs and worms, in shad and bluegill colors. Zaras, Pop-Rs, and Rapalas are good for topwater.

Primary Structure: Look for bait and deep water access near points. Largemouth concentrate around the wood in suitable areas, smallmouth orient off points. Bass are shallow during the spawn, but move down close to 30 feet deep in summer.

Other: This lake has a slot limit, which is the primary reason why there is such a good population of quality bass. All bass between 12 and 15 inches long must be released immediately. Five fish over or under the limit may be kept.

Largemouth at Oroville will suspend in trees in deep water.

OTAY LAKE

Lower Otay, a San Diego City Lake, is famous for producing lots of large Florida-strain bass. When the bite is good, experienced locals can hook a five fish limit on five casts. Even inexperienced fishermen are practically guaranteed of limit when the bite is on. Rowan Stone summed up Lower Otay when he said, "It's a real fisherman's lake, because it has all kinds of great structure. Some days when the shad are busting, you can see hundreds of fish caught in a few hours. But, when the bite is off, it can be tough."

As on any lake that is famous for both quantity and quality of bass, there is bad news. Otay gets pounded. Crowds are a fact of life on Southern California lakes, and Otay is no exception. During opening week and on weekends early in the year, it is hard to find a fishing spot on the 1,266 acre lake. The lake is at its best in early fall when there are fewer fishermen.

Otay holds almost every type of structure that bass fishermen could ask for. There are extensive brush piles, good points, broken rock, flats, and tules along the banks. Active fish are found in less than 20 feet of water throughout the year, and though there may be deeper suspended fish, a relatively shallow water pattern will almost always pay off. There is also a good bite on jerkbaits and surface lures when the shad are busting.

Four- to six-inch plastic worms are the lures to use 90 percent of the time.

"When the lake opens in January it isn't a wide open bite," said Joe Mazzurco, "because the water is so cold. But, bait fishermen do real well, mostly on crawdads and shiners. Sometimes we'll get 14 and 15 pounders in the first couple of weeks. As the water warms up, the fish start moving up to the tules and aquatic vegetation. They take shiners well and you can get a limit in about 20 minutes. But, by February the bass get pretty easy to catch on artificials too."

Even with the cold water, the locals don't fish much below 20 feet. A mid-winter pattern should concentrate on steep points in areas with vegetation nearby. By mid-February the fish are holding right along the weed lines and outside of the tules, and worms work well. Mazzurco and Zimmerlee both prefer to split-shot worms on Otay, but Stone goes with a Texas-rig, because it helps him avoid snagging on brush. "Ninety percent of the time at Otay you are worming," said David Zimmerlee, "with four- to six-inch worms or three-inch Reepers."

By the end of February or the first week in March, the bass will have moved onto the spawning beds. Mazzurco said, "There is so much aquatic vegetation, it is hard to find the spawners. I go with crankbaits and spinnerbaits at this time of year, like a Fat Rap or a medium-size spinnerbait, white with silver is the most consistent."

As fish move into the spawn, work flats that are from one to eight feet deep. Don't rely on spotting fish, because the vegetation will hide them. Fish anywhere along the banks where there is a shallow shelf and weed nearby. There are two primary arms on Otay, the Otay Arm and the Harvey Arm. The Otay arm warms more quickly and earlier in the year. A cold north wind blows down the Harvey arm and slows the spring warming trend. The Otay Arm is also known for better quality fish and its clear water, while the Harvey arm has greater quantities of bass and dirtier water. The shallow points by the docks are good with fish really bunched up on them, but the area is also well known to fishermen, and gets hit pretty hard.

By mid-morning, shallow bass that aren't guarding nests are forced off the flats by fishing pressure. This is true throughout the year, whenever there are a lot of boats on the lake. The pressure forces the bass to behave differently than they would on other lakes, given the same conditions. Yet, the bass are still predictable. They can be caught by observant fishermen who realize that fishermen pounding the banks drive the bass to offshore breaks.

"People pressure is more important than weather," Stone said. "On Otay you have to mix it up with the ledges and flats, 'cause fish will move back and forth a lot, all year-round. You can catch them on the taxi-way as they are coming in and going out."

The way it is done is move off the banks, beyond the casting distance of those fishermen working the shore. This provides a chance to hook the bass as they move to the safety of deeper water. Spinners, spoons and worms fished from five to twenty feet deep work best to take these moving bass. A lure that will fall through the entire range from shallow to deep provides the best chance of finding the depth fish are moving at. Once onto the migration depth for a particular day, catching fish is primarily a matter of tightening the pattern.

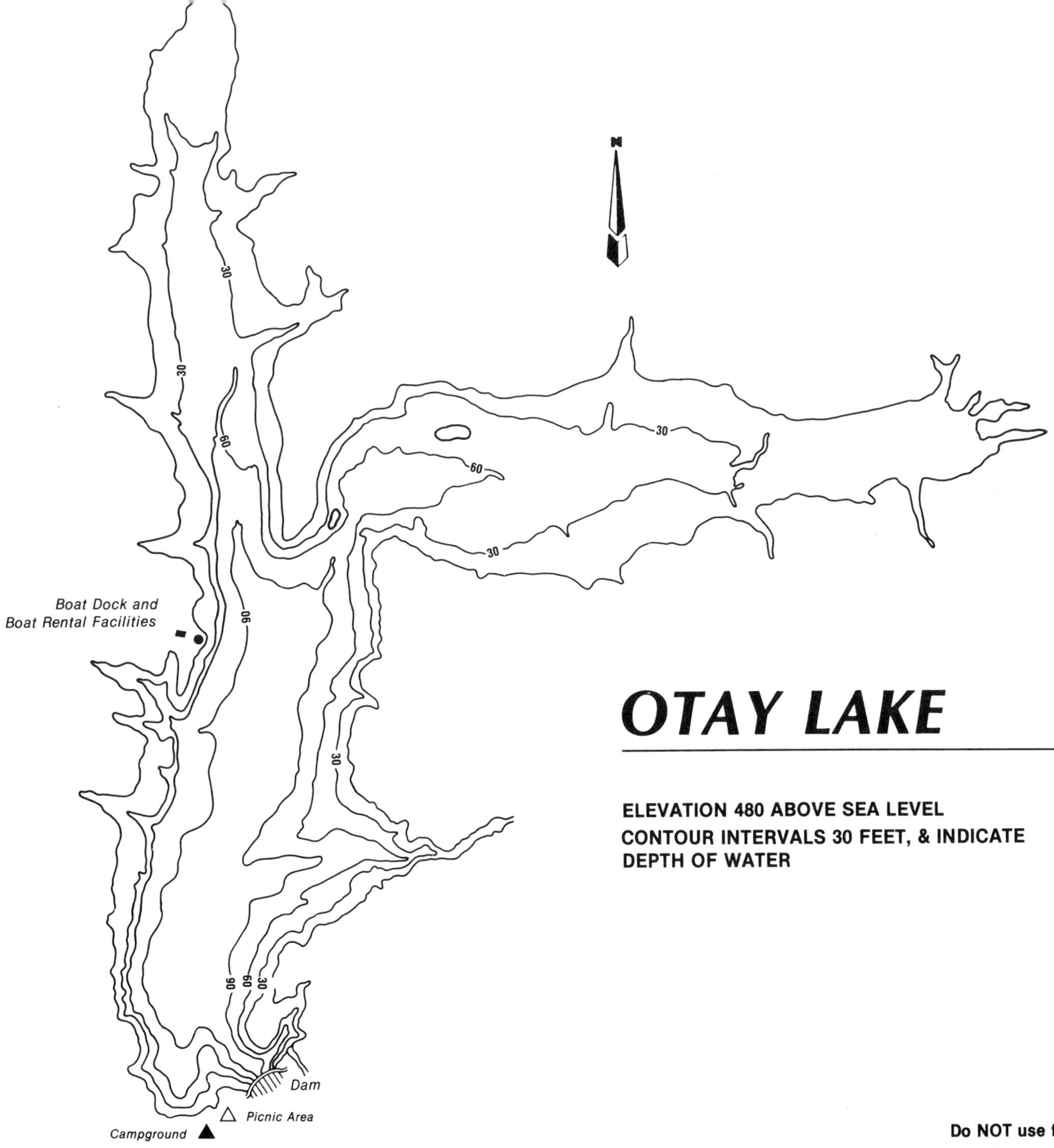

OTAY LAKE

ELEVATION 480 ABOVE SEA LEVEL
CONTOUR INTERVALS 30 FEET, & INDICATE
DEPTH OF WATER

30

30

60

30

30

60

30

06

30

60

90

Boat Dock and
Boat Rental Facilities

Dam

▲ Campground   △ Picnic Area

N

Do NOT use for Navigation Purposes

The most reliable summer pattern consists of fishing along weed lines with crankbaits and jerkbaits, in less than 15 feet of water. Throw ahead of the boat along the weed line, and bring the bait back with an erratic stop and start motion. "In heavier pockets of weed, go with a Johnson Minnow Spoon or a buzzbait," said Mazzurco. "Use it on the openings or on the edge of lines. We'll also pitch a worm into heavy pockets, it's like flipping but on 10-pound line. The best worms for this are six-inch curl-tails. Let them fall straight down and fish slow, since you have to drop the worms into the openings in the pockets, the fish has to come to the worm."

After the spawn, fish are pushing shad and there is a dynamite top-water bite. It lasts all through the summer. "You'll see the shad boiling," said Stone, "it looks like the water is alive. It only lasts a couple of hours a day and you never know where or when. But when it's on, you'll know cause you will see all the boats. We use spoons, Spooks, Rapalas, and sometimes blades to take these fish. Wait until you see fish boil, then cast to the boil and let the spoon sink right to the bottom. When the spoon hits the bottom in 20 to 30 feet, bring it back up. A lot of people don't let the lure fall far enough, they let it drop three or four feet, then reel in, but they should let it fall."

The final summer pattern is to go after suspended fish. The lake used to stratify in summer and fish would be found near the surface or suspended in fairly shallow water, far from any sign of structure. Now that there is an aeration system, there seem to be fewer suspended fish. Still there are always some and it can be a reliable summer pattern when top-water and weed lines won't produce.

To get suspended fish, they must first be located, and the only way to do it is with a good graph. Once they are found, jig spoons near the fish or swim a Reeper on a darthead. The suspended fish may hold in water anywhere from 10 to 100 feet deep, though they are usually in less than 20 feet of water. Mazzurco thinks the suspended fish are a little smaller on average than fish that orient to vegetation, though the suspended bass can be easier to catch.

Fall is the finest time to fish on Otay. Fall fishing doesn't require anything fancy. In about September the bait moves closer to the banks and the suspended fish come in after them. With fewer fishermen on the water, the fish stay in the shallows all day long, rather than being forced to the deeper ledges. The fishing is great along the weed lines and the edge of the tules. There is good top-water fishing back in the coves and cuts on Rapalas. At this time of year crankbaits and worms will produce double limits of bass, with fish that commonly weigh more than eight pounds and some that go better than 13 pounds.

All of the flipping in fall is done with worms. The local guides don't feel this is a good jig lake. The best worms are eight to twelve inches long in darker colors. The Otay Special is a brown worm with a black vein along its length. It has been consistent for the past 25 years, and will no doubt keep catching fish for another 25. Work the worms slow on the bottom at this time of year, split-shot the smaller worms and Texas-rig the large sizes. Finally, the locals won't go on the lake without a supply of salt and pepper Reepers that are

Jerkbaits are effective in spring and fall.

fished on a darthead hook. Between these two rigs, it is tough to go wrong.

The best part of fall fishing is the lack of crowds. There are usually fewer than one or two dozen boats on the lake and there is seldom a line to launch.

Otay is a fairly clear water lake, but a lot of the surface area is covered with green mossy slime and vegetation. For fishing in the clear water use line of less than 10-pound test. Fifteen-pound line is needed for flipping worms directly into the tules, but 10 pound is adequate for working in and around most of the vegetation.

The lake is closed through duck hunting season, from the end of October until the end of January. The rest of the year it is open only on Wednesday, Saturday and Sunday.

The main structure on the lake is tules, rock, moss, and trees.

OTAY GUIDES

Joe Mazzurco (619) 463-5202
Western Plastics, P.O. Box 1732, Lemon Grove, CA 92045
Joe has been a licensed guide for more than eight years, and is also the owner of Western Plastics, the makers of the Otay Special. He has placed in the top ten at professional bass tournaments many times, and has also qualified for many Tournaments of Champions.

Rowan Stone (619) 698-8826
2425 Massachusetts Ave., Lemon Grove, CA 92045
Rowan has been a licensed guide for eight years and has been fishing these lakes for bass for 20 years. He has been Hidden Valley Bassmasters Angler of the Year and has finished in the top ten of U.S. Bass a few times.

Dave Zimmerlee (619) 271-8726
8957 Helen James, San Diego, CA 92126
Dave caught the 3rd largest bass that has ever been officially recorded, out of Lake Miramar. He is active in tournament fishing in Southern California.

OTAY FACILITIES

Otay is controlled by the San Diego City Lake Department. There is no camping on the lake, but there are plenty of hotels, motels, campgrounds, stores for bait and tackle, and other services in San Diego. There is a fee to fish of $3.50 per bass fishermen, or $4.00 for trout fishermen. There is also a $4.00 launch fee. The lake tentatively opens at the end of January and closes in October. It is open only on Wednesday, Saturday and Sunday, call first. There is a hot line with current information, (619) 465-3474.

KEY TO OTAY LAKE

Best Season: Fall, the fish move shallow in September and October and there are fewer fishermen on the water to put the bass down. Other than that, spring. Try to go during the week to avoid the weekend rush.

Lures To Use: Four- to six-inch worms or three-inch Reepers are the lures to use 90 percent of the time. An eight- to twelve- inch Otay Special worm is good in fall. Also spoons, spinnerbaits, and Rapalas.

Primary Structure: Otay has all of the standard types of structure that bass fishermen look for. There are brush piles, points, broken rock, flats, tules, and moss. Look for combinations of these structure types near migration routes. When the lake is really getting pounded by fishermen, move offshore beyond the casting distance of the boats hitting the shore. Work the bass as they come off of the flats in their migration to the safety of deeper water. It isn't generally necessary to fish deeper than 20 feet on Otay at any time of year.

Other: Use lines of 10 to 15 pounds, or for open-water worming, go a little lighter. See facilities section for when the lake is open.

Submerged trees are good fishing areas.

PARDEE LAKE

Pardee, people fish for trout up there, don't they?
That's the kind of question a bass fishermen is likely to get asked when he mentions Pardee Lake. This lake is something of an undiscovered smallmouth bass hot spot. "You won't see five bass boats on the water in a day," said Jim Land. "All the people who come here are trout fisherman. About the only place you ever even see anyone at all, is up by the marina where they stock the trout."

In spite of its lack of notoriety, Pardee is an excellent smallmouth bass lake. There are largemouth too, but very few. The smallmouth on the other hand, are off of every point, and on the broken shale "nothing banks." The lake is loaded with two- to four-pound bass that nobody bothers to fish for. Those who know where and how to fish the lake, can land 15 to 20 quality smallmouth in a day.

Pardee is located just minutes from Lake Camanche, in the Sierra foothills east of Stockton. The lake has only 2,200 surface acres, but has 43 miles of fishable shoreline. Pardee Dam is one of the oldest dams in this part of the country, built in 1929. Because the lake is a drinking water supply for the East Bay area there is no swimming allowed, something of a bonus for fishermen seeking refuge from jet skis and ski boats. The

Pardee is predominatly a smallmouth lake and lure selection should target smallmouth.

lake is peacefully quiet and the facilities are well-maintained.

There is a spring fishing pattern, and a pattern for the rest of the year. On the surface, that doesn't sound very complex, but there is more to it. Small fish are a dime a dozen and can be caught off of almost every bank. Larger fish hold only in the prime spots.

Structure and river current are the most important keys to finding smallmouth bass on this lake. Unlike many bass lakes, in which bass follow the migrations of shad, the bass at Pardee are homebodies, they move only short distances throughout the year. There are no shad in this lake, so bass have no incentive to move around a lot. The primary forage species are: trout, kokanee, bluegill and crawdads.

"This lake is perfectly suited for smallmouth bass," Tony Fox said. "There are lots of long shale banks and deep water. A classic smallmouth point is long and sloping, flat on top, with broken rock near steep banks and creek channels. There should be suitable spawning areas nearby as well, within at least one-quarter to one-half mile of the area you are fishing in, no matter what the time of year. Those are the kinds of things you have to look for with smallmouth. They won't be on any one thing, you have to look for the combination."

There are lots of points that meet all Fox's criteria for a perfect bass spot, more than could be thoroughly fished in a long day on Pardee. Water movement helps to further isolate the best fishing spots. "There is a pretty good current running through the lake most of the time," Fox added. "The fish relate to the current of the river and creek channels, because the moving water brings food and oxygen. That is why it is so important to find points that are close to the main flow of current."

Points and islands on the outside of bends in the river are among Fox's favorite spots. Pardee Lake has a long, oval shape, with an extensive river arm flowing into the eastern bank of the oval. Within the river arm there are good bass points, especially on the points where the river flows into the main body of the lake.

There is almost no wood or weed structure in the lake. The water district maintenance workers remove any trees or debris that finds its way into the water. This means that the only thing the bass have to relate to is bottom characteristics. What a smallmouth considers a good break can be subtle, for instance the line where a rock covered ledge changes from uniformly large rock to small pea gravel, may have the same effect on fish as a tree or change in depth. Fox said, "You gotta fish the bottom. Fish always relate more to the bottom than any other kind of structure."

Pardee opens in the second half of February. The smallmouth will already be on a pre-spawn pattern. Look for fish around the spawning banks near the flat sloping points that Fox describes as perfect smallmouth spots for the rest of the year. The bass aren't as likely to be back in the large deep coves, they will spawn in the smaller coves near the main body of the lake and river arm. Once the spawn gets underway, fish hold in two to ten feet of water. They are easy to see with polaroid glasses.

By the time the water hits 70 degrees, in about June, the smallmouth will have moved to the humps, points, and underwater islands. This is where the fish stay for the rest of

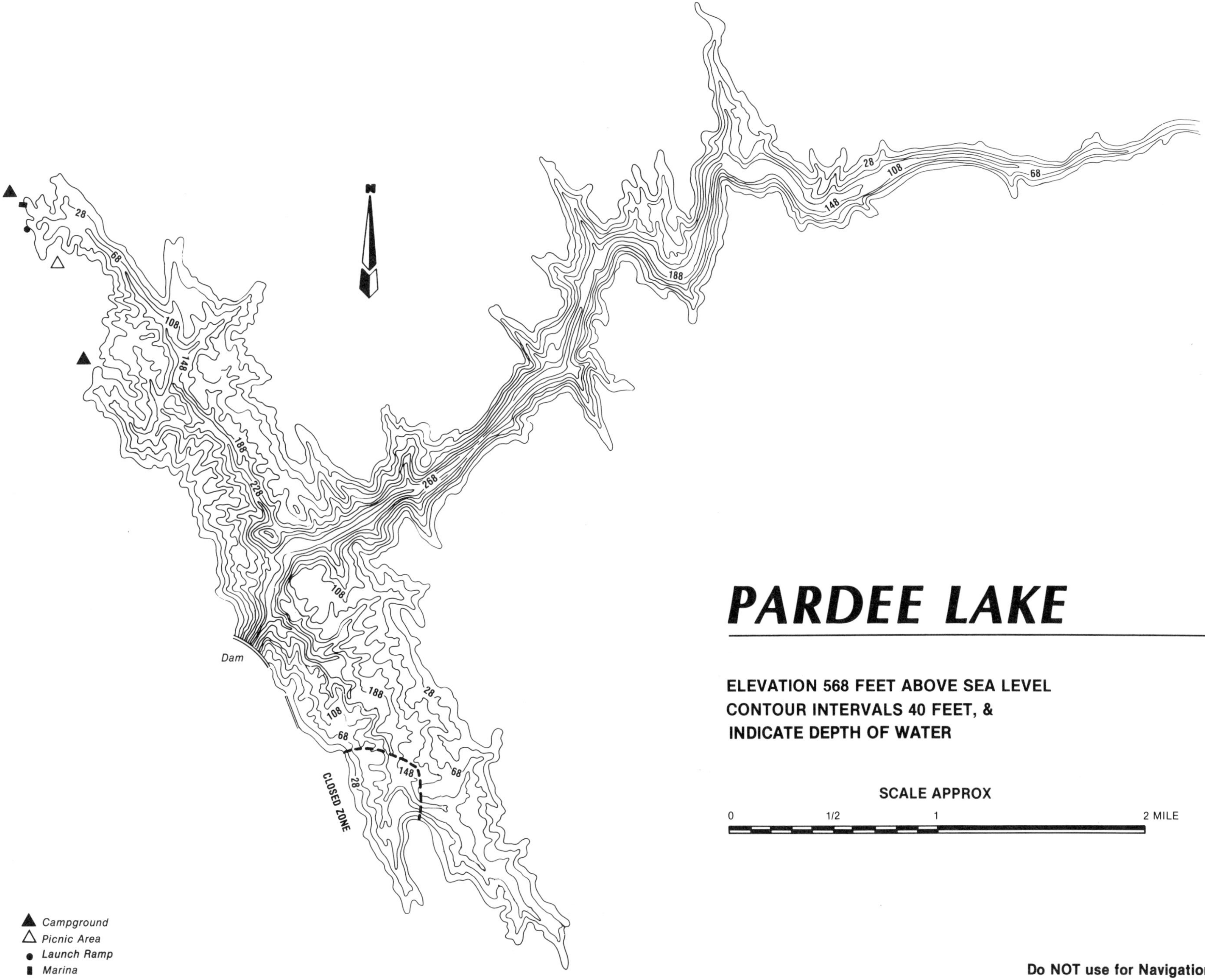

PARDEE LAKE

ELEVATION 568 FEET ABOVE SEA LEVEL
CONTOUR INTERVALS 40 FEET, &
INDICATE DEPTH OF WATER

SCALE APPROX

0   1/2   1   2 MILE

Do NOT use for Navigation Purposes

68

108

28

148

188

188

228

148

108

68

28

268

106

188

188

228

148

108

68

28

68

148

28

108

68

28

CLOSED ZONE

Dam

▲ Campground
△ Picnic Area
● Launch Ramp
■ Marina

Paradee is not crowded like many of California's lakes.

the year, right through fall until the lake closes to fishing on the first Sunday in November.

When it is hot and sunny, work the shady side of the points. In a lake with so little cover, bass utilize the shade cast by points. Even during the brightest hours of the day, Fox and Land don't find bass deeper than 25 feet on Pardee. Fox said, "The bass feed heavily on the bluegill and catfish spawns, which occur later than the bass spawn, and I think that this easily available food keeps the bass shallow."

"Normally, when you find one good smallmouth, fish the area hard because there are probably others," said Land. "Usually they group by size. The little ones hang out with the little guys. The big guys with the big guys. When you find the little ones shallow, move out about 10 feet and you often find big ones."

Don't overlook top-water fishing. "We always start out top-water," said Land, "especially in spring. You'll get a lot of fish on surface lures fished slow. No matter what time of day we get on the lake, even in summer and fall, we always go with top-water first. Then we will go to cranks, and finally jigs or worms."

Fish slow. Land and Fox think that smallmouth are more inclined to take a slow moving bait than a fast one. With largemouth, fishermen usually like to give their jigs a little action. For smallmouth it is better to let a lure rest on the bottom and watch the line for slight motion. The smallmouth strike can range from a pounding attack, to a take that is so gentle, it can't be felt. Watch the line. Fox said, "You won't usually get hurt fishing slow, but you can get hurt by fishing too fast."

For lures, both Fox and Land prefer smaller baits. They'll use 1/8-ounce to 1/4-once hair jigs. They also like four-inch worms and smaller surface plugs. For colors, brown, green and red are the best in worms and jigs. Shad patterns are good for plugs. They seldom use spinnerbaits or buzzbaits, though they will use these lures after heavy rains with a lot of run-off that muddies the water.

Under ordinary circumstances, this is a very clear water lake. Lines of four to eight pounds are recommended. Fortunately, there isn't much wood or brush to loose a fish in. Fox said, "Give the fish line and let them go, because smallmouth pull hard. If you are used to largemouth you'll swear that every fish you have on must be at least five pounds before you get it into the boat. You can't force them in, or they'll break you off. I think fishing for smallmouth can make you a better fisherman, you have to use patience to get them."

Land added, "After you have been into a few three or four pound smallmouth, that's all you want. Nothing else will do it."

PARDEE GUIDES

Tony Fox (209) 223-4153
205 Anita St., Jackson, CA 95642
Tony is a licensed guide who has fished the mother lode lakes for seven years. He specializes on Pardee because it is a smallmouth lake and, well, he prefers smallmouth.
Jim Land (209) 223-2238
Jim's Bait and Tackle
603 S. Highway 49, Jackson, CA 95642
Jim owns the bait and tackle store in Jackson. He has fished for bass since he was a kid in San Diego, and has been fishing Pardee for the past two years, since moving to the area.

A smallmouth over three pounds is not uncommon.

PARDEE FACILITIES

Pardee Lake Resort (209) 772-1472
4900 Stony Creek Rd., Ione, CA 95640
Pardee Lake is a drinking water reservoir; no body contact with the water is permitted. The resort offers: bait and tackle, coffee shop, marina, boat rental, and swimming pool. There are 100 campsites, 87 with full hookups, in addition to a small trailer park; $8 a day to camp, $13 a day in the trailer park, reservation are accepted only for the trailer park. The day use fee is $3 per car, $3 per boat, and $1 per dog. There is also a $2 per person fee for fishing. The lake is closed from mid-November to mid-February.

Glory Hole Sporting Goods: Offers complete bait and tackle as well as other sporting goods. Located at 2892 South Highway 49, Angels Camp, CA 95222, just before the turn off to the Glory Hole Campground. Call (209) 736-4333.

Rocky shorelines near deep water are places to try a top water bait like the Tiny Torpedo.

KEY TO PARDEE

Best Season: March to October. There are only two basic patterns. Fish are shallow during the spawn in March, then move out to 15 or 25 feet after June.
Lures To Use: Top-water plugs, Rapalas, Tiny Torpedos, and Baby Spooks. Small hair jigs and four-inch worms in brown, green, and red.
Primary Structure: This is the real key for smallmouth. First off, look for major points on the outside bends of the river channel where there is some current flow and deep water nearby. Then work the subtle breaks at 15 to 25 feet, which could be humps, a steep drop, a change in the bottom composition, a small cut, or rocks. Also concentrate on the shaded side of the points. That is the pattern for all seasons except the spawn. During the spawn, move to the gravel flats, within a few hundred yards of the best points. There is almost no wood or vegetation in the lake.
Other: Very clear water, use four- to eight-pound line. Work slow and always start with top-water.

Trees that hang over the bank and into the water are definitely worth fishing. Wood is generally removed by the Municipal Water District. When you see it take advantage like the fish do.

PERRIS RESERVOIR

The biggest attraction at Lake Perris is the number of world-record spotted bass this small lake has produced. Perris holds the current world record, as well as at least four of the largest spotted bass ever caught in the world. Take a look at the IGFA record book, five out of seven current line-class records are from Perris, with only the 16- and 20-pound line class records held by other lakes. The world record was broken twice on Perris in January of 1987, with Steve West taking a spotted bass that weighed nine pounds, four ounces. This record was tied in April of 1987 on Perris, by Gilbert Rowe. Another world record could be waiting at Perris right now.

If the chance of catching a world record isn't exciting enough, good fishing throughout the year just might be. The winter action isn't as fast as in summer and the fish are harder to find; but one of the nice things about spotted bass, is they don't stop feeding in cold water.

In spring, summer, and fall, the lake busts loose with an outstanding top-water bite. In these three seasons it doesn't take fantastic luck to catch more than 20 fish per rod in a morning. More than half of these fish may be small, but fishermen should easily catch and release at least four or five

If fish on Perris are deep use worms or spoons. If they are shallow in the trees go with a top-water bait like a Rapala.

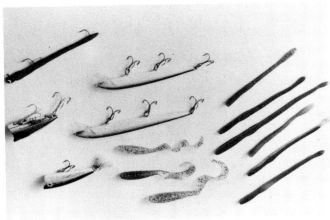

good-size fish. On Perris a legal fish has to be 15'', and fish of this length often top three pounds.

In years past, Perris was on the decline, then the Department of Fish and Game stepped in to restore the world-class fishery. Their efforts have been successful, as attested to by the recent string of world records. "A few years back, you couldn't buy a bite on Perris," said Maurice Holybee. "The number and quality of fish that we catch here now is testimony to Fish and Game's two fish limit and the 15'' minimum size. It really brought the lake back and I think it is now one of the best lakes in the state."

Lake Perris is a small, bowl-shaped lake, with only 2,200 surface acres; there are no extensive arms, few points, and for all intents and purposes, no bays or coves. The water is very clear, when the lake is calm the visibility through the water is at least 15 or 20 feet.

From spring through fall, the best fishing area is in the submerged brush and trees found on the southeast side of the lake. This area is about two miles long and forms a wide belt of cover that extends 100 to 200 feet from the shore. It looks like spinnerbait heaven, but the guides prefer lures like Rapalas, Spooks, buzzbaits, Gitzits, and worms.

Conventional wisdom has it that spotted bass orient to rocks and boulders, while largemouth prefer timber. But, at Perris where rocks and brush are mixed, a school of spotties may be only 10 or 12 feet from a good largemouth area. "I don't target one species over the other," said Dave Mitchell. "Both species are utilizing the same areas lately. Which is sort of a surprise because before everybody thought the spots wouldn't use the brush, but they are right in there with the largemouth."

"One trick to finding spotties is this," Woody Woodruff said. "Go to rocky, brushy areas in six to fifteen feet of water, this is during the spawn to mid-summer. In all that thick brush there will be places where there isn't any brush at all, they look like holes. The reason there is no brush, is that there are rocks on the bottom. So you cast into those holes and a lot of the time, there you go. You'll catch spots. Cast into the brush on the other side of the boat, and you'll catch largemouth."

This doesn't mean that the whole two-mile stretch of brush-line is going to produce bass. On any given day, there will be a few areas, only 20 to 30 yards wide, where the bass are active. This is especially true of the spotted bass that school and move more than largemouth. Mitchell suggested trying places with both vegetation and structure. Rocks with moss growing on them are also a good sign.

Holybee added, "In deep water, if you find a spot with fish on it, mark it with a buoy. You may want to make another couple of passes after throwing the marker, to verify the exact position of the fish in relation to the marker. Now, you fish exactly where the fish are. I have noticed that quite often when an angler finds a good looking spot he fishes around it, but spends little time actually fishing on 'the spot.' In the shallows, the same thing happens, a guy passes a particular section of trees, he catches a fish, then moves on. Those comparatively small sections are where the fish are, not 20 or 40 feet away. It only makes sense to me, to fish exactly where the fish are, spending very little time on the in-between spots."

At Perris, the tactics for catching both largemouth and spotted bass are similar. Anytime from March until late November, use top-water lures in sizes that are standard for largemouth bass, and smaller plastics that are good on clear water lakes throughout the West.

During spring, summer and fall the surface bite can be good even through the middle of the day, although it is usually best in the morning and evening. But, guides have seen fish caught on top-water at midday, even on bright sunny days. As long as the pattern works, go with it. Holybee and Woodruff use the rule of about one fish per hour in the boat. This lake is popular with skiers in summer, so plan on getting the serious fishing in before 9:00 or 10:00 a.m.

For surface fishing, Holybee uses a "slammin'" technique, with Rapalas. Think of slammin', as a way to make the lure dart and then appear to die just under the surface. Holybee makes short casts close to the trees and brush; then with a hard downward jerk of the rod, he retrieves the lure two or three feet, pulling it down beneath the surface. Then he takes up the slack line, while the lure floats to the surface, then slams it again.

Woody likes to use Rapalas, Baby and Chugger Spooks, and Pop-Rs, around the trees. However he twitches the bait back to the boat in a more conventional fashion and doesn't think slammin' is all that much more successful. Fishermen should try both tactics and go with what works. Mitchell uses bigger baits in fall, like full-size Zara Spooks and buzzbaits, adding, "Those are about the only two lures I'll throw in fall."

If the top-water bite doesn't produce fish, Mitchell recommends moving off-shore from the brush line, into water 10 to 20 feet deep. Look for drop-offs with rock structure, like a small peak for instance, and use a 3/4-ounce jig, a Garland jig, or a plastic worm.

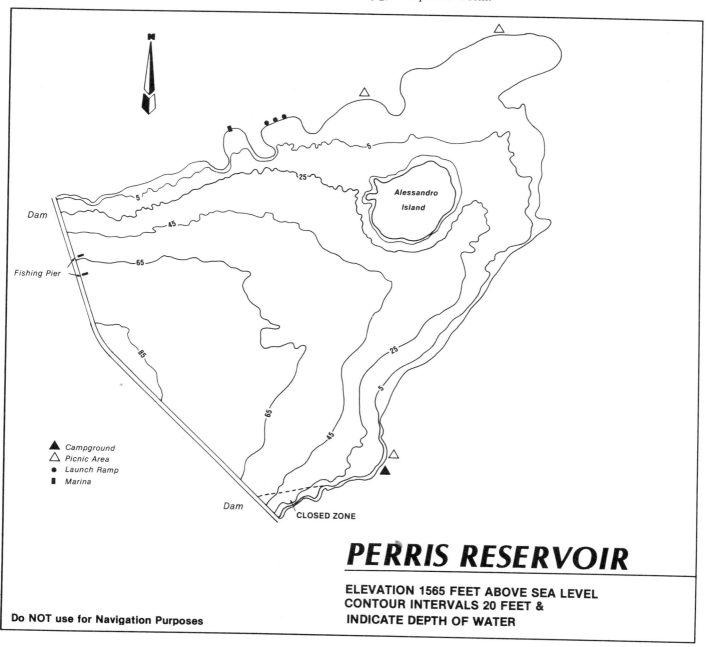

PERRIS RESERVOIR

**ELEVATION 1565 FEET ABOVE SEA LEVEL
CONTOUR INTERVALS 20 FEET &
INDICATE DEPTH OF WATER**

Do NOT use for Navigation Purposes

Structure fishing on this lake is either shallow trees or deep water breaks.

A popular worm is the "Lake Perris Special," manufactured by Workin' Girl Worms. The Special is a four-inch, paddle-tail worm, in moss green with a black vein. Holybee caught a former world record spotted bass on a Special. Other popular worm colors are: almost any variation of moss green, salt and pepper, and chartreuse sparkle. Occasionally people catch fish on an eight- inch Workin' Girl worm, in Cin-a-melon color. It is a good lure when the bass are in shallow water around the trees.

The guides on Perris like to fish worms with an open hook whenever they can get away with it; the only time they rig weedless is in the very thickest brush. As far as hooks and weights, they use everything, from dartheads, to bullet sinkers, egg sinkers, and split shot. For ordinary shallow worm fishing, small light wire hooks are the rule, with as little weight as possible. Lines need to be light, from six to ten pounds, because of the clear water and small baits.

For worm fishing in deeper water, Holybee and Woodruff like to use a pea-head weight with a 3/0 Eagle Claw hook on a four inch Perris Special worm. "It's a giant hook for a little worm," said Holybee, "but it doesn't bother the fish."

They fish this rig with an adaptation of Iovino's doodling technique, that they call "diggin' in." Fish the worm on the bottom, and shake the rod tip fast; if it is done right, the line feels like it is beating against the weight of the lure as the slack comes up. The idea is to let the head of the hook dig into the soft bottom, creating a big silt cloud with the tail of the worm wriggling around in it, like a creature trying to dig into the mud.

For winter fishing, concentrate on catching spotted bass in 30 to 60 feet of water. These fish often school near structure, like tire reefs, pipes, ledges, and rock piles, although spotties sometimes hold in areas where the bottom is almost barren. Occasionally trophy fish are caught in less than 20 feet of water, in January and February. Look for these big fish around huge rocks that extend into the water, after four or five days of warm weather.

To catch spots in winter, you should have a very good paper graph, such as the Lowrance X16. Search the deeper lake structure to graph several bass in an area. They may not look like typical fish arches, the spotted bass sometimes hold so tight to the bottom they graph like tortoise shells. It is tough to distinguish them from rocks, but there is a good chance that the arches with gaps beneath them are spotties.

Spoons are good in winter. When all else fails, turn to deep water spooning on the tire reefs or at the northern end of the dam. Work the spoon slow, hopping it over the bottom or jigging vertically. To keep from constantly loosing spoons on the rocks, substitute a light wire hook for the hook that comes on a regular 3/4-ounce spoon. Try a Mustad 3551, No. four for a 1/2-ounce spoon, or the No. two for 3/4-ounce spoons. The lighter wire will bend out if the hook snags, so the spoon can be retrieved if it catches on structure.

The lethargic spotted bass bite very lightly in winter. Barbs must be super sharp and fished with a light drag. The combination of light line and a light drag will get more bites and few fish will break-off if they are worked gently.

130

When the bite is really slow in winter, live crawdads may be the only thing the fish will hit. Fish them with the minimum amount of split shot that will take the crawdad to the bottom, and a No. four Mustad 33637, plastic worm hook, or the equivalent by another manufacturer. Target the tire reefs and deep rocky drop-offs and let the crawdads do the work. Most of the time, artificials produce the best, but in those tougher months, live bait may be the only way to go.

One word about the tire reefs. The bait balls on this reef can be 20 feet thick. It is a place that any fisherman would look at and surmise; bass must come here to feed. Well, they may be feeding, but it isn't on artificial lures. It is tough to get bass on the tire reef to hit an artificial at all, perhaps because there is so much readily available bait in the water. On Perris, the bass in the shallows are usually a better bet for fishermen.

Perhaps the best spotted bass lake in the world, Perris has produced four world records.

PERRIS GUIDES

Maurice Holybee (714) 785-7336
Bass Connection
7755 California Ave., Riverside, CA 92504
Maurice held the former All-Tackle Record for spotted bass, with a fish caught at Perris in 1988. He owns The Bass Connection and is an expert on fishing Perris. He also designs and manufactures Workin' Girl Worms. Many of these worms are created for the conditions at Perris. The Bass Connection can refer customers to guides on the lake.

Dave Mitchell
Dave has been fishing tournaments since 1976 and his home lake is Perris. In the Red Man Colorado Division he took 9th for the year in 1986, and 10th for the year n 1987. Dave is on the Pro Staff at Anglers Marine for Champion Boats and he is also sponsored by: Berkley Trilene, Daiwa, Haddock Lures, and Executive Tackle.

Woody Woodruff (714) 689-3514
Woody was guiding for Steve West when West caught the current All-Tackle Record spotted bass, with a fish from Perris that weighed 9 pounds, 14 ounces. Woody is a well-known bass expert, has been fishing since he was seven years old, and was formerly a saltwater guide (before he got so wrapped up in bass fishing). He currently guides on Lake Perris.

LAKE PERRIS FACILITIES

Perris is close to Riverside and there are plenty of motels, restaurants, and other services on the freeways leading to the lake.

Lake Perris State Park is a popular camping and day use facility. There is a complete marina with a small store, bait and tackle shop, launch ramps, gas, snack bar, and hot showers. There are 254 campsites with hookups for $16 a night; 167 without hookups for $10 per night. The day use fee is $4 per car. Call (714) 657-0676 for information. For reservations through Mistix call (800) 444-7275.

The Bass Connection, 7755 California Ave., Riverside, CA 92504. (714) 785-7336, for complete bait, tackle and fishing information on Perris.

KEY TO LAKE PERRIS

Best Season: Spring, summer and fall all offer good fishing and a great top-water bite. The lake is popular with skiers in summer, plan on getting off the water by 9:00 or 10:00 a.m.

Lures To Use: Four- to six-inch worms. Go with mossy green, brown, crawdad colors, and chartreuse flake. For top-water they'll all work, Pop-Rs, Spooks, buzzbaits, jerkbaits, it isn't particularly important, choose the lure for the structure. In winter or deep-water, use spoons, jigs, and worms.

Primary Structure: The trees and brush that line the shore, for topwater. Areas with rock and brush for fishing on the bottom, and the big rock boulders for shallow fishing in winter. For deep water, look for breaks, but they can be only a few feet high. The spotted bass may orient over flats that don't look like they would hold bass at all; it takes a good graph to find them.

Other: This lake is the place to be for world record spotted bass. There is a two fish limit, and bass must be at least 15 inches long.

Two happy anglers with Lake Perris bass.

PINE FLAT RESERVOIR

Pine Flat is a lake on the rebound. As Bob Perry said, "Back in the mid-'70s, Pine Flat was the pits. Now, it's very good."

The lake is a 21 mile long, deep canyon lake, on the Kings River, in the foothills east of Fresno. There are major bends in the lake, following the contour of the old riverbed. There is very little timber or vegetation in Pine Flat, though when the water is high there may be bass cover in willows and grassbeds, especially above Trimmer Marina. The prime fishing spots are on pronounced points along the main river channel, and in the coves formed by creek channels. At Pine Flat, fishermen need to know how to use a graph and fish the bottom.

The rebirth of Pine Flat is due in part to the introduction of spotted bass. In the six years that spotted bass have been in the lake, they have done very well and increased their numbers, primarily at the expense of the smallmouth bass. Spotted bass over seven pounds have already been caught and there is a strong population of spots of all year classes.

Spotties were considered a good choice for this lake, because of drastic water level fluctuations. The reservoir water is used primarily for agriculture resulting in draw-downs each spring, at the height of the largemouth spawn.

The most reliable way to catch fish at Pine Flats throughout the year is by using soft plastics and small jigs.

Spotted bass spawn deeper and earlier giving them a decided advantage over the largemouth. Also, the rocky habitat and clear water are ideal for a spotted bass fishery. The success of the spots may come at the expense of largemouth and smallmouth, but both these species were declining with current water management policies. At least the spotted bass have a fighting chance of holding there own.

Pine Flat is a finesse fisherman's lake. Small baits are the rule on Pine Flat. Small four-inch worms, on 1/16- to 1/32-ounce jig heads or split shot, produce 99 percent of the bass. Clear worms with flake for a little color are good. Four- to eight- pound lines are essential.

The key is to fish slow. Then slow it down some more. A proper retrieve of a worm can take more than two or three minutes. These bass take lures very gently, almost imperceptibly. The sign of a fish may be no more than a sideways motion or the faintest feeling of pressure at the end of the line. Keith Lienau calls it a "wet leaf bite."

In mid-March, the spotted bass begin to spawn. "They'll move onto major points in the main body of the lake, and then migrate back into the nearby coves," said Perry. "You want to fish down to 20 feet for spotted bass in the spawn. The largemouth spawn about a month later, primarily above Trimmer. They'll be in the big coves, on flats near deep water creek channels."

A good pattern for largemouth in early spring is to fish in the river current, just above and below obstructions. "This is assuming that the current isn't a super-cold ice-melt," said Lienau. "They'll hold in those still water pockets in two to three feet of water and then they will move off to the spawning beds. This is an unusual pattern and something most fishermen don't look for. But flipping jig and pigs of 1/2 to 5/8 ounce, right into those pockets can produce some really nice bass."

While the largemouth are spawning, almost any lure that attracts their attention will work. For the spotted bass straight-tail worms and grubs are the way to go. At this time of year, Lienau likes to fish his worms on a 1/8- to 1/16-ounce jig head, worked extremely slow. "With fish moving up to make a nest," he said, "they'll move the lure and spit it out once it is off the nest. You'll miss that kind of motion with a split shot. On a jig head you have a direct line to the lure."

In summer, there is often a top-water bite early in the morning and late in the evening. The surface fishing is best where water-skiers have muddied the water, over long tapering points with broken rock. Use Tiny Torpedos and Pop-Rs in the smaller sizes, even the larger fish hit small top-water baits.

There are two distinct patterns for finding bass in summer. "If the lake level is stable or rising, the bass will hit top-water early in the morning on cuts and over brush tops," Lienau said. "They will also hit a split-shot worm, rigged on a floating jig head. Fish this over newly submerged grass and they'll murder it. That's a lot of fun, because ordinarily the bite is very light.

"If the lake is falling, throw off points, as much as 50 yards off of the points. The fish may be suspended, holding in shallow water over a deep bottom. Look for long tapering points, not steep, but with deep water on each side. Put the boat up on the bank and cast offshore."

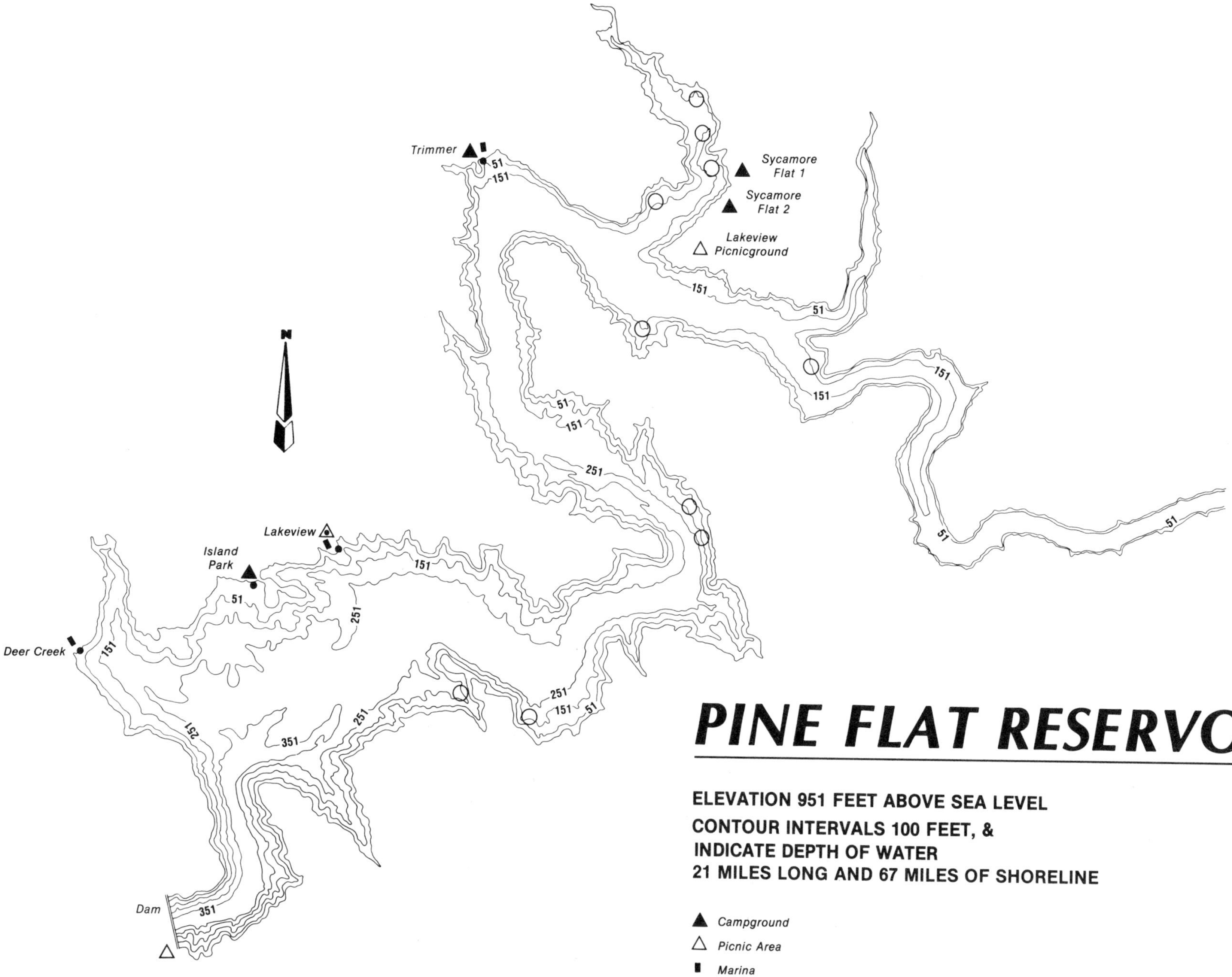

PINE FLAT RESERVOIR

ELEVATION 951 FEET ABOVE SEA LEVEL
CONTOUR INTERVALS 100 FEET, &
INDICATE DEPTH OF WATER
21 MILES LONG AND 67 MILES OF SHORELINE

▲ Campground
△ Picnic Area
■ Marina
⬙ Resort
◯ Boat Mooring Area
● Launch Ramp

Sycamore Flat 1
Sycamore Flat 2
Lakeview Picnicground

Trimmer

Lakeview

Island Park

Deer Creek

Dam

N

51
151
251
351

Do Not Use for Navigation Purposes

During the heat of the day, look for the mud-lines created by the wave action of wind and water-skiers. Also fish the points and walls, near deep water, the fish will bite all day, but they might be deep.

The best summer fishing is at night. The bass come out of the 20 to 35 foot range that they hold in during the day and feed near the banks in less than 10 feet of water. Perry likes to use a spinnerbait at night, or flip a Texas-rigged ringworm. He uses heavier line at night, up to 14-pound test.

By October, the fish are on a fall pattern. "It gets tough then," Perry said. "The largemouth bite dies. But, the spots still hit. They can always be found off of walls and in deep coves. They run in schools by size. Find a concentration of spots, and you'll catch them. Keep moving until you find a school of decent-sized fish, that's the key."

The bass may come up into water about 15 feet deep or so for a brief time in fall, depending on the water temperature, but there are more and better fish at depths between 20 and 25 feet. As the water gets cooler, go slower, and use split-shot rigs more than jig heads. The bass hold on steeper banks, but not on the vertical walls. Look for broken rock, especially on off-shore humps and islands.

One good thing about spotted bass, they keep biting in winter. It may be a soft bite, but it is a bite. Both the largemouth and the spotted bass are bunched up off of the major points. Look for points with large boulders, the bigger the better. Rock absorbs heat from the sun, and that attracts the bass.

"Split shotting is most popular in winter," Perry said. "Fish the cuts on steep walls. When the water is in the low 50s, the spots hold at 55 to 65 feet, or even down to 70. The largemouth are usually above them, in water of 15 to 35 feet."

"On this lake I like to 'shitbank' it," Lienau added. "Especially in a big tournament, because if the area looks even remotely good, it'll get pounded. So I shitbank, go for the most nothing banks that look really ugly. There may be a few cuts, they may be just straight, but they are covered with broken, scraggly looking rocks. In one tournament, my partner and I had 23 fish before 7:00 a.m., by fishing one of those banks that didn't look like it would hold anything.

"Pay attention to the river channel, fish on the outside of the wide bends. You can fish all along the channel, but those outside bends and the adjacent coves are going to hold more bass."

You can often catch quality fish on this lake from structure—free banks.

PINE FLAT GUIDES

Keith Lienau (209) 439-4391
6674 N. Alva, Fresno, CA 93711
Keith has been fishing tournaments on the West Coast for 14 years. In the West Coast Bass Team Circuit he and his partner took Anglers of the Year; out of 500 possible points, they had 493. Keith's sponsors are: Budweiser, Ranger Boats, Tru-turn, Richard Neal's Worms, Bass Specialties and Thermo Batteries.

Bob Perry (209) 431-5449 or (209) 224-4546
3210 E. Shields, Fresno, CA 93726
Bob is a licensed guide and has fished tournaments since 1972. He provides on the water instruction, exclusively for bass.

Keith Lienau with a spotted bass.

PINE FLAT FACILITIES

The Army Corps Of Engineers, operate a total of four launch ramps and two campsites on the lake. Three of the launch ramps offer complete marinas with stores, tackle, and boat rentals, through concessionaires. They are usually open year-round, though in winter the services may close during the week. The 4th launch ramp is at Island Park. Call (209) 787-2589.

Island Park has 52 regular spaces and 52 overflow spaces, with hot showers, and a launch ramp. There is a store on private property next to the campground. The fee is $8 per night between April 1 and September 31; there is no charge the rest of the year.

Deer Creek Group, there are two separate group sites, they are accessible only by boat and require reservations.

The U.S. Forest Service runs two campgrounds at the headwaters and upriver of the lake. They are primitive, with no launch ramps, water, or electricity. The flip-side is, there is no fee and they are open year-round. (209) 855-8321.

Sycamore has 20 sites, and a group site.
Kirch Flat has 19 sites, and a group site, it is on the river.
Fresno County, has three campgrounds below the dam of the lake. The fees are $9 per night for the first vehicle, $4 for the second. (209) 488-3004.
Choinumni, 75 sites, with running water and restrooms.
Pine Flat, has 52 sites, with running water and restrooms, plus a group site by reservation only.
Misty, is strictly a group site by reservation only.
Lombardo's: A private facility, with campgrounds for tents and RVs, and an eight room motel. Directly above the launch ramp at Lakeview, at the headwaters of Pine Flat.
Doyle's Store: Bait, tackle, and convenience items. Open seven days a week, year-round. 25425 Trimmer Springs Rd., Piedra, on the way to the lake. (209) 787-2387.

KEY TO PINE FLAT

Best Season: Spotted bass start to come on in mid-March, followed closely by smallmouth. The largemouth won't spawn until a month later. Summer is good, early in the morning and at night. The spots bite decently in winter. Fall is tough.
Lures To Use: Small finesse baits, four-inch straight tails in winter, four-inch curl tails in summer. Light colors are best. Tiny Torpedos are good for top-water, use anything else and it's a waste of time.
Primary Structure: Fish along the main river channel; the largest and the most fish will be on the outside bends of the river. Target the small cuts, especially for the spotted bass that school by size, all the good fish will be packed onto one tiny little cut or variation in the rock. Largemouth are up above Trimmer if there is enough water, and they'll be on flats or in the eddies formed by obstructions.
Other: A finesse lake. Be ready for a "wet leaf" bite, it is very light. Fish slow, slow, slow.

Calm day on Pine Flat.

PIRU LAKE

Piru is a top-water fisherman's lake. It's an action lake. The strictly northern-strain bass aren't going to rank with the biggest in the world, but they can definitely provide plenty of excitement.

There are those fishermen who would take top-water action on decent-sized fish over the possibility of a lunker; these are the fishermen who should head for Piru in the spring. On this lake, fishermen could work buzzbaits all day and never go more than 15 minutes without a bite.

"I've had guide trips for customers on Piru, where we had 67 fish in a day, all on buzzbaits and spinnerbaits," said Ron Glover. "And those people had never fished a spinnerbait before. Piru bass aren't big fish, but there is a lot of action."

This is an untalked about, overlooked, bass lake. The reasons for Piru's lack of fame are obvious; the lake is located off Hwy 126, midway between Lake Casitas and Lake Castaic, two of the most talked about bass lakes in the county. How can a 1200 acre lake that produces lots of one to five pounders, compete with two lakes fighting for the next world record? Only by virtue of solitude and fishing action. Piru's other negative, is that the lake is popular with skiers in summer. To avoid the wash from ski boats, plan on getting off the water by 10:00 or 11:00 a.m. on hot summer days.

Top-water baits are great on this lake. If the fish are not up go to a plastic worm.

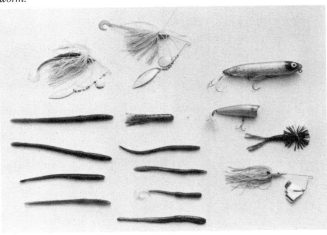

The best thing about Piru is that it is an easy lake to fish. As Glover said, "When you find lakes with pure northerns in them, just go back to the basics. They aren't as finicky as Floridas, it is a lot easier to catch them."

By basics, Glover means fishing near the shoreline in less than 25 feet of water. No fancy stuff. Fishermen should look for vegetation, stick-up, and walls, and choose a lure according to the season and time of day. In a sense, this is a great lake for beginning bass fishermen, because the fish behave in predictable patterns. Find a spot that looks good, cast an appropriate lure, and the odds are high of landing a fish. It's that simple. Nothing builds confidence like catching fish.

The best time to be on Piru is spring, starting in about March. At this time of year, the bass may still be on a pre-spawn pattern. They are likely to hold in 15 to 25 feet of water, on the migration routes from deep water to shallow flats, especially the flats at the top of the lake. Jig and pig is an excellent lure for pre-spawn bass. The smaller jigs, like the Skinny Bear designed for smallmouth bass fishing, have proven to be top lures for largemouth on any clear-water lake.

By April, fish are on the beds in the shallows. If the water is high enough to cover the shoreline vegetation, fish around the stick-up. There are good flats in the three coves of the lake, as well as in the headwaters. All of these areas will hold spawning bass. The tactic for finding bass is to cruise the shoreline, looking for flats near cuts with structure, then cast onto them.

Use any surface lure that will come through the brush. Glover recommends buzzbaits. The buzzbait bite holds up all day in spring, even on sunny days. For better quality fish, Glover likes to use the Zara Spook and standard Rapalas for top-water. But, the buzzbait gets good fish and comes through the stick-up that hold bass on Piru.

Glover recommends varying the speed of the retrieve on top-water lures according to the conditions. When fish are shallow and can see the lure easily, fish the lures a little faster. When the bass hold in deeper water, it may be necessary to slow down, to give them time to come up and get the bait. If a bass holding at 20 feet can see a surface lure, he'll come up and hit, provided the lure is fished slow enough to give him a chance to react. It may even take several casts over the same point to get the fish to bite. The important thing to remember is, don't rush it. Give the fish time to react.

If the top-water doesn't produce, the next lure to move to is a spinnerbait with a willow-leaf blade, and a thin curl-tail worm of 3 1/2 to 4 inches as a trailer. "The nice thing about the spinnerbait," Glover said, "is they're very versatile. You can fish them on top or on the bottom. They also come right through the stick-up without snagging."

When the bite is tough, which doesn't happen often in spring, turn to plastic worms, fished on either split shot or Texas-rig. Glover recommends four- to six-inch worms, in purple, salt and pepper, and salt and pepper with a chartreuse tail. Three-inch Yamamoto grubs, in salt and pepper, and root beer are also good. The key to effective worm fishing is to go slow. It is fine to fish at a medium speed when covering water, but on spots that look like they should hold bass, slow it way down. Keep in mind that when the fish are aggressive

LAKE PIRU

ELEVATION 1055 FEET ABOVE SEA LEVEL
CONTOUR INTERVAL INDICATES DEPTH OF WATER
SURFACE AREA RANGES FROM A MAXIMUM OF
1200 ACRES TO A MINIMUM OF 750 ACRES

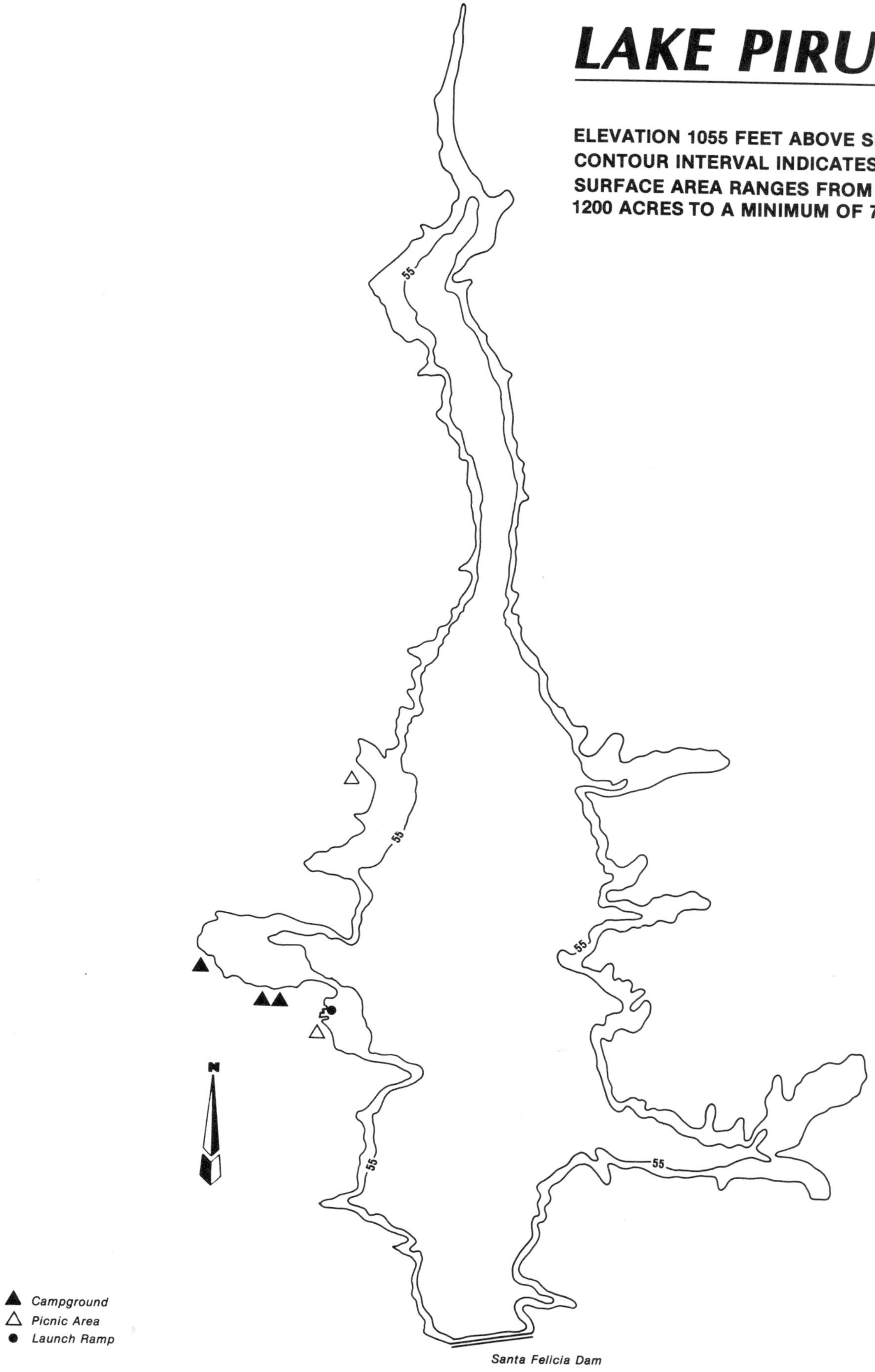

55

55

55

55

55

N

▲ Campground
△ Picnic Area
● Launch Ramp

Santa Felicia Dam

Do Not Use for Navigation Purposes

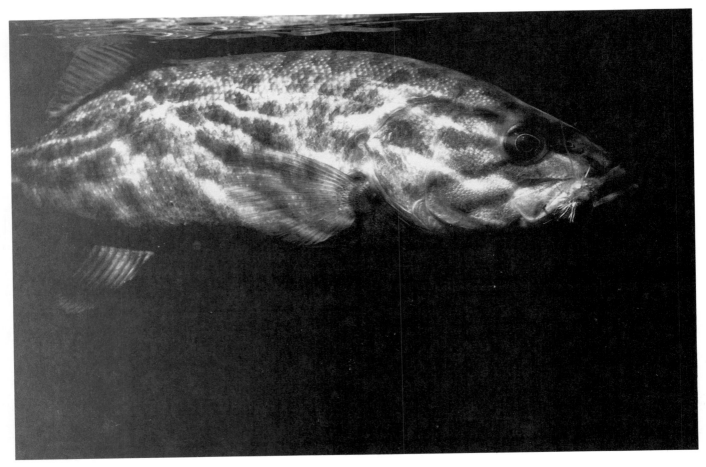

Smallmouth, arguably, fight harder than largemouth.

on Piru, it would be better to use a top-water lure or a spinnerbait. Since the only time fishermen are going to turn to worms is when the fish are dormant, it is important to slow down enough to give half-interested fish a chance to strike.

By summer, worms are the main lure to use during the heat of the day. Glover likes shad colors better in the summer. Salt and pepper blue flake is his top producer. Work the worms on split shot in about 20 to 25 feet of water. Look for steep rocky points and walls. Glover said, "A lot of the time I'll throw the worm up on the bank and work it out until I find out what depth they are concentrating at. You don't loose anything by doing that."

Early and late in the day, there is still an excellent buzzbait bite, right through the summer. If the stick-up is still submerged, keep working it as in spring, but look for areas with deep water access. If the stick-up is out of the water, fish over points and near vertical walls. It doesn't matter if the bottom is 10 feet deep or 30 feet deep, when the fish are feeding, they'll come to the lure. Casting surface plugs across points can often be the best pattern, just alter the speed according to the depth of the fish.

"Fall is a continuation of summer," said Glover. "You still have a good surface bite. It is better on buzzbaits at that time of year, whereas in summer you might have done better on a floating plug. You'll still get fish on worms and jigs,

anywhere from 15 to 25 feet. In fall, you want to fish a lot of points and across points, throw into pockets and that kind of thing. Because the fish are schooling up."

Winter is tough. Some fishermen do all right by fishing with jigs and spoons, over concentrations of fish. But, it means a lot of time graphing the bottom and slow fishing. Truth is, from December to January, fishermen would probably do better to go to another lake.

Piru is a clear water lake, use lines of eight pounds or less for all subsurface fishing. For top-water lures Glover likes to use line of about 14 pounds. The thicker diameter line helps the lure to float and the fish aren't as likely to be line shy on a top-water bait, as they would be on subsurface lures.

The primary forage in the lake is shad and crawdad, along with stocked trout. Though there are a lot of crawdads in the lake, Glover still thinks either shad-colored lures, or purple and black worms and jigs, work better than red and brown lures.

This can be a dynamite lake to go and have fun on, either flipping the brush or working a top-water lure. It is a consistent lake, one of those spots that is ideal for fishing with novice bass fishermen or christening a new boat or rod. Unlike at many of the famous trophy lakes, on Piru your chances are very good of catching bass just about every day out, and lots of them too.

PIRU GUIDES

Ron Glover (818) 349-1757

Ron has been a licensed guide for the past four years, though he has fished Southern California lakes since he was a kid. He has fished tournaments for 11 years, and in 1988 took Angler of the Year for the Southern River Circuit in WON Bass. His sponsors are, North Hollywood Marine, D.K. Spinnerbaits, B.C. Tackle, and C & L Tackle.

Ron Glover with a healthy looking fish.

FACILITIES AT PIRU

Piru Recreation Park, has a good launch ramp and marina. There are boat rentals and a bait and tackle shop. The campground has 200 campsites, of which 61 have electric hookups, no reservations accepted. There are hot showers and flush toilets. The entry fee for a boat is $4, camping is $11 without hookups and $14 with hookups. Open year-round. Call (805) 521-1500 for information.

Other: There are motels, restaurants and stores in Fillmore, seven miles west on Hwy 126. Castaic Junction is 11 miles east on Hwy 126, and has motels, restaurants, and boat repair shops.

KEY TO PIRU

Best Season: The fish are in pre-spawn by March and in the shallows by April. Excellent top-water fishing from April through June. In summer, the fishing is reasonably good, use top-water early and late in the day, fish worms at midday. Fall is a continuation of summer. The buzzbait bite stays good through Indian summer, and bass still hit worms and jigs.

Lures To Use: Buzzbaits, Zara Spooks and floating Rapalas. Willow spinnerbaits with a 3 1/2- to 4-inch curl-tail worm as a trailer. Four- to six-inch worms in shad colors, on either split shot or Texas-rig. In winter and early spring, very good jig lake, especially for smaller jigs.

Primary Structure: If the water rises in the spring, there is brushy stick-up on all the flats in the lake. There are three large coves that are excellent in early spring. This is the place to look for bass through spring. Later in the year, move to rocky points and steep vertical walls.

Other: A clear water lake when the run-off isn't heavy. Use six- to eight-pound line for sub-surface baits.

Ron likes to fish the flats at Piru with top-water baits and blades.

PUDDINGSTONE LAKE

Gregg Silks said, "The thing about Puddingstone is that it has always been there, since back in the 1930s. It's an old lake, but it still produces bass; good quality bass on a regular basis. It's been there since every bass fisherman was a kid, and every bass guide in Southern California has fished it at one time or another. It is kind of nostalgic, 'cause even after fishing all over the country, we all still go fish the old mud puddle now and then."

Puddingstone breaks almost every rule. This lake covers only 250 acres, and it is located at the junction of Interstate 10 and the 210. The lake is within a short drive of about 26 million people, yet during the week, from December to March, the lake is uncrowded. Then again, lakes are supposed to peak after 10 or 15 years, but Puddingstone is still going strong after almost 60 years.

More important, small lakes in the middle of town don't generally turn out big bass, but the Puddingstone lake record is 14 pounds, 12 ounces. On top of that, small lakes that produce lunkers are supposed to hold only a few bass, that have eaten all of the other fish that were under three pounds; this is the old quality versus quantity problem. But, at Puddingstone limits are fairly easy to land from January to April, while eight to ten pounders are caught on a fairly regular

Lure selection for Puddingstone.

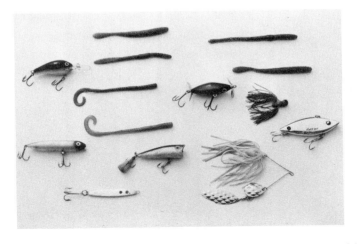

basis. Scott Burright said, "The average fisherman should be able to catch bass, darn near every single day of the year. This is a real consistent lake."

There aren't a lot of tricks to fishing on Puddingstone. The forage base is diverse, including shad, bluegill, crawdads, turtles, frogs, and just about everything else that can survive in a California lake. That gives fishermen a lot of options in terms of the type of lures that are going to produce bass. This is a good lake to experiment on with all types of lures, from crankbaits, to spinnerbaits, to plastic worms. One of the nice things about a small lake, is that there is plenty of time to run through all of the lure possibilities on each spot. Because it is easy to fish the whole lake in a single day, there shouldn't be much question of having been on the wrong spot. At the end of a day on Puddingstone, it is easy to determine which lures worked and which didn't.

The prime time of year to fish on Puddingstone is from December to April. That includes the winter and most of the spawning season. The largest and most fish are caught from late January through April. The reason the winter is considered good among fishermen who know the lake, is that there are almost no skiers; in fact during the week in winter there is hardly anybody on the lake at all.

There is relatively little vegetation on Puddingstone. In the old days, there were a lot of lily pads, tules, and willows. Now the lake is managed as a park, and most of the shoreline vegetation was removed to make room for skiers and picnic-types. On the other hand, a tire reef was placed in 50 feet of water, for deep water structure, and 200 Christmas trees were recently put in the lake. There is also an aerator, to prevent a strong thermocline from developing. Burright said, "We are making a real effort to make this a fisherman's lake. We are doing a lot of stocking and creating structure. It's been paying off already."

The bass are in pre-spawn by the beginning of February, and spawning by March. They come from the deep water holding areas at 40 to 60 feet that they used in winter, into water less than 15 feet deep.

Split-shotting four-inch plastics, in salt and pepper, and brown colors, is the most consistent method from spawn through pre-spawn, though this is by no means the only way to go. Use slower lures early in the year when the water is below 55 degrees. As the temperature rises into the optimum spawning temperature range, experiment with spinnerbaits, Gitzits, and crawdad-colored cranks.

Burright suggests working the steep cliff areas and the docks. Both areas are good in late winter and early spring. The bass hold off the shelves of the cliffs, as they work up into shallower water. By the beginning of April, the bass are all over the shoreline, on the shallow water beds. They'll stay shallow until May.

Summer presents a couple of problems for fishermen. First off, the fish may come shallow only at night and in the early morning; during the day they hold in deep water sanctuaries. According to Silks, the fish moving deeper doesn't matter much, because there is a larger problem at midday when the lake is completely taken over by water-skiers and drag boat racers.

The only way to fish Puddingstone in summer, is to get on the water at dawn, and fish until 10:00 a.m., then go home.

The lake management doesn't allow fast boating on the lake until 10:00, so the water is fishable in the early morning, and the crowds aren't too bad then.

In early summer, split-shotting plastic worms in 15 to 20 feet of water works well almost anywhere on the lake with deep water nearby. Later on in the year, by August or so, start using crankbaits. "Medium-size crankbaits work real well," said Burright, "I generally prefer shad colors, though to be quite honest, a wide variety of colors work out here. I find the Rat-L-Traps in chrome and silver work real well."

Around the end of September, fishing slacks off, though how much depends on the weather. In a warm fall the fishing remains good for another couple of months. There isn't any fall feeding frenzy. The bass just slow down and move deeper. In fact, the fall and winter bite are almost identical.

"In fall and winter, bass are anywhere from 40 to 60 feet," said Silks. They hold on the deeper structure and off the cliffs. Black plastic worms fished on the tire reef work well. Jig and pigs are also reliable on all types of deep structure when the water is cool. This is a good winter lake, because the water seldom drops much below 50 degrees, also because it is fairly small, fish are not hard to find and can't move super-deep.

Puddingstone is fed entirely by run-off from the surrounding hills, and when it rains, the lake becomes chocolate brown. This isn't great for the fishing, but the bass may still hit lures like spinnerbaits, that put a lot of vibration in the water.

The real trick is to avoid the crowds, and not get too disgruntled about trash, noise, chop, and other problems that go with metropolitan lakes. Take advantage of the quiet seasons, when the only people on the lake are other fishermen. And remember, Puddingstone is one spot where the fish bite well, almost every day.

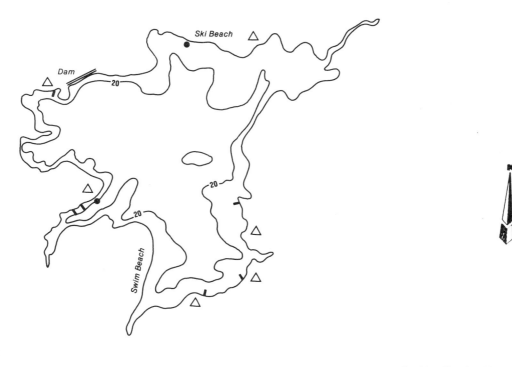

PUDDINGSTONE LAKE

ELEVATION 941 FEET ABOVE SEA LEVEL
CONTOUR INTERVAL INDICATES DEPTH OF WATER
SURFACE AREA 250 ACRES

Ski Beach

Dam

20

20

20

Swim Beach

△ Picnic Area
● Launch Ramp
❘ Fishing Pier

Do Not Use for Navigation Purposes

141

This lake has typical Southern California structure.

The background scenery is wonderful on Puddingstone.

PUDDINGSTONE GUIDES

Scott Burright (714) 599-2667
Bonnelli Park
120 Via Verde, San Dimas, CA 91773
Scott has been living in this area and fishing Puddingstone since the late 1970s. He has worked at the lake since 1981, and is now the manager of all the park concessions, including the bait and tackle shop.

Gregg Silks (714) 987-7721
P.O. Box Altaloma, Ca 91701
Silks is a licensed guide. He lives 22 minutes from Puddingstone and fishes it frequently during the quiet seasons. He has fished on this lake since he was old enough to wind a reel. His sponsors are, Berkley, Cotton/Cordell, Bomber, Heddon, Cannon Downriggers, Plano, Daiwa, Rebel, Poe's, Wall's and Outdoor Apparel.

Landing a nice bass is always fun.

PUDDINGSTONE FACILITIES

Bonelli Park, is a day use park with launch ramps, boat rentals, bait and tackle, snack bars, and picnic areas. The lake is open to fishing all year from sunrise to sunset and the

park stays open till 10:00 p.m. in the summer. The boat rental and tackle shop are closed Tuesday and Wednesday in the winter. Fees are, $4 day use, $4 launching. Call, (714) 599-8411.

East Shore Campground, does not have launching facilities. The campground has 543 RV sites with hookups at $19 and $22 a night. There are also 54 tent campsites. They have a grocery store and swimming pools. Reservations are necessary during most of the year because they get booked solid, months in advance. Call (714) 599-8355.

Steep cliffs and deep waters are good areas to fish.

KEY TO PUDDINGSTONE

Best Season: December through April, when the water-fun crowds are not on the lake. The real fishing peak is, late January through May. In summer, fish the lake early in the morning, then get off the water by 10:00 a.m., when the lake is taken over by water-skiers.

Lures To Use: Anything and everything, a good lake to experiment with new lures and to practice techniques. The most reliable fish catching lures are probably plastic worms, salt and pepper, browns, and black.

Primary Structure: The lake is small, so all of the water can easily be covered in a day. Good areas are the cliffs, which have shelves and deep water, the docks, the Christmas trees, and the tire reef, marked with a buoy in 55 feet of water.

Other: The lake tends toward the murky side, especially after rains. Go with line from six to twelve pounds, depending on the type of bait being used.

RUTH LAKE

Ruth Lake is close to perfect. It is an isolated, serene, 1200-acre lake, surrounded by mountains that are covered with pines. Though the lake is small, it doesn't seem so because it is long and narrow, with dozens of secluded bays and estuaries fed by mountain creeks. All this provides plenty of almost private fishing spots.

Of more interest to fishermen, the lake is loaded with bass. The lake holds northern-strain largemouth up to nine pounds, with a good population of fish over five pounds. When the water is clear and the fish are shallow, bass can be seen all around the lake, grouped in the backs of creek cuts, as well as near structure and stick-up.

Better yet, there are few fishermen on the lake. During the week, while school is in session, there won't be another boat on the water. In summer and on weekends, there might be two dozen other fishermen; this is what they call a crowd in these parts.

The only drawback to this perfect set-up is relatively poor access. Ruth Lake is in Trinity County, well over an hour inland from the coastal town, Fortuna. All access is via logging roads, with hair-pin turns that wind through mountain passes.

This is a typical bass lake. Lure choices should be made according to the time of year. No fancy tricks needed to catch fish on this lake.

But, don't get the idea that this lake isn't worth the drive; it is. This is one spot where 50 fish days are plain old reality. When Lorin Fleming came out to do the photos for this book, he fished for about five mintutes and in that short time he landed a three-pound bass. "It's going to be tough today," he said. "This is really terrible."

It's easy to get spoiled.

Ruth is a narrow canyon lake, about 11 miles long, and less than a mile wide, formed by a dam on the Mad River. The upper third of the lake is all one big shallow flat; largemouth spawn up there in spring, though the flats go dry in fall. The other two-thirds of the lake shoreline is steep walls. The guides claim the lake was clear-cut before the dam was built, but there are still quite a few stumps, and plenty of vegetation along the shoreline in places where the slope of the bank is less than 45 degrees.

There are largemouth and smallmouth in the lake. The smallies were introduced about five years ago and they are already beginning to take over the banks in the steeper portion of the lake. The largemouth still dominate in the shallow flats at the headwaters, as well as the bays and coves.

The key to fishing on Ruth is temperature. All of the guides in this area plan their fishing strategy with the aid of a temperature gauge.

The bass start moving up to the shallows when the water temperature reaches 45 degrees, sometime in March. There is a tremendous pre-spawn move on the part of the largemouth, as fish move from the deep end of the lake to the shallow flats at the upper end. Look for fish on the migration channels in early spring, in the waters that receive sun all day, primarily on the northeast side of the lake. Work all of the main points and areas with shallow water near deep water. This pattern should pay off in plenty of bass. But, the fish are still fairly inactive, don't go ripping lures through the good spots. Go slow until the water temperature climbs a little higher.

"In pre-spawn, we like to use cranks, like a Mann's Deep 15," said Mike Turner. "The fish will be eight to eleven feet down, so I use a Big Bomber or a Poe, anything that will go down that far. Run it really slow. Take it down and keep it on the bottom, go as slow as possible." In muddy water, and it is usually muddy in early spring, the guides prefer a rattling lure. When the water clears a bit, they use crawdad or chartreuse Wiggle Warts, for better action. The spring bite is best in the afternoon, peaking at around 1:00 or 2:00 p.m.

"When the water hits 50 degrees, both largemouth and smallmouth will be up," said Pat Murphy. "Jigs in black and brown, with pork, will catch both of them."

"When it gets into the high 50s to the low 60s," Turner added, "I am seriously flipping a jig or throwing a spinnerbait around wood. We're talking the sunny side of the lake now, that's the key. Fishing on a bush, tree or stump, you'll catch bass like crazy in April."

"When the fish start spawning, at about 60 degrees, you can catch them on top-water around any stump and on flats," said Fleming. "I don't know why, but the smallmouth seem to spawn around wood. You'll catch the largemouth on top-water, too, stazting a few weeks later. All spring, I always have at least one top-water plug on my rods. A Rapala and a salt and pepper grub will do good all the time. The bass won't hit crankbaits as much once they start spawning.''

Night fishing is the most reliable summer pattern. Use spinnerbaits, jig and pig, and jitterbugs, all in black, in less than 10 feet of water. It is a lot easier to keep track of your lure with pearlescent line and a black light on board; this equipment will make six-pound line look as big as a rope in the water.

During the summer days shiners will be moving in the grass beds. A Rapala thrown into that action can be deadly. As the grass gets really matted, fishermen have to concentrate on the open pockets. Fleming said, "Look for grass areas with moss growing around it. A combination of moss and grass with open patches is best."

By mid-June, bass move onto major points, channels, and steep rocky bluffs, especially when the wind kicks up. Fleming still works at less than 10 feet, but Turner will move down a little, and throw jigs and worms in 10 to 20 feet of water. "Work your jigs on the main points when the sun is high on the water," said Turner, "but don't forget top-water early and late in the day."

When the lake is drawn down in fall, the shallow flats at the top of the lake go dry and the largemouth are forced into the main body of the lake along with the smallmouth. Fleming says that for about three to four weeks, the fish will come shallow again, and can be caught in the same ways as in spring. As the water drops to 55 degrees, the smallmouth move shallow and hold tight against the banks where there is broken rock.

Later in fall, bass hold along the main river channel. Murphy said, "The flats on the edge of the channel are between 20 and 30 feet deep. In the middle of the river channel the depth is 50 to 60 feet. Largemouth are going to hold on the lip of the channel. You'll also find them on points, in 20 to 30 feet of water."

Ruth can have a terrific winter bite. Murphy says that it all happens along the river channel, where fish were biting in fall. Because the lake is falling, the largemouth concentrate in this deep, nutrient-rich water. "The whole thing about winter fishing is that it all depends on if the lake stays clear or not. If the lake is clear, the fishing is excellent, if it's mud-

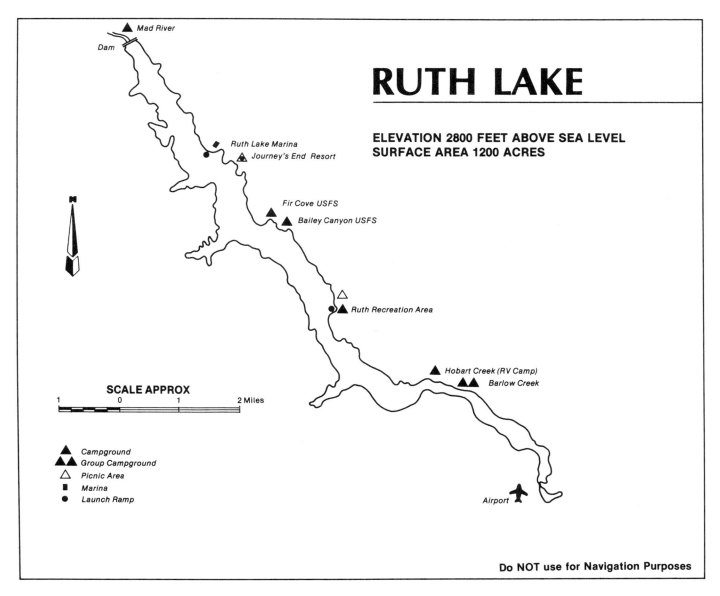

145

dy, stay home. There is about a fifty-fifty chance, so call first to check the conditions. You get two kinds of murky: a greenish tint is okay, it is the yellow mud color that destroys the fishing."

Fleming recommends four primary winter spots: the needle point off the marina, the vertical wall directly across from the marina, the dam, and the river channel. Use marker buoys when fishing the channel. For winter fishing, he'll use spoons, jigs and Little Georges. The Little George is a favorite of all the guides because it can be worked deep like a jig, but the small rotating blade flutters as the lure falls.

"If you graph fish in, or on the top of the river channel, vertically jig them," said Turner. "Work only fish holding right on the channel. Because if they are well above it, then they are suspended. On this lake, suspended fish won't eat. They are just looking for a nice water temperature."

Don't bother cruising the lake trying to graph big bait balls, this may be standard practice on many lakes in winter, but it doesn't do much good on Ruth. There are no shad in Ruth, only shiners, and the shiners don't ball up in large dense schools. The other primary forage species are crawdads and bluegill, with stocker trout for the big bass.

The guides on Ruth almost never fish line heavier than 10 pounds, and six-pound line is used when the water is clear. Always carry a good supply of top-water plugs.

The weather conditions change fast at Ruth Lake, it can snow in May, or top 90 degrees. when camping at the campgrounds around the lake, be prepared for any type of weather, since there are only two lodges with rooms near the lake. And as far as the fish go, no matter what the weather is they'll bite — with one big if. "What I look for," said Fleming, "is three days of consistent weather. It doesn't matter what type of weather, just so it is three days of the same. Then the fishing will be good."

Smallmouth are becoming dominant. There is still an excellent population of largemouth, some over 10-pounds have been caught.

The largemouth hold better on the flats, in the tree stumps and around the vegetation.

RUTH LAKE GUIDES

Lorin Fleming (707) 574-6359
Star Route Box 155, Bridgeville, CA 95526.
Fleming is not currently a licensed guide, but he did guide at Ruth for about four years. He has been fishing Ruth Lake for 15 years. He has also fished pro tournaments and placed in the money many times.

Pat Murphy (707) 764-3709
655 Rigby Ave., Rio Dell, CA 95526
Murphy has fished Ruth Lake his whole life, and fished major tournaments all over the West. He has qualified for many Tournaments of Champions, and taken many top ten spots in major tournaments.

Mike Turner (707) 574-6378
P.O.Box 191, Mad River, CA 95552
Turner has fished Ruth Lake since 1973. He currently fishes about three days a week on the lake, and maybe even two nights a week if he gets the chance. He has taken fourth in a U.S. Bass team tournament at Shasta.

RUTH LAKE FACILITIES

Ruth Lake Community Service District Campgrounds: The service district runs a public launch ramp, open year-round with a marina, courtesy dock, and picnic area — there is no fee for day use. They also operate the following three campgrounds that are open from Memorial Day to Labor Day. Reservations are accepted only at Barlow, because it is a group site. There are no hookups at any of the campsites. For more information call, (707) 574-6332.

Ruth Recreation Park: 50 sites, 18 of them on the water, hot showers, paved launch ramp. $5 fee per car for camping, launching at no charge.

Hobart Creek: 20 sites, running water and a dirt launch ramp. $5 fee per car for camping.

Barlow: a reservation only, group campground. There is a kitchen and group bathrooms, not directly on the water. The fee is $35.

Forest Service: There are two Forest Service Campgrounds. Fir Cove and Bailey Canyon have 20 campsites each, without hookups or launch ramps. The fee is $5 per night. These campgrounds are usually open from May 15 to October 15, depending on the weather. Reservations are not accepted, except for large groups; (707) 574-6233.

Journey's End: This motel, restaurant, bar, tackle shop, and gas station, is directly across the street from the public launch ramp. In the past year owners Tom and Marilyn Stevens have expanded; the restaurant now serves pizza and a wide assortment of "down-home gourmet" dishes, at reasonable prices. The tackle shop and general store carry all the basics for fishermen and campers. And they are now open seven days a week, year-round, barring bad weather. The price for rooms is $32 to $35 dollars a night, but ask about the fishermen's special discounts. Call, (707) 574-6441.

Flying AA Dude Ranch: A dude ranch about 10 miles from the lake, caters primarily to fly-in guests. Offers a coffee shop, bar, pool, and horse-back riding. The AA is now open year-round. Price is $50 a night for rooms. Call, (707) 574-6227.

KEY TO RUTH

Best Season: Good all year-round, best after three days of consistent weather. It doesn't matter if it is freezing or boiling, the rare cases of consistent weather make this lake turn on. In the heat of summer, fish at night. a very good winter lake.

Lures To Use: The guides use all of the standard lure-types at some time during the year, they match the kind of lure they use to the temperature. Cranks are good prior to the spawn when the water is cold. Later go with jigs and worms. As the spawn really gets going, use spinnerbaits, buzzbaits, and top-water plugs. During summer, use more worms. For deep water fishing, try a Little George.

Primary Structure: This lake has points, flats, coves, vegetation and wood. All of it can hold bass. The largemouth hold mostly on the flats at the headwaters and in the shallower coves on the south side of the lake. Smallmouth are on the steeper rocky walls. In winter, fish along the lip of the main river channel for both species.

Other: Line weights should be light, six to eight pounds usually. The access roads aren't great, the lake is only about 45 miles from towns on the major highways, but the drive takes one to two hours.

The smallmouth hold on rock walls.

SAN VICENTE LAKE

San Vicente is not an easy lake to fish, but it is definitely a consistent lake. Just about any time of year, it is going to take work to boat a limit of bass; on the other hand, almost every day of the year the average fisherman will catch at least a few. The action is pretty average all the time, without huge peaks and slumps.

The exciting thing about fishing on San Vicente is that it is a great lake for trophy bass. Joe Mazzurco said, "We know for a fact there are world record fish in San Vicente. We know it from Fish and Game surveys. When you fish on that lake, you always have to be thinking that any cast could be the next world record."

The best part is, Sav Vicente hasn't reached its peak yet. The average size of bass is in the three-pound range, but the total number of bass is still increasing, as is the average size of the fish. An aerator was added a few years back with funds provided by the Southern California Bass Council. The aerator prevents an extreme thermocline from forming and allows fish and bait to disperse throughout a greater volume of water. This creates a better overall environment, and by making a larger area of the water acceptable to bass, the lake can support a greater total number of fish.

Plastic worms are the most popular bait on this lake.

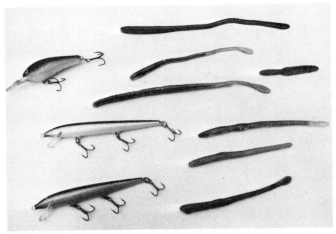

Part of the reason that San Vicente has such large fish, is due to its abundant food supply consisting of massive crappie, crawdads, shad, and trout. Mazzurco said, "We more or less feed trophy bass with the trout."

San Vicente is a steep-sided, clear water lake. There are huge boulders and rock piles around the lake, but only some of them will hold concentrations of bass. The trick is to identify the rocks that are made of decomposing granite, or "DG." From a distance DG looks very smooth and rounded, but close-up, it appears porous, with lots of indentations the size of sand-grains. This type of rock does a couple of things, first it absorbs heat well. In addition, all those little holes trap organic particles; that feed tiny plants and animals; that attract baitfish; that attract bass. The largemouth pack onto DG in early spring.

There are also weed beds around the edges of the lake and all over the flats. These are fairly new to the lake, but fishermen have already found that they hold bass. At times the top-water bite is tremendous over the weed beds in water from 15 to 25 feet deep.

"In fall, when the lake opens to fishing, there can be an excellent top-water bite," said Bobby Sandberg. "It depends on the weather, if we have a hot summer that continues through fall, use top-water early in the morning and in the evening. I use a No. 13 Rapala, Pop-R, or Zara. Take the Rapala and fish it parallel to the bank over the grassbeds that are in 15 to 35 feet of water. This pattern is going to work until we get real cold nights. It produces nice fish."

Later in the day, move away from the weeds and look for rock piles in water from 20 to 50 feet deep. Work the rocks slow, with Texas-rigged worms, on six- to eight-pound line. San Vicente is not a good jig lake. There is a healthy crawdad population, a sign that often points toward jig fishing, but for some reason jigs don't produce well at San Vicente.

For the most part, with the exception of the top-water bite, the most reliable lures throughout the year are soft plastics. But, these aren't the standard finesse baits that are so popular on all of the Southern California lakes. Mazzurco uses worms from three to twelve inches long. "Go for the extremes," said Mazzurco. "Use little baits, like a three-inch Reeper or a four- inch worm; or get out a big nine- to eleven-inch worm. With the smaller baits, put the split shot on 24 inches above the hook, for more action. With the larger worms, move the weight down to 12 or 15 inches from the hook. Let the fish dictate what they want in terms of size. Early in the year, the smaller worms are more consistent, but the really big fish will go for a big bait at any time."

Mazzurco suggests cinn-a-melon pepper for the larger worms, because it has a flake in the plastic that breaks up the appearance of the body line. Smokes, and salt and pepper are also consistent colors, in both the large and small worms.

Sandberg uses worms up to 18 inches long on San Vicente. He fishes straight-tails in mossy green and brown, on 1/0 or 2/0 hooks. He said, "Work them very slow, and let the fish eat the big worms for a while before setting the hook. Don't set it right away. They have to get the whole worm into their mouth, before you move it."

By the end of December, the fishing gets tough. The bass are in the winter mode. They may hold as deep as 60 feet, though 30 to 50 feet is the norm. Use very small worms, Texas-rigged, and crawled over the bottom, slow as a snail. Mazzurco likes the darker-colored worms in winter, such as electric grape.

Fish worms uphill from winter through the spring. Hold the boat on the edge of the bank and cast out into the lake. Many fishermen simply beach their boats on this lake and walk the banks. Both Sandberg and Mazzurco agree that the fish on Vicente are very selective in terms of uphill or downhill presentations. In winter and spring, fishermen improve their catch rates by as much as 50 percent by fishing uphill.

To catch bass that suspend away from structure, beneath the schools of shad, try Hopkins spoons. They work best jigged vertically near the bottom and edges of shad concentrations.

The early pre-spawn bite is underway by February. "It is good fishing by then on crawdads, shiners, plastic worms and Reepers," said Sandberg. "You'll get very nice fish out of water from 35 to 40 foot deep, over rocky points. Fish the crawdads without any weight, on 10-pound line, with a size 6 hook."

Both Texas-rig and split-shot worms, in the smaller sizes, are likely to produce fish during the pre-spawn. Continue to work them slow while the waters are cool. Look for the bays and coves with warmer water temperatures. The DG rock warms the adjacent water, concentrating pre-spawn fish early in the year.

Fish around rocks that get sun throughout the morning and early afternoon. Sandberg fishes with the sun at his back in the morning, and faces into the sun in the late afternoon. Mazzurco said, "In early spring, there may be 30 fish in a 10 or 15 foot stretch of the DG rock. It gets the water real warm, and the bass pack on tight."

After two or three warm sunny days, the bite can improve dramatically in early spring. Basically, a warm spell is what they are waiting for, while staging in deeper water. That boost in temperature brings them onto the beds.

Fish are in the shallows by the middle of March. There aren't a lot of flats on San Vicente, the few spawning areas are easy to locate. Mazzurco said, "When bass are in the shallow coves, split shotting and Rapalas can be deadly."

After the spawn, plastic worms become the dominant lure. Bass are usually shallow in the morning, but they'll move out

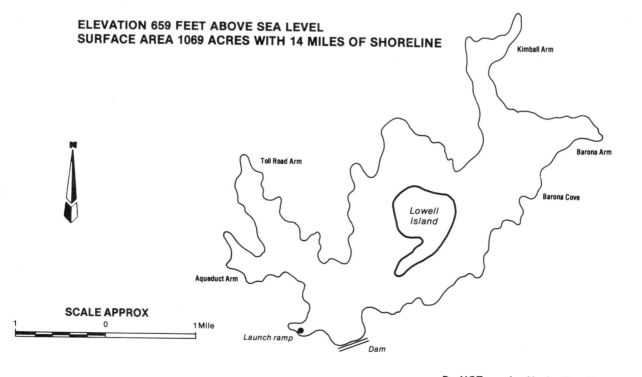

LAKE SAN VICENTE

ELEVATION 659 FEET ABOVE SEA LEVEL
SURFACE AREA 1069 ACRES WITH 14 MILES OF SHORELINE

Kimball Arm

Barona Arm

Toll Road Arm

Barona Cove

Lowell Island

Aqueduct Arm

SCALE APPROX

1   0   1 Mile

Launch ramp

Dam

Do NOT use for Navigation Purposes

during the day to 20 or 25 feet of water. During post-spawn the bass disperse all over the lake; in the mornings they are caught off the shallow water along almost the entire shoreline. Later in the day, follow the bait and look for long sloping points.

The bass continue to bite well after the spawn, even when they have moved out to deeper water. There can be a very good Rapala bite along the weed lines, up until the time when the lake closes for the summer.

"When you find a good area," Sandberg said, "stay on it for a long period. Be patient and fish it thoroughly. This is an excellent lake for trophy bass. These fish are very fat and pretty."

Like all San Diego Lakes, San Vicente is closed part of the year, usually from May to November. In addition, it is open only on Thursday, Saturday and Sunday. Actually, it is open to skiing in the summer, but not to fishing.

Bass like this one can be easy to come by.

Rocky banks are great fishing areas.

SAN VICENTE GUIDES

Joe Mazzurco (619) 463-5202
Western Plastics
P.O. Box 1732, Lemon Grove, CA 92045
Joe is the owner and founder of Western Plastics, a hand-poured worm manufacturing and distribution company based in San Diego. He has been a licensed guide for more than eight years. He has also fished professional tournaments, and has qualified for many Tournaments of Champions.

Bobby Sandberg (619) 226-2805
1878 Chatsworth Blvd., San Diego, CA 92107
Bobby is a licensed guide and has fished for bass since he was about 10 years old. He has been a pro tournament fisherman since 1971 and has qualified for the Tournament of Champions 13 times. He has won major tournaments at Lake Mead twice and at Lake Roosevelt twice. His sponsors are, Yamaha, Ranger, Kunnan fishing rods, and Space Savers Construction.

A lot of anglers get out of their boats so that they can work worms up hill.

Another bass tricked by a plastic worm.

SAN VICENTE FACILITIES

San Vicente Lake, is run by the San Diego City Lakes Department. There is a launch ramp, marina, snack bar, and bait and tackle at the lake, through a concessionaire. The fee to launch is $4. There is also a fishing fee of $3.50 per rod for bass fishing, and $4.00 per rod for trout. The lake is open to fishermen from November to May, on Thursday, Saturday and Sunday only. Of course these dates are tentative, and subject to change. Call the Hot line for the current schedule, (619) 465-3474.

Other: There are motels, restaurants, sporting goods and tackle stores in San Diego and the neighboring cities.

KEY TO SAN VICENTE

Best Season: Spring and fall. From the middle of February to April is the best. Closed to fishing in summer.

Lures To Use: Plastic worms, either the small three-inch Reepers and four-inch worms, or nine- to eighteen-inch straight-tail worms on 2/0 hooks. Brown, cinn-a-melon, smoke, salt and pepper, and moss green are all good colors. Also, Rapalas and Zaras for top-water. Crankbaits and spinnerbaits catch fish sporadically. Not a good lake for jigs.

Primary Structure: Decomposing granite: the large boulders and rock walls that look smooth from a distance, but have tiny holes all over the surface. They are great spots for bass. also, the weed lines, especially when fish are at depths of less than 35 feet. There isn't a lost of wood in the lake, with the exception of some very deep trees that are only good in the winter when fish move deep. Most of the time, the granite rocks and weed lines are it.

Other: A clear water lake, use six- to eight-pound line. San Vicente is a trophy bass lake, be ready for a lunker on every cast.

Fishing points is always a good tactic on San Vicente.

SHASTA LAKE

S hasta is a big lake with a lot of fish, it is famous for producing incredible numbers of bass. "In spring, you can catch 50 to 60 keeper fish per boat, per day, on top-water," Eric Lovelace said. "You can catch 50 fish a day in the summertime too, but the fishing is a little slower and only about half of the summer bass will be keepers."

Fishermen describe smallmouth and spotted bass stacked up on structure like piles of cord-wood. This lake is something of a bass factory. The lake holds largemouth, smallmouth and spotted bass. The down side of fishing Shasta is that though there are lots of bass weighing from one to three pounds, there are relatively few trophy fish. It's a catching lake, not a wall-mount lake. But, when the catching side of the picture is this good, few fishermen would complain.

Shasta covers 29,500 surface acres and is the largest man-made lake in California. The lake is located north of Red Bluff, at the northern end of the Sacramento Valley. Shasta is very deep and clear, with five river arms; Backbone, Sacramento Arm, McCloud River Arm, Squaw Creek Arm and the Pit River Arm. This is a steep canyon lake, with vertical walls and lots of feeder creeks, cuts and coves. The

Shasta is thought by many to be the best bass lake in California. There certainly are large numbers of fish so at any given time, any lure will catch fish out of Shasta Lake.

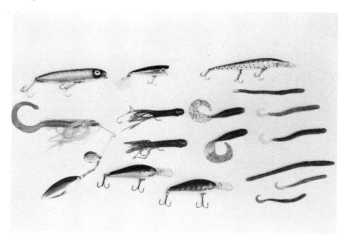

primary bass structure is almost exclusively rock and points; the only exception is the Pit River Arm, which holds most of the timber. Not surprisingly, the Pit Arm is the place to head for largemouth.

The spring bite is on from late March through May. Look for spawning bass in the backs of creeks and coves, where the water is warmer. The spawning smallmouth and spotted bass may be as deep as 20 feet, over pea-gravel near rocky points. The largemouth spawn in less than 10 feet of water and hold tight in the submerged manzanita trees.

"The top-water bite on Shasta is the best in California," Lovelace said. "I use a medium-size Pop-R in black and silver, or a 1/2-ounce buzzbait. Fish areas with a lot of rock, in the backs of coves and on shallow points. At Shasta I can catch fish all day long on top-water."

Dan Hannum fishes the submerged manzanita trees when the water is high or rising to pick up largemouth. "When fishing manzanita in the lake, use a spinnerbait or a Texas-rig worm. Most of the time I fish with six- to eight-pound line, but in the wood you need to go with 14 pound, or you'll never get the fish out. The newly submerged grassbeds are good for plastic Reepers and worms. The fish seem to like mossy greens and crawdad colors on this lake."

When the water level is falling fish the very steep points, with immediate access to deep water — the bass may suspend. Look for points surrounded by deep water. The smallmouth and spotted bass may spawn on narrow ledges at 15 to 20 feet, where their fry are not as vulnerable to falling water, as they would be on long, sloping flats.

The key in spring and fall is to cover a lot of water to find active shallow fish. The bass will be up, it is simply a matter of finding the right structure pattern. After a warm spring rain, "the fish go bananas," Lovelace said. "They'll hit anything you throw. Same in summer. It can't get better than fishing Shasta after a warm rain."

Though the fishing slows down in summer, it is still a long way from what most fishermen would consider a tough bite. From June to September, the fish move off points. They hold in 25 to 40 feet of water, on the steep points near the main body of the lake where the water is deeper and cooler. This is the time to split-shot Green Weenies on six-pound line.

There is a top-water bite early in the day, off of the same steep points that are good for worming in summer. These are the places where the bass have quick access to deeper water after sunrise. "The fish will hit surface lures in the middle of the day," said Hannum, "but the trick is to fish on vertical banks, where the water drops to 40 or 50 feet, within two or three feet of the bank. Work a Tiny Torpedo parallel to the bank and the bass will come up from the deeper water and hammer it."

Crankbaits can work in the mud-lines on the main body of the lake. On an otherwise clear water lake, that off-color water can draw a lot of fish into an area. Ripping a Rapala through the dirty water or working a crawdad colored Fat Rap, can result in a limit of keeper bass, real fast. Look for mud-lines where there is wave action from boat traffic or wind on banks of red clay.

Fall fishing patterns are similar to spring. The bass are active, shallow and feeding, from October to November, or in a warm year even into January. The fish hold on big bluffs with

SHASTA LAKE

ELEVATION 1067 FEET ABOVE SEA LEVEL
SURFACE AREA 29500 ACRES WITH 370 MILES OF SHORELINE
700 FEET DEPTH APPROX

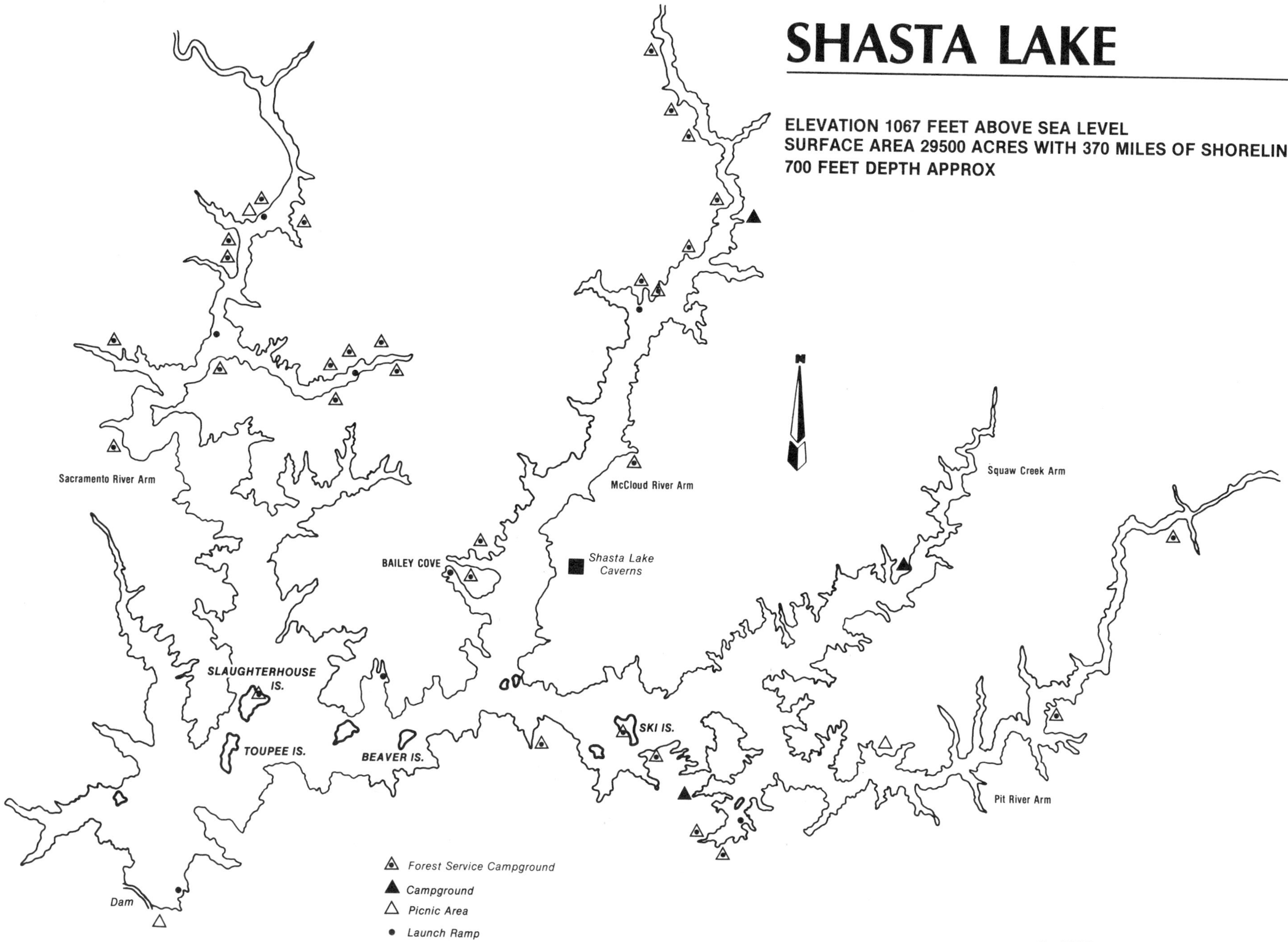
N
Sacramento River Arm
McCloud River Arm
Squaw Creek Arm
Pit River Arm
BAILEY COVE
Shasta Lake Caverns
SLAUGHTERHOUSE IS.
TOUPEE IS.
BEAVER IS.
SKI IS.
Dam
Forest Service Campground
Campground
Picnic Area
Launch Ramp

Do NOT use for Navigation Purposes

lots of outcroppings, where they are suspended at shallow depths against steep walls.

"Fish the walls with white spinnerbaits or cranks," said Lovelace. "I like a white spinnerbait with a single No. 5 Colorado blade, or a shad or crawdad colored Fat Rap. Just work parallel to the bank with a medium retrieve; throw right along the edge of the wall. I catch most of my fish in about 10 feet of water. We do a lot of ripping too, off of shallow secondary points."

Eric Lovelace, a young, up and coming California basser displays a Shasta Lake smallmouth.

When the fall bite slows and the bass are less active, use a root beer Gitzit on a 3/0 hook, with a 1/4-ounce weight. Gitzits are a good all season bait, especially at times when the bite is tough. They are the top producers from the fall transition into winter. Fish Gitzits at medium speeds while the water is warmer and as the water gets cooler slow them way down.

From January to March, the bass hold in deep water at 45 to 65 feet. There are old bridge pilings in the Sacramento River Arm that hold fish, but otherwise winter fishing is almost exclusively in the main body of the lake. Look for spotted and smallmouth on long deep points and boulder piles. It takes a graph to find the reliable winter fishing spots. The bite is very soft in winter, use finesse lures, and fish slow.

Spoons work well for vertical jigging along walls near bait balls. Lovelace also likes to use Iovino's doodling technique with brown, and salt and pepper worms. Lovelace said, "It is really important that you use that glass bead. Go with the technique exactly the way it is shown in the videos, it'll catch these bass in winter."

Jigs are good on the rock piles. Hannum uses tarantula jigs that he ties himself. This is a 1/8-ounce jig, with rubber material wrapped around the shank. The soft, fat body feels more life-like to the fish, giving them something that feels natural to hold onto. Using lures that bass hold onto is the key to fishing a soft bite in deep water.

The Bridge Bay Resort Area is a real good spot for people who are just learning the lake," said Hannum. "All the big tournaments weigh-in and release their fish up there. You can catch a lot of quality fish in this area. There is also Silver Thorn on the McCloud River, but it is real clear, so you have to be cautious that you don't spook fish. The main body of the lake is a reliable area for spotted and smallmouth bass, all year long."

"You can go out on Shasta almost anytime and catch fish," Lovelace added. "It is just unreal. Even when the water is super low, or it is cold out, you can always count on catching bass at Shasta."

The backs of cuts where wood reaches into the water is a perfect place to throw a top water bait and catch a black bass out of Shasta Lake.

SHASTA GUIDES

Dan Hannum (916) 541-8801
P.O. Box 822
South Lake Tahoe, CA 95705
Hannum has been a licensed guide for the past five years. He guides on Shasta during the spring and fall. He also guides on Tahoe and Clear Lake. Hannum is a field tester for DuPont, Stren.
Eric Lovelace Store (916) 275-8553 Home (916) 275-6693
Hidden Valley Market
7013 Hidden Valley Dr., Redding, CA 96003
Lovelace is a licensed guide who has fished and lived near Shasta for four years. He fished professional tournaments for the last nine years, frequently finishing in the top 10. His sponsors are Berkley, and Hidden Valley Market, the family-owned bait and tackle store.

SHASTA LAKE FACILITIES

There are dozens, amybe hundreds of boat launches, campgrounds, and lodging facilities on Shasta Lake, what follows is a very short list. For more information contact: The Shasta Lake Information Center, (916) 275-1587.

Public Launch Ramps: There are six public launch ramps, that charge no fee. They are: Antlers, Hirz Bay, Bailey Cove, Packers Bay, Centimundi, and Jones Valley. Some of these may be closed when the water level is low, call the Information Center (916) 275-1587, to see which ramps are operating.

Fishing Resorts: Again, this is only a partial list.

• Antlers Resort Marina has boat rentals, gas, cabin rentals, showers, laundry, and bait and tackle. There is a public launch ramp nearby. Located at Antler's Road, Lakehead; call (916) 238-2553.

• Bridge Bay Resort has a boat ramp, boat rentals, gas, motel, restaurant, lounge, groceries, and bait and tackle. Located at Bridge Bay, take the Bridge Bay exit off 15, 10300 Bridge Bay Rd. Call (916) 275-3021.

• Holiday Harbor Resort has a complete marina and launch ramp, boat rentals, bait and tackle, gas, campgrounds with hookups, showers, laundry, and groceries. Located on Shasta Caverns Rd., O'Brien. Call (916) 238-2383.

• Sugarloaf Marina Resort has a marina, launch ramp, boat rentals, gas, bait and tackle, campsites with hookups and showers. Lakeshore Dr., Sugarloaf. Call (916) 243-4353.

• Silverthorn Marina Resort has a complete marina, launch ramp, boat rentals, cabin rentals, restaurant, lounge, bait and tackle. On Bear Mountain Rd., via Oasis. Call (916) 275-1571.

• Hidden Valley Market: Sells groceries and a large selection of bait and tackle. 7013 Hidden Valley Dr., Redding. (916) 275-8553.

SHASTA KEY

Best Seasons: March through May is the spawn with the best fishing of the year. The air temperature gets hot on Shasta in summer, but plenty of fish are still caught, though the average size drops a bit. In winter, it's cold, tough and deep.

Lures To Use: Root beer Gitzit, reliable all year-round, also standard worm colors in four to eight inch sizes. Crawdad and shad colored crankbaits, as well as Tiny Torpedos for top-water.

Primary Structure: In the Pit River Arm, fish around the wood for largemouth. Rocky points and creek channels in the arms are good for smallies and spots in spring and fall, especially over pea-gravel in spring. For winter move out to deep water in the main body of lake.

Other: There are a lot of fish in Shasta and there is no single hot spot or best arm of the lake. Fish are dispersed all over the place, though fishermen will find that each of the species stakes out a particular type of habitat. But, the whole lake holds fish.

Rock points like this are a good place to worm fish or throw cranks if the top water bite is not happening.

SILVERWOOD LAKE

Silverwood is a skill building lake. There is a good population of eight- to twelve-pound largemouth bass in the lake, though bass that weighed more than 16 pounds have been caught. Because the lake water comes directly from the Delta, via the aqueduct, there is an extremely rich food supply, that results in fat healthy bass. However, learning to fish on Silverwood takes time, persistence, and sharply honed techniques. Gregg Silks said, "You have to use all your abilities at this lake."

There is a pay-off for serious bass fishermen. "If you can learn to fish Silverwood, you can fish any lake there is," said Gregg Silks. "I have fished all over the country and caught bass using the same techniques that I developed at Silverwood. The lake has largemouth and stripers. It has current, deep water, shallow water, trees, cliffs, rock piles, it is alpine and desert; Silverwood has everything there is. The Delta waters have brought stripers into the lake, as well as several species of minnow and two types of shrimp that provide forage for the shad; the crawdads are native.

Lures used on Silverwood.

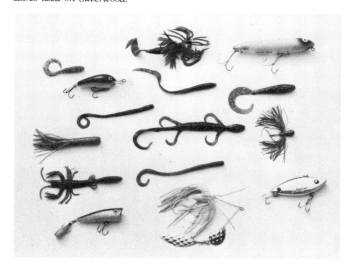

This is an unusual lake, in that it has almost every type of structure that bass fishermen will ever encounter, packed into a mere 950 surface acres. At an elevation of 3,000 feet, the lake's water goes through dramatic temperature fluctuations, ranging from below 50 degrees in winter to the mid-70s in summer. The water level also fluctuates, sometimes as much as 20 or 30 feet in a week. The lake is on the edge of the Mojave Desert and Sierra pine. One end of the lake is in forest, the other in desert. Silverwood is a lake of challenging contrast.

The spring bite begins about three or four weeks later on Silverwood than on lowland lakes. Being deeper and at a higher elevation than the lowland reservoirs, it takes longer for the water to warm. "During spring, I pick up on the outside points," said Rick Stivers, "the major points off creek channels. In this lake it is an absolute must to have a bathymetric map."

The key in early spring is water temperature, look for the warmest water in the lake. The standard rule on most lakes is the northwest factor, which states that because the northwest flats get the most sun, they will warm first. This does not always hold true on Silverwood, because the aqueduct spills into the lake at the northern end. If it is freezing in the San Joaquin Valley, where the aqueduct water comes from, the lake water in the north end of may be colder than the water at the south. A thermometer is essential to determine where the water is warmest.

By the time the water temperature reaches 57 degrees, the bass become active. Below 57 degrees use jigs and spoons, above 57 go with jigs and crankbaits. Work these baits along the major migration routes from deep water to the flats. As the water continues to warm, the fish will move back along the creek channels to the spawning beds. At 60 degrees, it is time to start throwing spinnerbaits and worms near the spawning areas.

"The fish spawn from March through June," said Silks. "You will see them on the beds when the water is between 63 and 72 degrees. Look for them to be on flats near a creek channel, because that provides an escape route if the water level or temperature suddenly changes. Spinnerbaits are deadly. Basically you can use anything that looks like it threatens their nests, buzzbaits and stickbaits are real good."

As summer comes on, the bass may be shallow early and late in the day, but they move down to about 20 feet in the middle of the day. When the sun is low, the bass push schools of shad and it is a good time to fish top-water baits.

When the sun is high and the bass are deeper, finding schools of shad is critical to catching fish. In fact, Stivers feels that this is always a primary concern for fishermen on Silverwood. He said, "If you are having trouble locating shad, look for ducks and grebes. If you can fish within 100 feet of a grebe, you'll be fishing on bait."

He adds that the better quality bass tend to hold at a fairly constant depth, between 15 and 30 feet deep throughout the year. For short periods the fish may go deeper or shallower, but because of the constant changes in weather and water level, the large fish generally stake out a territory at a moderate depth and stay there.

Rather than changing the depth he works at, Stivers changes his tactics, primarily by working uphill or downhill.

In early spring and during the spawn, times when the fish are moving from deep to shallow water, work lures downhill. When the water level is falling and the fish are moving out, hold the boat tight to the shore and fish uphill.

"The Yamamoto rig is ideal on Silverwood," Stivers added. "You need a special hook, called a Yamamoto hook, that is like a tuna hook for live bait fishing in the ocean. You rig it with a four-inch grub, hooked through the head so it hangs off the end of an exposed hook. It is like a live bait rig for calico bass fishing. The same rig works with worms and Gitzits too.

"The only thing you have to remember is that you don't want to set the hook. Which is real good at Silverwood because the fish don't attack the bait. When a fish is on, you just sweep back, the fish hooks itself. The harder the fish fights, the deeper the hook penetrates. The first thing people say when they look at this rig is, 'no way.' But, it works well. When fishing deep, nine times out of ten you won't know fish are there, with this rig the fish hook themselves."

During fall, there is often fog on the lake, caused by warm water and cool nights. This brings on an excellent top-water bite in the morning. And with fog on the water, the bass won't go quite as deep later on in the day. The fall pattern closely echoes the spring pattern, with bass holding on migration routes in the shallows, but they face into the main body of the lake, so uphill fishing techniques work best.

Snow usually hits the lake about Christmas, and this officially marks the onset of winter fishing. The lake turns over sometime in late December or January; fishing is extremely tough during the turn-over. The best plan at this time is to go fish another lake. Other than during the turn-over, fishing can be good at Silverwood, even during the cold months. It is an excellent time to go fishing, because very few boats are on the water.

"I graph on ledges and try to find balls of bait first," said Silks. "I look to see what depth bait is holding at and then I work that level. Sometimes you get a split level, where shad are at 20 or 30 feet and also at 80 or 90 feet. Then I work

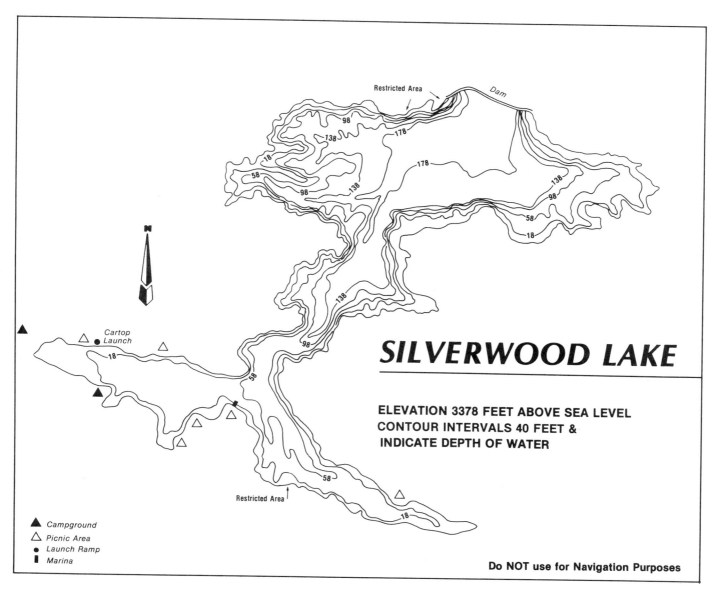

SILVERWOOD LAKE

**ELEVATION 3378 FEET ABOVE SEA LEVEL
CONTOUR INTERVALS 40 FEET &
INDICATE DEPTH OF WATER**

▲ Campground
△ Picnic Area
● Launch Ramp
▌ Marina

Do NOT use for Navigation Purposes

While Silverwood supports stripped bass it also holds a good population of black bass with a few every year caught over the 10-pound mark.

both levels. When you see this pattern, slow down a lot. Don't be afraid to throw a one-ounce jig down there and just work it slow over rock piles. For winter, I use at least a 3/4-ounce spoon or a jig."

Blue, green and white are the most popular colors for baits at Silverwood. Silks uses any worm with a little sparkle in it, in four inches when the water is cool and eight to twelve inches when the water is warm. Stivers prefers to use a four-inch worm throughout the year. They both recommend six- to eight-pound test for finesse lures, and 12- to 17-pound test for top-water and jig fishing.

"The only way to be really effective at Silverwood," said Stivers, "is to record everything you do and every condition. The guys that fish the lake a lot keep a good record, and it will be fairly consistent from year to year."

"Don't worry about what to throw at the fish," Silks added. "Worry about finding them. Then you can throw anything you like until you find something that works. Be there when the fish are feeding. Learn the habits of the fish before you go out. If you put in your time on this lake, it will make you a better fisherman."

SILVERWOOD GUIDES

Gregg Silks (714) 987-7721
P.O. Box 712
Altaloma, CA 91701
Silks is a licensed guide and has fished Silverwood for 13 years. He has been fishing since he was a kid, and has studied marine biology, which gives him a good perspective on fish behavior. He manufactures fishing tackle under the company name, Zoomer Products. His sponsors are: Berkley, Cotton/Cordell, Bomber, Heddon, Cannon Downriggers, Plano, Daiwa, Rebel, Poe's, Walls and Outdoor Apparel.

Rick Stivers (714) 243-2906
11269 Evans Crt., Moreno, CA 92360
Stivers has been a licensed guide for three years. He has fished on Silverwood since 1969 and now fishes the lake close to 150 days a year. He also fishes Lake Perris on a very regular basis.

Structure consists of rocky points and wood.

SILVERWOOD FACILITIES

There is a State Park at Silverwood, it is open year-round, with campsites and a marina. There are 128 campsites, without hookups. The charge is $10 per night. Launching is $5 for motor boats, $2 for boats without motors. There is a lake store with fishing tackle, gas, and rental boats. Reservations are taken through the Mistix service, (800) 444-PARK.

There are no hotels or much of anything else right on the lake, with the exception of the State Park. The closest tackle shop is in Hesperia.

KEY TO SILVERWOOD

Best Season: The spawn is from late March to June. Summer offers decent fishing early in the day, look for bait when the sun is high. Fall brings an excellent top-water bite, and the fishing stays good until November. Don't go fishing as the lake turns over, usually in December or January.

Lures To Use: Yamamoto rigs are excellent whenever fish are below 20 feet. Four-inch plastics are good all the time. Spinnerbaits and buzzbaits during the spawn, jigs and spoons in winter.

Primary Structure: Early in the year use a thermometer to locate the flats with the warmest water. Look for bites near structure in summer. Creek channels, rock piles and migration routes are the most reliable areas. Also, the Ski Arm is good because fewer fishermen bother with it.

Other: A difficult lake to learn, there is plenty of food so the fish are not pushed into hitting lures out of hunger. Also, the elevation causes the spawning season to occur about three weeks later than on lowland lakes. Go with six- to eight-pound test for finesse lures, and 12 to 17 for top-water and jig fishing.

Evening is often the most enjoyable time to fish.

SUCCESS LAKE

Lake Success is on the brink; it is a lake in transition. Over the next few years, the fishery will either boom or bust, it is a toss-up as to which is more likely to happen.

In 1988, Success was poisoned with rotenone to remove carp and goldfish that were destroying the bass fishery. Poisoning the lake sounds like a pretty drastic measure, but consider these numbers. Prior to treatment, local sportsmen's clubs and the Department of Fish and Game removed 10,000 game fish, including bass, catfish, crappie and bluegill. They figure they saved about half of these desirable fish, which were placed in holding ponds above the lake. While there were an estimated 20,000 game fish in the lake, there were 300 *tons* of carp and goldfish.

Excessive numbers of carp do several things to a bass fishery. First they compete with the bass for food and space and eat the bass fry. Second, they stir up the bottom sediments; the lake was mud-brown all year long. High levels of sediments in the water lower the oxygen carrying capacity, which isn't good for bass, especially in a small, shallow warm-water lake. The final result was a lake completely out of balance and over-run with carp.

Lures for Success Lake.

These days, Lake Success is clear, with visibility better than 20 feet. The lake was immediately restocked when the water level rose and flooded the holding ponds. The introduction of Florida-strain bass should produce much larger fish in the future.

"The verdict is still out on how the fishery will be affected," said Calvin Foster. "One thing we do know, is there are a tremendous number of fry. They are growing fast, maybe as much as an inch a month. They are short and fat, and reaching 11 or 12 inches in a single year. This has always been a very productive fishery, with large numbers of fish that are easily caught. Now that the carp have been removed, it should be dynamite."

Located above Porterville, Lake Success is a shallow lowland fishery, surrounded by rolling hills, and the bottom of the lake consists almost entirely of long, extended flats. Most of the primary fishing structure is vegetation of one sort or another. When full the lake covers about 2500 surface acres; it is as deep as 110 feet, however, that deep water is only in a few holes that are remnants of the construction of the dam. The lake is drawn down 65 to 70 feet every fall for flood control purposes, leaving only 320 surface acres with an average depth of 30 feet. Obviously, water level fluctuation has an effect on fishing tactics. The positive side of this is that the water level fluctuation is fairly predictable so fishermen can plan around it, the water rises in spring and is drawn to minimum pool by fall.

"The bass are in pre-spawn by the end of January or beginning of February," said Foster, "when the water starts to rise and gets to 60 degrees. By the second week in February, fish are up and more active. We'll be fishing on the northern banks in 15 to 20 feet of water. During feeding cycles, they'll be up in six or eight feet."

When the water is high enough to reach the coves, bass move into the cockleburs, which makes up 95 percent of the newly submerged vegetation and provides great cover for bass. A split- shot worm is just about the only lure that will come through this stuff, and even that lure is going to get snagged a good deal of the time. But on a split shot, the worm floats up out of the vegetation where the fish can see it easily.

During the recent drought, willows have grown thick in the South Fork. "This is traditionally a very good spawning area," said Foster. "If we ever get a full lake again, it will be a great place to flip pork and worms."

For pre-spawn bass, go with six-inch plastic worms on split shot. Surface lures can be good, as well as single-blade spinnerbaits worked slowly around the trees and newly submerged brush. The key is to work the warmer flats near deeper water, there is plenty of vegetation all around the lake.

By March, the spawn is in full swing. Bass on the beds hit grubs, worms, and jigs. Those fish that are still roaming, are very aggressive and attack Rattlin' Spots and Rat-L-Traps. When the bite is on, these lures can produce a fish almost every cast. "Another good lure is the Heddon Sonar," Foster added. "Be willing to lose that bait. Your productivity with this lure will increase 75% if you fish it right on the bottom."

"Surface lures are real good too," said Borwick. "We use mostly Rebels. This is pretty much a morning and evening bite, though it depends on the weather. Work the surface over the northern flats, around the trees and stumps. Sometimes in spring, they'll stay on top-water all day long, so be ready for it.''

By the time the spawn is over the water temperature reaches 70 or 80 degrees. When the water is this warm the fishing is good early and late in the day on crankbaits, buzzbaits, Zaras, and spinnerbaits, worked in shallow water. After the sun has been on the water for more than two hours, the bass move down to 15 or 20 feet. At midday, the only reliable lures are soft plastics, and even those are not going to be very productive in the heat of the day.

"Your best bet is to fish at night," said Borwick. I like spinnerbaits and plastic worms. Work the spinnerbaits fast at night. You'll find fish along the banks near deep water. They stay deep all day and at night come into the shallows to feed. This pattern lasts through August.''

The water level begins to fall by the first of June, and it continues to drop through September. It drops slowly, only six to eight inches per day, so it doesn't shut the fish off during the summer; the heat has a much greater effect. But, low water can have a big impact on the fall fishing. Foster said, "In a low water year, the trouble we get in about October is low oxygen levels. The water doesn't fluctuate much after September, so it is low but stable. But, if the lake doesn't fill in the spring, the oxygen becomes a real problem and in some years we can get a fish kill in the fall.''

In September and October, the bass are actively feeding in 12 to 15 feet of water. Because there are not many points, creek channels, or other break-type structures, the key to finding bass in fall (when the vegetation is left high and dry), is to look for hard clay on the bottom. The fish relate to the flat patches of hard clay, surrounded by soft mud and silt, as if they were real breaks.

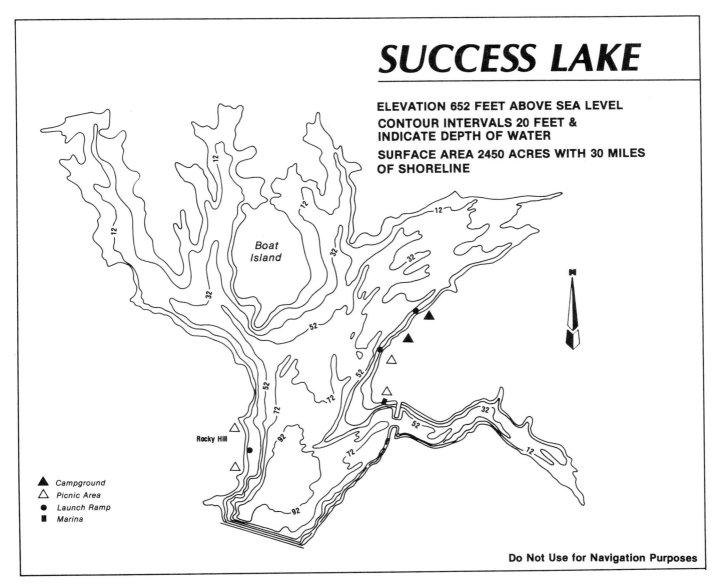

SUCCESS LAKE

ELEVATION 652 FEET ABOVE SEA LEVEL

CONTOUR INTERVALS 20 FEET & INDICATE DEPTH OF WATER

SURFACE AREA 2450 ACRES WITH 30 MILES OF SHORELINE

Boat Island

Rocky Hill

▲ Campground
△ Picnic Area
● Launch Ramp
■ Marina

Do Not Use for Navigation Purposes

Summer time around the weed beds can be great for top water baits.

Success used to be known as the bass factory.

To find these areas, use a flasher. Over the hard bottom the flasher indicates a double echo as two separate bands. Turn down the sensitivity so that the second band is faint over the clay, now the second band will disappear completely when the boat drifts off the clay and onto soft bottom. "You want to stay on these harder surfaces," said Foster. "Fish will relate to these and hold real close to the bottom. It doesn't look like they are holding on anything at first, it took me a while to figure out that the key was the change in bottom composition. Again, when fishing on these areas, plastic worms are the most productive. Green Weenies have been real good in this lake."

Borwick added that the bass may go into a flurry of surface feeding in the fall if the conditions are right. Look for shad busting on the surface and cast medium-sized Torpedoes. He doesn't like to use the smaller ones, because they are harder to cast long distances and the bass near the surface spook easily.

Once the water temperature drops below 50 degrees, usually in late October, the fishing slows down. The bass are inactive, and fishermen can't rely on a consistent pattern developing. "The fish get deeper and deeper," Foster said, "and it seems like the deeper they go, the less active they are. The only thing to do is fish at 30 to 40 feet with plastic worms, worked very, very slow."

There isn't a lot of structure when fish are off the banks, look for hard clay bottom, tiny drop-offs, and small rock piles. By the end of January, the bass become active again.

SUCCESS GUIDES

John Borwick (209) 781-2078
33283 Globe Dr., Springville, CA 93265
John has worked at Lake Success for the past 12 years. For the past 13 years he has fished on the lake as a licensed guide.

Calvin Foster (209) 784-2551
1016 N. Cobb, Porterville, CA 93257
Calvin has fished Success very actively for the past 15 years. He is President of the Lake Success Bass Club, and Chairman of the Valley Bass Council. He has worked at the lake for 17 years with the Army Corps of Engineers.

Rocky points are the prime structure on the lake.

Split shot worms are the most reliable way to catch fish year round at Success.

LAKE SUCCESS FACILITIES

Lake Success Park, has 104 campsites, with running water, hot showers, and 15 primitive campsites. There is a launch ramp, and a full-service marina with boat rentals, bait and tackle, and basic groceries. The camping fee is $8 from April 1 to September 31, there is no fee in the off-season. Call (209) 784-0215 for information.

Other: There are motels, restaurants, and sporting goods stores in nearby Springville and Porterville.

KEY TO SUCCESS

Best Season: February to the end of May, the spring period. Summer is good for shallow water night fishing as well as early and late in the day.

Lures To Use: Small plastic worms and grubs; the Green Weenie has been very good on this lake. Also single-blade spinnerbaits, crankbaits, Rattlin' Spots, and jig and pig for larger fish. While shad colors used to be the best producers prior to treatment of the lake, now that crawdads and panfish are the primary forage; brown, green and reddish lures may be better.

Primary Structure: Vegetation-covered flats, willows in the South Fork and cockleburs in the northern coves. Very few substantial breaks or deep creek channels. When fish are deep, look for hard clay on the bottom.

Other: Formerly, the water was muddy brown with visibility of just about zero, now the clarity approaches 20 feet. The clear water and smaller baits require light line and finesse tactics throughout most of the year.

TRINITY LAKE

Trinity is a mountain lake, with deep, clear, blue water and steep, rocky banks, surrounded by pine-covered mountains. Both the largemouth and smallmouth bass do well here. When the bite is on, it isn't unusual to catch and release 20 fish in a morning, and all the bass will weigh between two and four pounds. Every spring the store at Trinity Center practically covers a bulletin board with photographs of the seven- and eight-pound smallmouth caught by their customers. The lake has the potential to produce a world record smallmouth; it has already claimed the State Record with a fish of 9 pounds, 1 ounces.

Trinity is also known as Clair Engle Lake. It covers over 17,000 surface acres, with 145 miles of shoreline. Though it barely qualifies as a mountain lake at an elevation of only 2,400 feet, because it is at the base of the Trinity Alps, the weather patterns are more like those of lakes at much higher elevations. There is often snow around the lake in winter, and even in summer, nights are cool. However, the main feature of the weather is a lack of predictability. The guides note that the fish will bite just fine, no matter what the weather does, so long as the pattern has been stable for three days in a row. That happens less often than one would think.

Some of the lures to use on Trinity.

"In early spring, when the water is about 43 to 45 degrees, the smallmouth bite starts," said Pat Murphy. "If the water is clear, fish breaks or points, at about 8 to 15 or even 20 feet, with jigs or grubs. If you can find a little discolored water, the crankbait bite will be good for smallmouth. Fish from the bank down, around stump banks and flats near ledges."

The head end of the lake and Stewart's Fork are loaded with cuts and dredger tailings. There is very little wood or vegetation on Trinity, just some manzanita stumps on the flats, and willows that were planted with the help of the local bass fishermen. The rock structure is the primary feature of the lake. A graph is practically indispensable for effective fishing.

"There are a lot of hydraulic cuts on the lake," said Lorin Fleming. "In the old days they did a lot of mining up here, they cut into the canyon walls with water pressure. These cuts might be three or four feet deep at the top, and drop down to 10 or 15 feet. They are real good for both largemouth and smallmouth. That's the key at Trinity, fish the cuts and the dingy, muddy water."

By the time the water gets to 50 or 55 degrees, usually in early April, the largemouth will be coming on. They'll hit crankbaits and jigs fished in fairly shallow water. Jigs and spinnerbaits are good in the willows. The majority of the largemouth are in the head end of the lake. "By mid-April, the willows come up around the headwaters of the lake," said Fleming. "It's real shallow. You can catch a largemouth in there practically every cast. Squirrel Gulch is good too, the farther you go up there, the better it gets, it is just loaded with tailings."

"In spring, the south end of the lake warms first," Jim Roszell added. "You'll find fish spawning all around the lake on red clay banks, nothing banks is what they are called. There is gravel in here, but the fish still prefer the clay."

This is a small bait lake. The guides prefer to use crankbaits of about 2 1/2 inches long. Worms and grubs are usually less than four inches. They will use six- to eight-inch worms, if they are fishing in the tailings, where the broken rock makes a slightly larger worm easier for the fish to detect. The best colors are crawdad imitations in browns, reds and greens. There are kokanee salmon in the lake too; crankbaits with white bellies and black backs make a good imitation. Because the water is so clear, six-pound line is standard, though 10- or 12-pound line might be used when jigging in deeper water over rock.

When the water temperature hits 60 degrees, the bite is wide open. Bass hit just about everything. It is a good time for top-water, with three- to four-inch jerkbaits. Fish top-water lures around the spawning grounds and on steep banks. Fleming said, "The top-water bite holds up all through May."

By the time the water hits 65 to 68 degrees, the fishing gets tougher. The largemouth are in post-spawn and the smallmouth migrate to deeper water. Almost any lure is as good as any other, but the bites don't come quickly.

Summer is the slow season on Trinity. The bite is best early and late in the day, and at night. Murphy said, "smallmouth can be caught off breaks of eight to twenty feet at night, during the day they stay below 20 feet. The largemouth fishing is good on top-water, early and late in the

TRINITY LAKE

ELEVATION 2200 FEET ABOVE SEA LEVEL
SURFACE AREA 17000 ACRES WITH 145 MILES OF SHORELINE

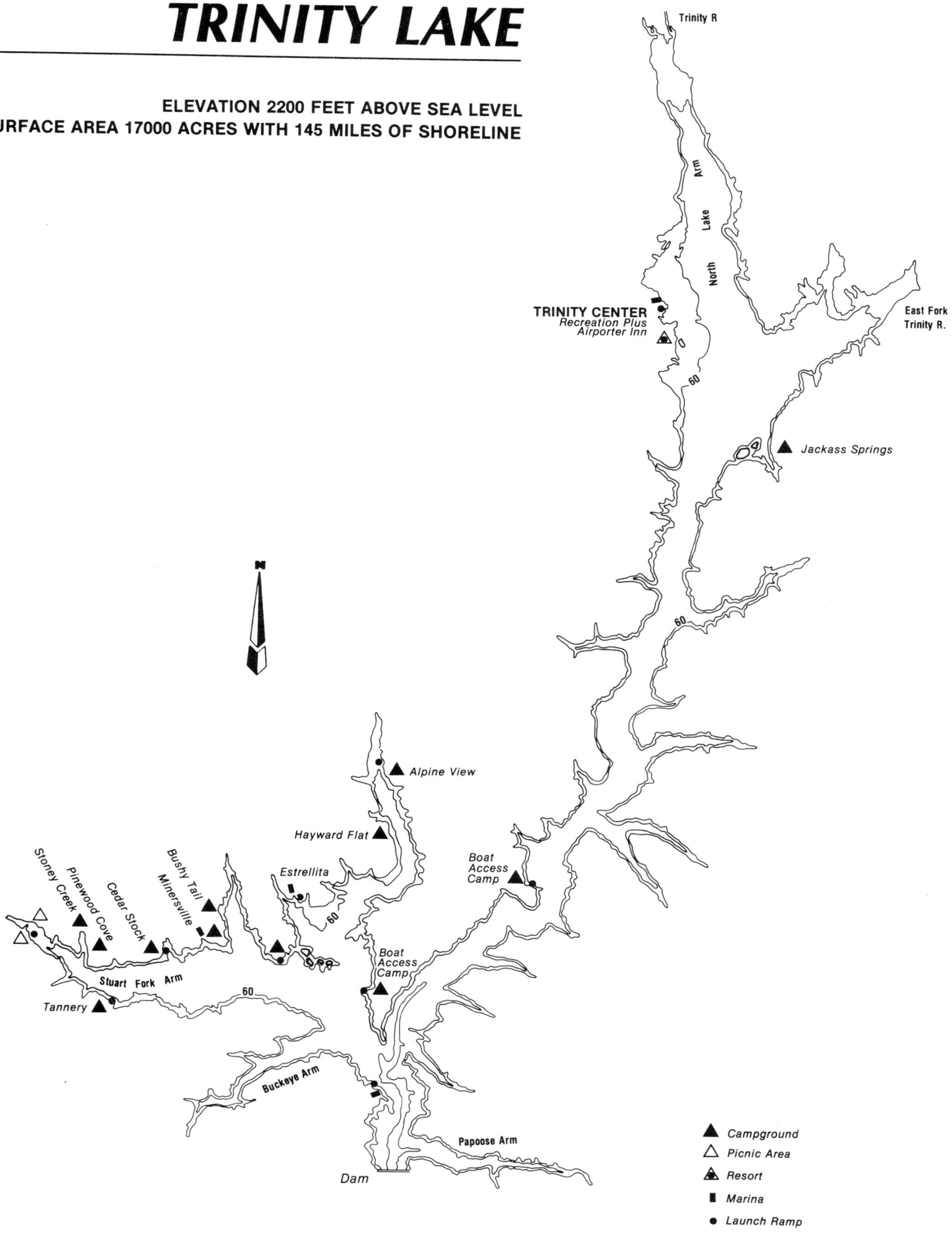

Trinity R

North Lake Arm

East Fork
Trinity R.

TRINITY CENTER
Recreation Plus
Airporter Inn

60

▲ Jackass Springs

60

▲ Alpine View

Hayward Flat ▲

Estrellita

60

Boat
Access
Camp

Boat
Access
Camp

Stoney Creek
Pinewood Cove
Cedar Stock
Bushy Tail
Minersville

Stuart Fork Arm

60

Tannery ▲

Buckeye Arm

Papoose Arm

Dam

▲ Campground
△ Picnic Area
▲ Resort
▌ Marina
● Launch Ramp

Do NOT use for Navigation Purposes

Dredger tailings and cuts from previous mining operations are a primary structure on the lake, especially Squirrel Gulch and Stewarts Fork.

day. By midday you have to move to deeper points, rock piles and tailing piles, in about 20 feet and fish with worms and jigs.''

Fleming recommends concentrating on the largemouth during summer, since they are more active than the smallmouth in warm water. The largemouth move into the brushy structure late in the evening. He also prefers to fish the lake at night with buzzbaits, grubs or worms, in dark colors. A black lantern on board the boat, makes the line look as fat as a rope, and that makes it a lot easier to detect bites.

"Fall is a pretty fine time to fish Trinity," said Roszell. "The forage come shallow and so do the bass. You get a final top-water fling.'' Work top-water around the main points, and cuts or brush. The bass will only be in shallow water that is adjacent to water that is a least 20 feet deep.

If the bass aren't taking top-water, move out to the main points and the well-defined cuts. Concentrate on the water deeper than 15 feet. Little Georges, worms, jigs, and spoons are good. The Little George is an ideal winter bait, because it has a weighted head that allows it to fall fast and stay near the bottom like a jig, but a small blade on the shank creates a fluttering vibration even at slow speeds.

Trinity might be cold in winter, but this is a great time of year to fish the lake. It isn't a fast action bite, but winter fish

are quality fish. On a day with only two strikes, both of the fish could easily weigh better than three or four pounds.

"Use a do-nothing lure for winter fishing," said Roszell. "Like split-shot worms, Gitzits, or jigs. You know, small baits with almost no motion. Or if it is a nice sunny day, cast onto the snow-covered banks with a crankbait. Slide it into the lake noiselessly and you'll get bit.''

The lake is often windy in winter, and the waves get above five feet. In bad weather, head for Bowerman, it is very sheltered and a boat can almost always be launched. There are good cuts back in Bowerman that hold plenty of fish. And it isn't as if it will be crowded with all of the normal boat traffic concentrated in one area, because few people fish Trinity in winter at all.

There are State Park campgrounds and private resorts on the west shore of Trinity. The resorts range from simple tent campgrounds, to full-service lodges, with horseback riding, swimming pools and restaurants. The Trinity Alps Wilderness Area is located on the west side of the lake, with hiking trails, trout fishing, and hunting for deer and bear.

There is a limit of two bass in the spring on Trinity, to protect the spawn. The rest of the year the limit is the standard five fish per person.

TRINITY GUIDES

Lorin Fleming (707) 574-6359
Star Route Box 155, Bridgeville, CA 95526
Lorin has been fishing Trinity for 15 years. He is on the water three or four days a week on average. He has been a licensed guide in the past.

Pat Murphy (707) 764-3709
655 Rigby Ave., Rio Dell, CA 95526
Pat does not guide, but he has fished on Trinity his whole life. He has qualified for many Tournaments of Champions, and placed in the top ten in many major tournaments.

Jim Roszell (916) 623-4356
Box 934, Weaverville, CA 96093
Jim has guided on Trinity for four years, he is on the water 100 days a year. Jim enjoys teaching people how to fish. He also fishes tournaments throughout Northern California.

In many bays there seems to be no structure; putting on a small crankbait and covering water fast may bring in a limit.

TRINITY LAKE FACILITIES

There are many well-developed campsites and lodges around Trinity Lake. The towns nearby can also provide additional services. This is a short list.

U.S. Forest Service, operates five boat launches that are open to the public for no fee. The only ramp that is open when the water is very low, is Minersville.

The USFS also operates 28 different campgrounds, for a total of approximately 600 sites. There are no hookups at any of these camps and in the off-season some are closed, though at least a few are open year-round. The price is $5 to $8 a night. No reservations taken. Call, (916) 623-2121 for information, ask for the Weaverville Ranger Station.

Reservations are taken only at Tannery Gulch and Hayward Flat because they are run by private concessions. Their prices are $8 and $12 per night. Both take reservations through Mistix (800) 444- 7275.

• Wyntoon Resort, has 300 campsites and 19 cottages. They also have a complete store with bait and tackle, laundry facilities and boat rentals. The launch ramp is on public property, right next door to the resort. Prices as follows; cottages $60, RVs $14.50 to $16, tent campsites $12. Write, P.O.Box 70, Trinity Center, CA 90061. (916) 266-3337.

KEY TO TRINITY

Best Season: Spring, especially the month of April. The smallmouth bite peaks when the water temperature is between 50 and 55 degrees. The largemouth peaks when the temperature is about 60 degrees. Fall brings on a feeding frenzy, and winter holds up well too. Summer is slow.

Lures To Use: Smaller baits. Cranks should be 2 1/2 inches long, worms and grubs less than four inches. Crawdad and kokanee fry imitations are good choices for colors. Three- to four-inch jerkbaits are good for top-water. Smaller spinnerbaits work well around willows. Little George and jigs are used in winter.

Primary Structure: Dredger tailings and cuts are all over the lake from defunct mining operations, especially around Squirrel Gulch and the Stewart's Fork. There is not a lot of wood in the lake, but the manzanita stumps that are in here will attract bass. Newly submerged willows are good too.

Other: Weather is a primary factor. Consistency is the key, after three days of consistent weather, go fishing. Even though the lake is only at 2,400 feet, it gets cold up here; in winter there can be snow on the banks. This is a clear water lake, use light lines.

Jim Roszell, a top guide on the lake, landing a smallmouth.

TULLOCH LAKE

Jon Walton said, "Tulloch is an excellent smallmouth lake, because of the clear sterile water. It is cold and rocky, and there is not as much cover as at some lakes, in terms of vegetation. That is not to say that it isn't a good largemouth lake. But it is a very, very good smallmouth lake."

Tulloch isn't big, but it holds a lot of fish. The lake is located 40 miles east of Stockton, directly below New Melones. The lake may not be large in terms of surface acreage, but it has more than 55 miles of shoreline. The four river channel arms are narrow and long, and account for most of the surface acreage. The arms provide miles upon miles of points, interspersed with shallow coves, that are perfect bass habitat. In addition to bass, Tulloch has produced crappie up to four pounds, but crappie numbers have been declining because of constant water level fluctuations.

The power generating plant on New Melones impacts the bass fishing on Tulloch in two ways. First off, Tulloch is filled by water released from New Melones. The water comes from the bottom of New Melones and it is much cooler than the surface water, therefore the water temperature in Tulloch remains cool all year, even in summer. When other lakes in the area have surface temperatures of 83 degrees, Tulloch won't rise above 73 degrees.

Lure selection on Tulloch definitely leans toward smallmouth bass but that's not to say it does not have some good largemouth.

Second, every 24 hours the water level on Tulloch rises and falls two or three feet, just like the tides on the Delta. They drop the lake level at night to generate electricity, then fill it during the day with water out of New Melones. If the "powers that be" coordinated the water releases, to let water in at the same time it is taken out, the level wouldn't change daily, but they don't.

"Things happen on this lake because of water release that don't happen on other lakes," said Wayne Brawley. "Take the river area that dumps out of Melones for example. When they turn the water loose, you get cold water on the bottom, it's a thermocline that the bass come up out of. Now you can go in there at 11:00 a.m. and the fish will be active. You should run in there every day in at midday, check it and throw some top-water lures. There is often great action above that thermocline layer."

All around the lake, there is good top-water action in spring, summer and fall. In the backs of the narrow coves, especially in the Black and Greenspring arms, there are grassbeds that hold fish. These are strictly top-water areas, use Zara Spooks, buzzbaits, and Tiny Torpedos. In water this clear, the fish will come up from 10 feet or more to attack a top-water lure.

Tulloch takes longer to warm than other lakes in the area, the real spawning action doesn't begin until April. An early spring pattern would target long tapering points near flats, work these areas with creakbaits or jigs. The fish hold at depths from 10 to 20 feet during pre-spawn. In a very clear lake, shallow is anything above 15 feet. One reason the smallmouth are doing better than the largemouth and crappie with the constant water fluctuation is that they spawn in deeper water.

A little later in spring, work over the flats near deep water. Start out with surface lures. If top-water doesn't produce, switch to a Texas-rigged worm on an open hook, worked over the gravel beds. Both Walton and Brawley like purple worms. Walton added, "Purple always seems good in clearwater, rocky lakes. It may imitate the shine that baitfish give off in deep water."

By June, bass are found off the main points, or they hold in the shade cast by docks during the heat of the day. "Rocks are good when there is no breeze to create a ripple on the water," said Brawley. "Then I go work the docks with a Rapala. You have to let the lure sit a lot, just twitch it a little and let it sit. A lot of people fish a Rapala too fast. You have to be patient. I throw it out and let the ripple disappear and then I just lift the line off the water, and that moves it a little. The bass will come and hit it when it isn't moving at all."

Walton uses shad-colored plastics to fish the docks, on very light weights. He uses only a 1/16- or 1/32-ounce weight, or sometimes no weight at all. The light weight allows the plastic to fall very slowly, and gives the bass time to respond to the bait. These bass under the docks are basically hanging out. They aren't actively feeding, so the lure has to be an easy target, one that they can't resist.

By far, the best summer fishing on Tulloch occurs at night. For one thing, the lake is a skiers circus during the day and there is no place to get away from the boat traffic. Also, when it is hot and the sun is bright, the fish stay deep during the day and come to feed only at night.

At night there is not much of a top-water bite. Brawley recommends a 3 1/2 inch, salt and pepper Kalin grub. Rig this grub with the hook exposed on a 1/4-ounce dart head hook. The Kalin grub has a large tail that creates vibration in the water. Throw the lure right onto the bank and work it down into about 10 feet of water. A moon-glow light makes it possible to "see every twitch when a bass hits it."

With the exception of night fishing, the lake is at its best in the middle of the day. "I catch more fish between 10:00 a.m. and 2:00 p.m., than at any other time of the day," said Brawley. "In summer, you can go out just before sunrise and catch a limit of fish on top, but the bite only lasts a short time, then it goes dead until 10:00 a.m., when you start fishing docks and cover. Overall, the best fishing is right in the middle of the day."

In many ways, fall is a continuation of summer, with excellent top-water action throughout the day. The bass may be a little more shallow until late in the season when the water gets very cold. "By late fall, the shad move up into creek channels," said Tony Foxe. "They'll be in areas with feeder streams. The bass will follow. Look for surface activity."

As the late fall transition comes on, the bass move toward the outside points, to deeper water. The shad will have moved to even deeper water of 55 to 65 feet and this draws the bass out of the shallow areas. Then the lake turns over, and the shad start dying. Around these shad balls is where the bass are easiest to catch, on Kastmasters and jigs. Look for fish over the rocks, at 25 to 35 feet. This will hold through the winter.

Late fall is also a prime time to land a big smallmouth. "Fish the rock ledges where there is a steep drop-off with a Zara," Brawley said. "That is a full-size Zara, black with white stripes. This is only for your big bronzeback, like a five, six or seven pounder. You can get a big one, if you work real hard. But, it is awful slow fishing. It is strictly trophy hunting. If you want a lot of fish, go deeper and work a jig."

On Tulloch, eight-pound line is the maximum weight, the water is too clear for heavier tackle. There is a healthy forage base of shad and crawdads in the lake. A good fisherman should be able to catch fish every single day on this lake. It is simply a matter of paying attention to the fundamentals. "The bass will utilize weed beds when they are available," said Walton. "And they need deep water nearby, as well as forage, shade and oxygen."

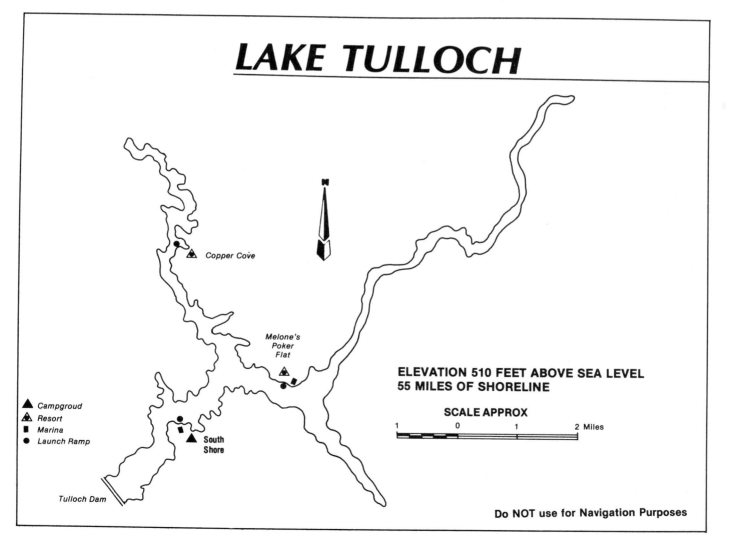

TULLOCH GUIDES

Wayne Brawley (209) 785-2818
137 Eagle Pt., Copperopolis, CA 95228
Wayne has been fishing Tulloch since the dam was built in 1960. He has lived at the lake for eight years. Wayne is the inventor of the Brawley Bass Bug, the original live-rubber jig. In other words, he was one of the founders of western bass fishing.

Jon Walton (415) 782-3932
Walton's Pond
23880 Hesperia Blvd., Hayward, CA 94546
Jon owns and runs Walton's Pond, a tackle shop specializing in black bass gear. He is not a guide himself, but can provide references through the shop. Jon teaches classes in fishing techniques through the store. He has been fishing for 30 years, and in the tackle business for 15.

Fishing surface lures around the docks in summer can be explosive.

LAKE TULLOCH FACILITIES

• Melones Poker Flat Resort, is a luxury bass fishing and water sports resort. There is a launch ramp, tackle shop and snack store, large bar overlooking the water, restaurant, and pool, with mooring slips included in the price of each room. Live entertainment in the bar on Friday and Saturday in season, off-season on Saturday only. Rooms are $55 in winter, $85 to $90 in summer. There is no charge for the launch ramp when staying in the resort, but for those who do not stay at Melone's, the launch fee is $5 in winter and $10 in summer. The resort is on the north side of the lake, down the road from Copperopolis. (209) 984-5248.

• Copper Cove, has a launch ramp, slips, gas, restaurant and bar. The cost to launch is $5. (209) 785-2240.

• Glory Hole Sporting Goods: Offers complete bait and tackle, as well as all sorts of sporting goods. Located at 2892 South Highway 49, Angel's Camp, CA 95222, near New Melones Lake. (209) 736-4333.

Other: There are additional tourist services in the nearby towns that cater to visitors who come to see the historical gold mining country.

Tulloch smallmouth are beautiful, clear water, hard fighting fish.

KEY TO TULLOCH

Best Season: April and May. Summer is good for night fishing. September/October fish top-water all day, over the same general areas that held fish in summer.

Lures To Use: Zara Spooks, Tiny Torpedos, and Rapalas for top-water fish. Purple ring-worms, and 3 1/2-inch salt and pepper Kalin grubs. Jigs are good too.

Primary Structure: Smallmouth hold off the points, near rocky breaks. There are grassbeds in the backs of the coves, especially in the Black and Greenspring arms. The entire lake is loaded with decent structure areas.

Other: Very clear water, go with line of about eight pounds or less. The water level rises and falls every 24 hours, it is almost like a tidal situation. Also, Tulloch is a cool water lake because it is filled from water at the bottom of New Melones. Look for spawning later than on other lakes in the area, and better summer fishing.

NOTES